WORKING AND
LIVING IN IRELAND

WORKING AND LIVING IN IRELAND

Eugenie Houston

Oak Tree Press
Dublin

Oak Tree Press
Merrion Building
Lower Merrion Street
Dublin 2, Ireland

A catalogue record of this book is
available from the British Library.

ISBN 1-86076-080-5

Printed in Ireland by Colour Books Ltd.

Contents

About the Author

Eugenie Houston is a graduate of Applied Languages at Dublin City University. During the past ten years, she has lived in France, Germany, the UK and Ireland, and her work has always involved dealing with people of many different cultures. Her work in the field of Human Resources has involved managing the expatriate programme for a global financial services firm in London, and being part of the start-up of a large pan-European call centre in Dublin as Human Resources Manager. She is presently Director of Human Resources at a leading telecommunications company.

About the Author

Acknowledgements

Anyone who doubts the effectiveness of teamwork should try to write a book in a short timeframe. Many people have been generous with their time and expertise in providing the research for this book. Without exception, those asked for help have responded with enormous enthusiasm and goodwill. Care has been taken to acknowledge these sources throughout. If anyone has been omitted, it is entirely unintentional. There are too many people to thank in this space; to all who have helped, I am extremely grateful. Particular gratitude must be extended to the companies who have contributed — despite year-end budgetary restrictions — to the section on **Who's Recruiting Now**. Many more have already asked to be included in next year's edition.

A few people must get special thanks. All at Oak Tree Press have been very generous with their encouragement and advice. Equal thanks to David Givens, Ciara Considine, Brian Langan, Jenna Dowds, and of course to Brian O'Kane, particularly for his contribution of the chapter **Setting Up in Business**. I am very grateful too to Mark Carter of Price Waterhouse and Liz Crehan of Inbucon, both of whom worked long and late to provide the most up-to-date material. And finally, thank goodness for the very best of friends and family who can always be relied upon for a sense of humour, great ideas, plenty of encouragement and the most down-to-earth approach to getting the job finished. They know how much they are valued.

In memory of Desmond and for Maureen

Introduction

The first thing to strike a returning emigrant five years ago would have been a country in the grip of Lotto fever as the twice-weekly spinning of a barrel of numbers on national television garnered pages of analysis, representing for many a single if remote prospect of prosperity. Participation in the National Lottery has not diminished but, in the first week of October 1997, news of whether or not the million has been won simply does not rank beside reports of the first Enterprise Ireland exhibition, swamped from the moment it opened by thousands of budding entrepreneurs keen to start their own businesses.

A cursory review of the newspapers in the same week sums up Ireland very well as it moves to the end of the century. An entire page of a respected Sunday paper is devoted to the lone male candidate in the presidential election with a blaring headline protesting that he is not "just a token male". Another equally respected publication devotes the same space on the same day to the chief executive of the Employment Equality Agency, highlighting her concern at the male/female pay gap. The same week has witnessed all sides, although not all parties, in the Northern Ireland peace process actually agreeing to participate in real talks, while in Dublin the debate continues about the fate of a government minister in the wake of yet another tribunal determined to flush out corruption. Mid-week reports of two Christian brothers charged with the abuse of children dating back some 50 years are duly reported, while the travelling community criticise their exclusion from consultation on a new project by the National Society for the Prevention of Cruelty to Children. Daily announcements of new companies starting up and expanding coincide nicely with news that unemployment has dropped below a quarter of a million people for the first time in six years. Meanwhile, economists, social groups and politicians battle it out for space to record their advice to the Minister for Finance on how he should use the available surplus funds in the forthcoming December budget.

Today, new arrivals will be greeted by a bustling economy with plenty of opportunity, while returning emigrants may well register their own disbelief at how much it has all changed. Rapid economic development has wrought significant changes in attitude in every age group. Far from bemoaning the way it used to be, Ireland's elder citizens are now more likely to be enjoying early retirement, while middle-aged people may well be busy raising the unexpected children of their own teenagers and the young immerse themselves in technology. There have been legislative changes as well. Divorce was introduced by the Family Law Act 1996 on 27 February 1997. Homosexuality was decriminalised under the Criminal Law (Sexual Offences) Act 1993 and the recent possibility that a well known senator who happens to be gay might have run for the office of president was greeted positively all round.

Reports of the rapid pace of development in Ireland may well be welcome news to the returning emigrant. However, if you set off years ago in a spirit of adventure and are returning now with a family, there are many things to consider. It has been the author's own experience that a gulf exists between the extensive coverage of all the good news of Ireland's growth and the essential factual information needed before an informed decision can be made to uproot a well-established and enjoyable life overseas and return home.

The aim of this book is to provide you with a realistic and accurate picture of working and living in Ireland in the last few years of the twentieth century, and to point you in the direction of further sources of information, where they exist. Expectations founded on an incomplete picture can end in disappointment.

The information contained here is intended to go a long way towards dispelling that possibility.

The book is divided into two sections: Working in Ireland and Living in Ireland. *Section One* focuses on working and details what you need to know about employment practices, employee rights, salaries and benefits. In addition, a number of the top companies based in Ireland have listed their employment opportunities for 1998.

Chapter 1, **Employment Outlook**, reviews developments in employment trends and inward investment. The electronics and software manufacturing sector has made a remarkable impact on Ireland's economy and, since 1980, 40 per cent of all US new inward investment in European electronics has come to Ireland. Recognising the long-term viability of this sector, the Government has approved an immediate capital investment of IR£5 million to meet the skills needs of high technology companies. IR£60 million has already been committed for a 50 per cent increase in the number of third-level places in computer science by the year 2001. Meanwhile, Dublin's International Financial Services Centre (IFSC) has developed into a significant world financial centre. A wide range of internationally traded financial services companies are licensed to trade there in activities ranging from banking and mutual fund management to corporate treasury and captive insurance. New jobs in this sector grew by almost 35 per cent in 1996, with 3,500 employed at year-end.

Thirteen of the world's top pharmaceutical companies and 10 of the world's top 15 medical products companies have operations in Ireland, and this is marked as the top growth area for the remainder of the century. Dubbed "Europe's back office" by *The Economist* earlier in 1997, Ireland is the top location in Europe for companies that provide telemarketing, customer support and technical services through call centres. In just two years, Ireland has emerged as the undisputed leader in the field of European call centres. In that time, over 40 major companies have chosen Ireland as the base for their new European call centres. The evidence is that the long-term unemployed are at last reaping the rewards of the (by now infamous) Celtic Tiger economy, while the opportunity to become Ireland's Information Age town is already transforming forever the prospects of a small tourist town near the south-west coast.

Chapter 2 provides advice on how to **How to Find a Job**, a process you should be able to start before you leave your current country, as Ireland is not large enough for recruitment to become regionalised, as it has elsewhere. Most recruiters will correspond with you electronically. Despite the current high demand for staff, standards are very high in the Irish employment market and being ill prepared can heighten the isolation of being a new arrival. A careful review of the contents of this chapter, together with the preparation outlined in Chapter 6 on **Interview Techniques**, will equip you well for a successful job search.

Chapter 3, **Who's Recruiting Now**, lists the top companies recruiting in 1998. From Fortune 500 multinationals to much smaller enterprises, they all have in common the need for world-class skills and experience and a shared recognition of the need to reach out, by whatever means possible, to the many emigrants who want to return home. This chapter serves a dual purpose. In addition to providing you with essential real career openings, the subscriptions made by these companies have enabled this book to be disseminated much more widely than would otherwise have been possible.

The level of **Salaries and Benefits**, covered in Chapter 4, will be a major factor in your decision to move to Ireland, and considerable emphasis is placed here on providing accurate market data. The methods of setting salaries are explained and examples across a range of functions are provided from the most rapidly expanding sectors, namely pharmaceuticals and health care, electronics and software manufacturing, and banking and finance. Categorising companies by size, the three best paid jobs in companies ranging from fewer than 50 to more than 500 employees are given. A special section on the information technology sector is included. You will find details of collective bargaining and a thorough analysis of contemporary benefits packages. And finally, because this book has something for everyone, a salary checklist that ranges from plumbers and truck drivers to chefs and chief executives is included as Appendix 1.

Your Rights as an Employee are outlined in Chapter 5 and merit careful consideration. It is important that you understand these before taking up a job in Ireland so that you know what to expect. Meanwhile, those of you interested in **Setting Up in Business** for yourselves will find extensive details in Chapter 7 of the points you need to consider and the places you should contact for more assistance.

Section Two on Living in Ireland covers the key areas that are central to your quality of life. Chapter 8 on **Moving to Ireland** provides advice on the practical things you need to think of when planning a move. Good planning will ease your relocation and once you start you will be surprised at how much is involved. Tips on what to take and what to leave behind, an explanation of the workings of customs and excise and guidelines on immigration and work permits are included. When you are settled here, **Transport and Travel** regulations and options are briefly explained in Chapter 16.

Once you are here, **Adjusting to Life in a New Country**, covered in Chapter 9, suddenly becomes more topical as the inevitable culture shock takes hold. This chapter explores why people are struck by differences in culture and suggests steps that you can take to minimise its effect on you. Research shows that returning emigrants can experience reverse culture shock, and experts suggest that commencing the transition process by saying your goodbyes well in your current country of residence can help.

When you have read Chapter 10 on **Finance and Taxation**, you will understand how the tax and social security systems work in Ireland and be able to calculate your own potential take-home pay or refer to the calculations provided. Analysis included in this chapter of net take-home pay after income tax and social security deductions in Ireland, the US, Canada, the UK, France and Germany shatters the perception that Ireland taxes prohibitively compared to other countries. Finally, this chapter compares the cost of living in Ireland to that in New York City, Paris, London and Frankfurt.

Having used this information to evaluate your potential financial worth in Ireland, Chapter 11 on **Housing** describes housing trends and prices, comparing renting to home ownership — a priority in Ireland where there are a million homeowners out of a total population of just over 3.5 million people. The home purchase process is explained, together with details of arranging finance, tax incentives and current interest rates. A county-by-county list of current house prices, ranging from mansions to cottages, is included in Appendix 2, and illustrates how widely the range spans. Spurred by rising house prices, the Government has ordered an evaluation of all the factors influencing the upward trend, while a local community group has proved that necessity is indeed the mother of invention with an innovative partnership with a building company that has resulted in quality housing in central Dublin for less than £50,000.

Personal circumstances dictate that not everyone moving to Ireland will end up working and details of **Social Welfare** provisions are outlined in Chapter 12. The range of benefits provided is extensive and no claim is made that this chapter covers all of them. Any of you seeking Social Welfare are advised to make enquiries of the authorities in your current country of residence to ensure that a missed formality does not result in a missed opportunity.

Family Matters in Chapter 13 touches on the areas that concern families in particular. Practicalities such as infant formula and childcare are covered, and a brief summary of legal matters such as adoption, marriage breakdown and making a will is included. There are tips too for retired people and suggestions about who to contact for more information.

The public and private **Health Care** systems are explained in Chapter 14, along with a summary of current health concerns and trends.

Education and Learning systems can vary greatly from country to country. Developments in Irish education are exciting and it would be tempting to provide three times the detail provided here. However, in keeping with the spirit of this publication in providing information that is relevant to relocating here, Chapter 15 explains how the system works at primary, secondary and third levels and includes additional information on adult and vocational learning.

Researching **Culture** is a pleasurable experience and Chapter 16 strives to provide a flavour of what is on offer, in the hope that you will enjoy sampling the wealth of offerings from theatre, music and dance to film, good conversation and the famous Irish *craic*.

The contents of this book are based on years of experience in dealing with over 700 people on the move in several countries. Bringing all of this information together in one place for the first time has been one of the most rewarding pieces of work I have ever undertaken. The enthusiasm and unconditional willingness to help encountered among the many people consulted for information has been tremendous. Plans are already in place for next year's edition, with many companies booking space in advance in the **Who's Recruiting Now** chapter. I expect there will be many changes to report during the year. A key aim is to keep information relevant to the needs of the readers, and I invite you to let me know of any ideas or suggestions you believe should be included next time. Correspondence should be sent to the address below. I look forward to hearing from you.

Eugenie Houston
Working and Living in Ireland
c/o Oak Tree Press
Merrion Building
Lower Merrion Street
Dublin 2

Part One

WORKING IN IRELAND

Chapter 1

Employment Outlook

Easily accessible, with the nearest airport just 30 minutes away by car, Information Age Town is a model of efficiency and high-tech communication. All public services make full use of the latest technologies. Every home, school, business and hospital is equipped and wired with the latest technology. Every home has a state-of-the-art telephone, with voice-mail and other services, every business a high-speed ISDN connection to the Internet and every child above the age of five has access to a computer and the World Wide Web. Silicon Valley or a sci-fi movie? Neither. If you know anyone of Irish extraction, the chances are that they know someone with links to this bustling County Clare town of 17,000 inhabitants, whose main activities centre around providing thousands of tourists with directions to the breathtaking Cliffs of Moher nearby and with plenty of culture and craic. Most leave having resolved to return, half-wishing that they could live there, were it not so quiet out of season.

Winner of the Telecom Eireann-sponsored Information Age Town Project, Ennis will shortly match the above description, for it has been chosen from among a shortlist of four provincial towns — the others were Castlebar, Kilkenny and Killarney — to become a showcase and guinea pig for the next wave of information technology. The competition attracted 46 initial entries from towns with between 5,000 and 30,000 inhabitants across the country in submissions that galvanised entire communities from the chambers of commerce to schools and the travellers' organisations. This is testament to just how widely the Celtic Tiger economy has impacted almost every corner of Ireland.

Clearly, one of the most important factors in your decision to move to Ireland must be employment — ironically so, if you are a returning emigrant, since this was likely to have been the main reason you left in the first place. Although Ireland still experiences unemployment of 12 per cent — down from 17 per cent in 1990 — the sustained growth in most sectors due to expansion of both indigenous firms and overseas companies, and a steady flow of greenfield start-ups, bodes well for the future. A total of 13,000 new jobs were created by IDA-backed companies in 1996, while indigenous Irish companies grew by 3 per cent (6 per cent in 1995).

Increased employment opportunities have been matched by a constant flow of returning economic emigrants and the arrival of new immigrants to Ireland. While welcoming this trend, there has been concern in the past that the long-term unemployed were missing out on the steady decline of the unemployment rate. However, recent figures show that this group is at last benefiting from the economic boom. According to a report by FÁS (the semi-state training and employment agency), unemployment rates among people out of work for more than three years are falling faster than the national average. In the year ending April 1997, the overall unemployment rate fell by 9.3 per cent, while the rate for the long-term unemployed fell by 11.2 per cent.

Strong links continue to be forged between indigenous firms and overseas companies based in Ireland. Purchasing of Irish-made components and raw materials has increased by 90 per cent over the past six years, and spending on Irish services by over 60 per cent.

Ireland has for the first time become the market leader for US companies undertaking greenfield investment into Europe, and 30 per cent of all such projects now come to Ireland. The perception has abated that such investment comes to Ireland because the financial package offered is too good to refuse. According to IDA figures, the cost of job creation is now only one-third of what it was ten years ago and Ireland has won investment against competition from much more generous packages in other countries.

So why the success? The key factors are: a strong economy where inflation has held steadily at low rates and is currently running at 1 per cent (the lowest in Europe); the high level of qualifications and skills of the workforce (the standard on completion of secondary school at 18 in Ireland is reputed to be equivalent to that achieved after two years in a third-level college in the US); 10 per cent rate of corporation tax where applicable; flexibility of the workforce; state-of-the-art telecommunications; sophisticated transport logistics; the attraction of existing blue-chip companies with successful operations here; and, of course, a good quality of life.

The Irish Government is acutely aware of the need for Ireland to remain competitive, particularly in the face of increasing competition from Eastern European countries for manufacturing projects. Considerable resources are dedicated to ensuring that the skills needed are available here. However, rapid investment and strong economic growth have resulted in shortages in certain key areas and, accordingly, there is a wealth of opportunities for anyone seeking a job in Ireland.

ELECTRONICS AND INFORMATION TECHNOLOGY (SOFTWARE, SERVICE, MANUFACTURING)

Most of the major global electronics companies are now represented in Ireland, citing its sub-supply base, excellent skills and low operating costs among the attractions for locating here. Since 1980, 40 per cent of all US new inward investment in European electronics has come to Ireland.

Over 300 companies are engaged in the development, marketing and manufacture of a wide range of leading edge products in a diversity of sectors, from wafer design and fabrication, systems, components and peripherals to communications, networks and software. These companies play a major role in Ireland's economy. Almost a third of the PCs sold in Europe come from companies based in Ireland. Exports of electronics products account for a third of Ireland's total exports.

Many electronics companies are increasingly engaged in complementary activities such as software development, technical support and customer care. Dell pioneered the trend by centralising its European logistics and customer support in Ireland, and companies such as Gateway 2000 have swiftly followed suit. IBM, Fujitsu, Motorola and DEC have seized the opportunity afforded by the availability in Ireland of highly skilled computer science graduates. Others with a presence here have adapted their operations to match the economy. For Electrolux, for example, it does not make sense to manufacture consumer durables in Ireland, but the company has begun to make logistical software for use by the group world-wide.

Recognising the long-term viability of this sector, the Government has approved an immediate capital investment of IR£5 million to meet the skills needs of high technology companies. IR£60 million has already been committed towards a 50 per cent increase in the number of third-level places in computer science by the year 2001. Places on post-graduate courses in computer applications are also on the increase and will rise by 50 per cent in 1997/98. In addition, the Department of Education has set up a task force to report by the end of 1997 on plans to provide adequate training to meet the expected increased in demand for electronic technicians.

With an expectation that 17,500 new jobs will be created in this sector within the next three years, companies are demonstrating their long-term commitment by co-funding training programmes for the long-term unemployed and for women who want to return to work. One such example is the EU-funded NOW Women in Electronics Programme, where, in conjunction with Tallaght Regional Technical College, leading companies including Intel, Hewlett-Packard and NEC invested in a variety of training programmes to promote the participation of females in the workforce and to upgrade existing skills of both male and female employees. Similar programmes are likely to continue, and the argument has been put forward in the UK, where women make up fewer than 5 per cent of the information technology sector, that this may be one approach to meeting the demands being made in preparation for the year 2000.

While Irish software companies are keen for the numbers returning to Ireland to increase, they are also capitalising on the high proportion of successful Irish executives working for financial institutions abroad, particularly in the UK. In September 1997, the Irish Trade Board held a unique "Irish in Banking" event in the UK to help penetrate this market. With Ireland the second largest software supplier in the world, second only to the US, the potential is clearly enormous.

- Leading **electronics companies** in Ireland include: Alps Electric, American Power Conversion, Analog Devices, Apple Computer, AST, AT&T, Avid Technology, Bourns, Cabletron, 3Com, Creative Labs, Dovatron, EICON, EMC, Ericsson, Fujitsu Isotec, General Electric, General Instruments, LG Group, Hitachi-Koki, Madge Networks, Matsushita Kotobuki, Maxtor, Mitsumi, Mitsubishi Chemical, Northern Telecom, Philips, Quantum, SCI, Seagate Technology, Sensormatic, Siemens, Stratus, Sun Microsystems, Westinghouse, Xilinx.

HEALTH CARE/PHARMACEUTICALS

Forecast as the biggest growth area for the remainder of the decade, expansion in this sector has already been dramatic, with 2,500 new jobs created in 1996 alone. Pharmaceutical and medical products companies from around the world use Ireland as a base for developing, manufacturing and marketing a diverse range of products, from analgesics to disposable contact lenses. Between them they generate US$6 billion of exports every year.

Thirteen of the world's top pharmaceutical companies and 10 of the world's top 15 medical products companies have operations in Ireland. They are attracted by the availability of highly skilled staff, the responsive attitude of regulatory authorities to their needs and the high quality of supply services. Many companies have shown their satisfaction with Ireland as a base in the most tangible way of all, by re-investing. American Home Products and Abbott Laboratories each have five operations in Ireland, while Johnson & Johnson and Pfizer each have three.

Among Irish companies, Elan has performed spectacularly and is now known globally for its products.

- **Pharmaceutical companies** include: Akzo Pharma, Bristol-Meyers Squibb, Elan, Eli Lilly, E. Merck, FMC, Forest Laboratories, Fujisawa, Ivax, Johnson & Johnson, Leo Laboratories, Merck, Nycomed, Pfizer, Pharmacia, Roche, RPR, Sandoz, Schering-Plough, SmithKline Beecham, Warner Lambert, Wyeth Medica, Yamanouchi.

- **Medical products companies** include: Abbott, Allergan, Bausch & Lomb, Baxter, Bayer Diagnostics, Braun, Becton Dickinson, Beiersdorf, Boston Scientific, CR Bard, Hollister, Howmedica, Mallinckrodt, Millipore, Olympus, Organon Teknika, Puritan Bennett, Sherwood Medical, Welch-Allyn American Home Products, Vistakon.

ENGINEERING

Automotive components and aerospace technology are two of the most important and rapidly growing sectors in Ireland today. Ireland exports close to US$1 billion worth of automotive components every year to customers in Europe, the US and the Far East. The products manufactured range from turbochargers by Allied Signal to cable harnesses by Kromberg & Schubert. In the aerospace sector, leading international companies with operations in Ireland include Pratt & Whitney, Westinghouse, Moog and Sifco Turbine. Their activities range from airframe and jet engine maintenance to sophisticated electronic sub-assemblies.

A highly trained and experienced workforce of designers, toolmakers and engineers, using the latest technology in

CAD/CAM and CNC equipment, has earned Ireland an international reputation for excellence in toolmaking and opportunities abound for this group.

- **Multinational companies** include: ABB, Alcatel Cable, Alcoa Fujikura, Allied Signal, AO Smith, Beru, Betatherm, Bijur Lubrication, Bruss, Cooper Industries, Crown Equipment, Dahlstrom, Donnelly Mirrors, Elasto Metall, Emerson Electric, General Monitors, General Motors, General Signal, Groschopp, Henniges, Jacobs Engineering, Kostal, Lapple, Legrand, Liebherr, Menvier Swaine, Mitsuboshi Belting, Moog, Ohshima, Packo, Pauwels, Pratt & Whitney, Radiac Abrasives, Sifco, Simon Engineering, Snap-Tite, Thermo King, Trac Tech, Volex, Wavin, Westinghouse, Wilo, Woco.

- **Indigenous Irish companies** have a growing presence in this sector. Moffett Engineering is an excellent example. From humble beginnings, the company developed steadily over the past decade and reported a 63 per cent pre-tax profit of IR£2.4 million for 1995. Not quite in that league just yet, but worth watching all the same, is electronics engineering company Acra Control Ltd., which exports its test equipment for the automotive aerospace industry to a global customer base.

FINANCIAL SERVICES

Established in 1987, Dublin's **International Financial Services Centre (IFSC)** has developed into a significant world financial centre. A wide range of internationally traded financial services companies are licensed to trade there in activities ranging from banking and mutual fund management to corporate treasury and captive insurance. New jobs in this sector grew by almost 35 per cent in 1996 with 3,500 employed at the end of that year.

The centre is serviced by an extensive network of major international banks, brokerage houses and professional advisors.

Leading corporates, such as IBM, Coca-Cola, Hewlett-Packard and Pfizer, have established operations there.

Altogether, over 400 of the world's leading financial institutions have set up new operations in the IFSC, with a further 350 managed entities carrying on business under the IFSC programme.

They include finance houses such as Citibank, Merrill Lynch, PFPC, Mitsubishi Trust & Bank, Daiwa, Deutsche, AIG and ABN Amro. IFSC operations benefit from a 10 per cent corporation tax rate which is supported by an excellent tax treaty network and an efficient regulatory environment.

Business & Finance magazine's 1997 IFSC Yearbook estimated that the size of the investment funds industry in Dublin exceeded US$100 billion as of 30 June 1996. The figures issued by the Central Bank of Ireland reported that lending by the 45 IFSC banks had increased to IR£25.5 billion by April 1996. The Department of Enterprise, Trade and Employment stated that the IFSC life insurance companies wrote IR£187 million worth of premiums in 1995, with the non-life insurance companies accounting for IR£183 million in the same period.

The success of the IFSC has also resulted in spin-off activities in the international services sector located outside the IFSC, such as Citibank's Regional Processing and Service Centre, which is expected to grow to a staff of 950 people, and Fidelity Investment's Technology Centre, which will employ 400 people at full production.

Aircraft Leasing

The number of aircraft leasing companies based in Ireland is now approximately 30. Among the notable new arrivals in 1996 were Kanematsu and Nichimen which joined their other Japanese colleagues such as Sumitomo, Nissho Iwai, Orix and Ryoshin. There has been plenty of leasing activity in recent months. Airbus Finance Company launched a successful commercial paper issue in the USA, restructured its term facility, acquired two A320 aircraft on lease to Mexicana and is hoping to acquire eleven new aircraft this year. Airbus Industries Financial Services acquired two new Beluga aircraft and established Irish joint venture companies with Iberia to finance four new A340s under Japanese leveraged leases.

Banking Sector

The banking sector at the International Financial Services Centre has been at the core of the centre's spectacular development. Most of the world's major international banks, as well as the principal Irish banking institutions, have established offices at the IFSC, which they have found to be an exceptionally profitable location from which to conduct their international activities. The IFSC has now developed as a leading global offshore location for activities such as asset financing/leasing, international banking and loan syndications, bank treasury operations, mutual fund management and administration, bond and commercial paper issuance, back office operations and management of client treasury functions.

- **Banking sector companies** operating in the IFSC include: ABN Amro, AIB Bank, Ansbacher, Bacob, Banco San Paolo, Bankinter, Bank of Liechtenstein, Bank of America, Bank of Bermuda, Bank of Ireland, Baring Brothers, BCI, BNP, Brown Brothers Harriman, Chase Manhattan, Chemical Bank, Citibank, Clydesdale Bank, Commerzbank, Credito Italiano, Daiwa, Deutsche Bank, Dresdner Bank, Generale Bank, Heleba, ICC, ING, Investors Bank & Trust, Kredietbank, MeesPierson, Mellon Bank, Merrill Lynch, Midland Bank, Mitsubishi Trust & Bank, Morgan Grenfell, National Irish Bank, Natwest, Paribas, PNC, Rabobank, Royal Bank of Scotland, Sanwa, Scotiabank, Sumitomo, Ulster Bank, West LB, Wuerttembuergische.

Mutual Funds

Since 1990 when the International Financial Services Centre was first opened to the mutual funds industry, the IFSC has emerged as one of Europe's leading offshore locations for the sector.

- **Mutual funds operations** include: ABN Amro, AIB, Banco Santander, Bank of Bermuda, Bank of Ireland, Bankers Trust, Baring Brothers, Brown Brothers Harriman, Citibank NA, Chase Manhattan, Chemical Bank, Commerzbank, Clydesdale, Daiwa Europe Bank, Deutsche Bank, Dresdner/Thornton, Dunedin Fund Managers, Gaiacorp, GAM Fund Management, Gandon Securities, FG Gestion, Global Fund Services, GT Asset Management, Hambros Bank, John Hancock, Henderson Crosthwaithe, IBT Trust & Custodial, Kemper, Kleinwort Benson, Lucky Securities, MeesPierson Fund Services, Mercury Asset Management, Merrill Lynch, Mitsubishi T&B, Morgan Grenfell, Natwest, Paribas, Pioneer Financial Services, PFPC, Premier Administration, R&H City Financial Ltd, Royal Bank of Scotland plc, Frank Russell, Salomon, Scottish Mutual, Smith Barney Shearson, Société Generale, Swiss Bank Corporation, Swiss Life, Ulster Bank.

Insurance Sector

The insurance sector provides one of the most important activities at the IFSC; activities include direct writing of insurance, life assurance, captive insurance management and international broking.

- **Insurance sector operations** in the IFSC are: Aachen, AIG, Alcan, Alexander & Alexander, All Nippon Airways, AON, BFC Insurance, BMW, Centre Reinsurance, Chubb Corp, Church & General, Coca-Cola, Codan Reinsurance, Cologne Reinsurance, Colonia, Coyle Hamilton, Eagle Star, Ericsson, Eurco Reinsurance, FBD, Hannover Reinsurance, Hansard, Hibernian, Interpolis, Irish Life, IRMG, London Life, McDonagh & Boland, Marsh & McLennan, Nat West Reinsurance, Old Mutual, J Rothschild International, Scottish Amicable, Scottish Mutual, Sedgwick, Sinser, Thomas Howell, Unison, Willis Corroon, Winterthur, XL Europe, Zurich.

Corporate Treasuries

The management of corporate treasuries is one of the most active sectors at the IFSC. Over 200 major international companies use the IFSC as a centre for global treasury activities such as inter-group lending/leasing, exchange and interest rate risk management, active management of group liquidity and the provision of sales aid financing.

• **Corporate treasury operations** in the IFSC are: Aer Lingus, AIG Financial Products, Airbus Industries, Analog Devices, Barlo Group, BCL Entertainment Corp, Black & Decker, British Land, Cadbury, Consolidated Press Holdings, CRH plc, Danisco, Ericsson, ESB, Gelderse Papiergroep, General Electric, Grafton Group, Grand Metropolitan, Guinness, Heinz, Hewlett-Packard, IBM Corporation, ITI, Kofisca Trading Co, Nutricia, Pfizer, Porsche, Securitas, Smurfit, Volkswagen.

INTERNATIONAL SERVICES

Dubbed "Europe's back office" by *The Economist* earlier in 1997, Ireland is the top location in Europe for companies which provide **telemarketing**, **customer support** and **technical services** through call centres. In just two years, Ireland has emerged as the undisputed leader in the field of European call centres. In that time, over 40 major companies have chosen Ireland as the base for their new European call centres.

The availability of well-educated and highly skilled young staff, language skills, competitively priced state-of-the-art telecommunications and generous tax incentives have made Ireland the preferred location for companies engaged in international services. These range from software development and production, multimedia and film to data processing, shared services, information services, laboratory and testing services.

As the number of organisations providing international services in software, teleservices and back office administration has mushroomed beyond all expectations, so too has the demand for skilled workers and a number of third-level courses have been developed at PLCs and other colleges to provide training for these areas. Applicants with excellent European language skills, including native speakers, are eagerly sought by all the companies operating in this sector and there is a lot of flexibility for those who want to work part-time.

Ireland can also boast the title "capital of Europe" for **software localisation and production**. Five of the world's top ten independent software companies have major operations in Ireland and today over 40 per cent of all PC package software and 60 per cent of business application software sold in Europe is produced here.

Recently Compaq, the world's largest PC maker, announced it was establishing a major multi-lingual European Care Centre in Dublin. This follows the influx of other pan-European service centres of leading Fortune 500 companies such as Merrill Lynch, Bankers Trust, AIG Insurance, Whirlpool and Becton Dickinson. Compaq's announcement means that four out of the world's top five PC manufacturers will have operations in Ireland. Also included in this list are: IBM (which some months ago announced a US$350 million investment in a 100-acre technology campus); Apple (manufacturing and related software); Hewlett-Packard (which in the latter part of 1996 announced a further investment of just under US$350 million investment in its inkjet manufacturing plant). Other major PC manufacturing companies here include Dell and Gateway, which also combine sales and support with their large manufacturing plants.

SAP, Germany's largest software company, has recently announced it is also setting up a Service and Support Centre in Dublin. The company's enterprise-wide solutions are used by seven out of the top 10 Fortune 500 companies.

- **International services operations**: Aldus, Andersen Consulting, Bankers Trust, Best Western, Cambridge Technology, CIGNA, Claris, Corel, DataEase, EDS, Funcom Dublin Ltd, Filenet, Gateway 2000, GFT Software, Global Reservations, Great-West Life Assurance, Hitachi, Hoskyns, IBM, Informix Software, ISOCOR, ITT Sheraton, KAO Corporation, Korean

Air, Lotus, Mass Mutual, McGraw-Hill, Microsoft, Murakami Wolf, New York Life, Novell, Oracle, Platinum Software, Point Info Systems, Quintiles, Radisson Hotels, Rand McNally, Software Spectrum, Symantec, UPS, Whirlpool, HW Wilson.

ENTERPRISE

Indigenous Irish enterprises continue to experience tremendous growth and their contribution to the success of the economy in recent years is finally being recognised. While the biggest success stories must be Esat Telecom and Iona Technologies, many more share the same entrepreneurial spirit. Between 1995 and 1997, small firms alone created almost 130,000 new jobs and it is estimated that an additional 100,000 will be created in the remaining two years before the new millennium.

In October 1997, Enterprise Ireland, an exhibition of more than 300 indigenous companies, attracted huge attendance amid estimates that up to 5,000 new small businesses might be founded as a result. Almost 40 per cent of all new businesses in 1997 were created by women. In total, some 16,000 new businesses were registered in 1997 alone, with job creation at around 50,000 for the year.

There are positive signs of enterprise and moves to fostering a more creative workforce in every sector. In some companies, all employees are encouraged to sell the company's products in some way, even if they are not part of the sales team. In the state-controlled broadcasting organisation, RTE, a prize fund of more than £50,000 has been allocated to reward suggestions from staff on how to grow the business or cut costs. Where an idea can be exploited commercially, the person who suggested it will be treated as a partner in the venture, irrespective of their usual role. Where an idea results in an on-going saving or the generation of on-going income, the suggester will be entitled to 10 per cent of the net amount saved or generated for three years, up to £10,000 per annum.

There is plenty happening too for young entrepreneurs. The Irish Times/Business 2000 Factfile is a free multi-media resource pack that links into the new school business curriculum. It provides profiles and other relevant information about 32 leading Irish and multinational companies as well as a reduced-price edition of the newspaper and a special helpdesk for teachers to contact. Numerous transition-year students at second level have already achieved success with business projects.

Recognising that tomorrow's entrepreneurs often find school dull because they are already ahead or are susceptible to bullying as a result of their abilities, Dublin City University's Centre for Talented Youth, Ireland, runs Saturday and summer courses in Dublin, Limerick and Cork for exceptionally talented young people. The centre's work is ahead of that in other European countries, many of whom are studying it to see how they can emulate its success.

At third level, the Graduate Enterprise Programme is a one-year incubation programme designed to provide business development and financial support to third-level graduates keen to start their own businesses. A joint initiative between Forbairt, local third-level colleges and other development organisations, the programme provides finance, business training and facilities to participants while they are researching their business ideas and developing them into business plans. The programmes run for twelve months; during that time, each participant is assigned an individual mentor to assist them with market research and prototype development. A key feature is that participants who cease employment to join the programme receive 50 per cent of their salary throughout, to a maximum of £15,000. Applications from returning emigrants are welcome, and further information is available from Forbairt's web page at www.forbairt.ie.

For more than 30 years, the Young Scientists' Exhibition has been one of the few opportunities for young people to showcase their innovation in the field of science and technology. Sponsored by Aer Lingus for 33 years and by Esat Telecom since May 1997, more than 23,000 young people, often working in teams, have displayed their projects to more than half a million visitors. Many of the winners have gone on to win prizes in European young scientist competitions.

TRAINING

As the economy has flourished, the demand for training has become much more sophisticated. There has been a noticeable, significant shift in the approach to training of many indigenous and multinational companies. In line with the move towards working in teams, there is a prevailing acceptance of the value of the individual and a recognition that the knowledge and skills of each individual employee has a direct impact on the achievement of company goals. The RTE example given above illustrates this point very well. When it comes to training, crude measurements of training activity are no longer enough. Companies focused on achieving competitive advantage are demanding a much greater level of sophistication and a different, more innovative approach. Much of this is driven by the pace of change in technology and the need to deal with change as a fact of life in modern business.

In addition to the question of identifying what skills and knowledge employees require in order to meet business goals, the priorities of training decision-makers include determining whether those skills are present and whether training is having any impact. Added to these are the challenges of providing training that enables participants to sustain knowledge in a changing environment, and doing so cost-effectively.

Training is of particular importance to companies in start-up phase and to those experiencing major organisational or cultural change. Further, human resources departments face pressure to produce results in training with sustainable benefits. While there is always the option of using one-dimensional measurements of training success — for example, number of people trained, cost per head and course satisfaction level — an increasing number of companies believe the solution lies in the application of technology to training.

In conjunction with its sister company, Octagon Technologies, which specialises in multimedia and web technology, the Computer Training Institute is breaking new ground in developing training tools and methodologies that enable client companies to develop skill-based job profiles which are linked to business processes. Individual performance is assessed against those profiles using on-line testing systems that are linked to specific, interactive, desktop-delivered training modules for the skills required.

Needless to say, the appeal to companies of sustaining the skills and effort invested in major training programmes is considerable. Among those which have worked with CTI and Octagon are: Hewlett-Packard (the development of a specialised IT induction training programme); Citibank (a major skills transfer from London to Dublin); Bord Fáilte (introduction of a nation-wide reservations system); Leo Laboratories (implementation of a major business planning system); and Elan Corporation (development of sustainable training programmes for SAP and other programmes).

Meanwhile, Irish Times Training reports a heavy demand for training in customer care skills. It has noticed a trend among its client companies to train employees in a wider range of skills regardless of their actual job function; for example, training courses in presentation skills and finance training for non-financial managers are very much in demand. Courses and workshops on managing people are their bestsellers.

The success of Galway-based Outdoor Innovations reflects the continuing demand for the skills needed in teamwork environments. Tailor-made residential courses with a significant outdoor team component in some of the beautiful parts of Ireland follow a company-specific needs analysis that involves the participants as well as their managers. This is indicative of a more focused approach to selecting training and an increased emphasis on achieving measurable results. Outdoor Innovations reports a marked increase in market share among multinationals, financial institutions and up-and-coming indigenous Irish companies that have dealings with business partners overseas.

Training initiatives are not restricted to private companies. In direct response to the needs of companies in the electronics sector, the Regional Technical College, Tallaght, under the EU-funded NOW (New Opportunities for Women) employment initiative 1996–1997 ran "Women in Electronics" (WIE) — a technical and personal skills training project designed to meet the needs of individual companies. The programme had two aims: to provide unemployed women with access to training and education with a view to getting jobs in the electronics sector (the Hewlett-Packard, Motorola and City of Dublin VEC programmes), and to provide a vehicle for people already working in the industry to access technical and personal development skills courses to help them progress within their organisations (the NEC and Intel programmes).

The success rate of those women who were unemployed has been high, with 95 per cent now working in a range of companies, including Motorola, Hewlett-Packard, Gateway 2000, 3Com, Applied Magnetics and Fujitsu Isotec.

Whilst much of the focus of the WIE project has been on training, the project is involved in other activities, including targeting senior management levels in the industry and working with training and employment organisations in France, the UK, Germany and the Netherlands as overseas partners. However, the co-operation with Plunket College has been one of the most significant successes of the project. This is shown by the decision of Plunket College and City of Dublin VEC to run a full-time electronics course from September 1997, based on the activities and lessons learned from the NOW project. This is a measure of how EU-funded programmes succeed, when pilot programmes such as Women in Electronics become mainstream training programmes, living on after the project has finished.

There is good news too on training for people with disabilities. To focus on just one organisation, the National Association for the Deaf has successfully campaigned for better facilities for the hard-of-hearing. Its achievements include the development of a Deaf-tech Resource Centre with interactive displays of adapted domestic equipment, News for the Deaf on national television, the establishment of Ahead (Association for Higher Education and Disability), job clubs with a high success rate and a wide range of training courses. These include courses for sign language interpreters and a new course to train teachers in lip-reading.

CONSTRUCTION INDUSTRY

The Irish construction industry has had a record-breaking year in 1997, and not before time, since the last real peak was in 1981. According to a report published by the Department of the Environment and Local Government, the value of output from this sector is expected to grow by 14 per cent to IR£7 billion (it grew by 23 per cent in 1996). The sector has experienced steady growth for the past couple of years and grew by 50 per cent between 1994 and 1996. Predictions are positive well into the next century.

The booming new housing sector is expected to account for more than half of the output from this sector in 1997, with infrastructural projects such as roads, airports and water treatment facilities accounting for another 20 per cent. Luas (the planned cross-Dublin rail service — possibly underground), the Northern Port Access Route, a new peat-fired power station, and possibly the Southern Cross Route are among the larger scale projects. According to the Department of the Environment and Local Government, investment in tourism projects is expected to decline from IR£238 million in 1996 to IR£207 million in 1997. After four years of steady increases, investment in agriculture is expected to fall from IR£299 million in 1996 to IR£246 million this year.

Despite the slow-down in some sectors, the overall boom in building is obviously good news for construction workers. While FÁS has set up an operation in the UK to entice Irish builders home, messages about the opportunities in this sector have gone out on the airways as far away as Australia. Those who do return should observe an increase in health and safety measures on construction sites as the provisions of the 1989 Safety, Health and

Welfare Act are ever more vigorously enforced, though it is acknowledged that the rate of accidents is still too high.

Many of the big construction companies do not hire directly, but work with sub-contractors. You will find details of agencies that deal with these in Chapter 2, **How to Find a Job**. Otherwise, contact the main companies and ask them which sub-contractors they use; also, refer to employment opportunities with John Sisk and Son Ltd., detailed in **Who's Recruiting Now**.

CONSUMER PRODUCTS

Although growth in this sector has waned compared to others, many international companies have taken advantage of Ireland's competitive cost and skill base for their own consumer product activities. In addition, Ireland's reputation for craftsmanship and attention to detail continues to withstand increasing competition, and Waterford Glass and other such companies continue to perform well. Success has come at a price, however; for example, Waterford Glass has exported production of certain new ranges to Eastern Europe, whilst Farah closed one of its plants in 1997, with the loss of 150 jobs.

- **Consumer products**: AT Cross, Asahi, Avon Products, Bose, Braun, Coca Cola, Farah, Fruit of the Loom, Giro Sport Design, Glen Dimplex, Hallmark Cards, Hanro, Hartman, Hasbro, Heinz, Huber Tricot, Huffy, Krups, Lowe Alpine, Moulinex, Noritake, Oriflame, Penn Athletic, Procter & Gamble, Rubbermaid, Saehan Media, Schiesser, Sea Ray Boats, Shopvac, Sram, Tarkett, Tretorn, Unifi, Waterford Glass, Yves Rocher.

TELECOMMUNICATIONS

Top quality telecommunications infrastructure is obviously a major consideration for new and expanding businesses. Returning emigrants to Ireland who have been away for more than a couple of years will find a vastly changed communications landscape.

Gone are the days of reliance on a single provider and waiting months for new telephone connections, thanks to competition. In 1994, two new telecommunications companies were started by Irish entrepreneurs to provide international and long-distance inland services to corporate customers. TCL, recently taken over by US telecommunications giant WorldCom, has about 700 customers, while Esat Telecom has almost 3,000.

There followed several years of battles between the new operators and Telecom Eireann, mainly concerning regulatory issues, and all sides welcomed the appointment of a Telecommunications Regulator in 1997.

With the corporate market already deregulated, and full deregulation looming by the year 2000, one of State-controlled Telecom Eireann's advantages has been that it has greater access to funds. TCL's takeover by Worldcom, and Esat Telecom's application for a listing on both the Nasdaq (the US Stock Exchange for small companies) and its European equivalent the Easdaq, following a successful bond issue in the US earlier in 1997, will put greater pressure on Telecom Eireann. Following a major review of its strategy in 1995, the latter has been under constant pressure to lower prices and costs and grow the volume of its business.

Over the past two years, mobile phone use has increased more than three-fold, bringing mobile use in Ireland to 9 per cent of the population — though it seems like more. Ireland also has the highest use of voice-mail in Europe, an indication of how ready the Irish marketplace is to adapt to new ways of using telecommunications technology. There is plenty of scope for competition too in the domestic market — with 81 telephone lines per 100 households, Ireland is presently well below the EU average.

Although Telecom Eireann's competitors guarantee lower costs, having to use the TE infrastructure network adds significantly to costs, something both TCL and Esat are in the process of changing. While Telecom Eireann is focusing on its Information Age Town, Esat Telecom is forging ahead with its own Information Highway — Ireland's first ever independent optic fibre network — using CIE's national rail network. The infrastructure, laid underground, is expected to be operational in the first quarter of 1998.

Competition has been good for Telecom Eireann's quality of service. New customers are connected, on average, within 10 days; the target is to bring this down to five days; all but three per cent of service faults are cleared within two working days; and all but five per cent of the country's 7,200 payphones are working at any given time. TE's challenge now is to try to minimise industrial unrest as it negotiates with unions on changed work practices. Current talks centre on selling some 15 per cent of the company to the employees, although TE's right to do so is contested by KPN/Telia, a Dutch/Swedish consortium that bought 20 per cent of Telecom Eireann in 1996. In any event, the Communications Workers Union — linked to the Teamsters in the States — do not want to pay cash for the shares. According to Telecom Eireann's annual report to April 1997, it must cut its payroll costs by a third over the next five years. Interesting times ahead.

AND THE REST . . .

With an economic boom in full steam, there are obviously opportunities in just about every sector. However, job seekers with no skills or training may not find immediate openings and should register at once with FÁS for training, particularly for computer skills. Overall, demand is high, and some small companies experience difficulties in attracting staff. A survey released by the Irish Small and Medium-Sized Enterprises Association (ISME) in September 1997 showed that 37 per cent of small or medium enterprises and 33 per cent of multinationals were experiencing labour shortages. In one of her last public addresses as President, Mary Robinson urged small companies to support more women in the workforce as a way of addressing these shortages.

In response to the growing concerns of employers, the Irish Business and Employers' Confederation (IBEC) piloted a survey in relation to filling vacancies in its West Region in April 1997.

A total of 57 per cent of companies surveyed reported recruitment difficulties. Non-exporting indigenous, distribution and service companies tended to be most concerned with recruitment difficulties. More than four out of 10 (41 per cent) ranked the tax and social welfare systems as the greatest areas of difficulty, indicating that they are by far the most important problems facing firms when recruiting employees. One in four (25 per cent) described "lack of skills" as the main problem.

Opticians with small practices, particularly in rural areas, face tough competition in attracting staff, as the big ophthalmic groups such as Vision Express can afford to pay very well.

The focus on **Education** is exemplified by the success of the Formative Fun educational advice centre in Dublin, which provides parents with advice on a huge range of educational toys. A brand new company, Forward Education and Training, will take a similar concept, including a Christmas club, right around the country from January 1998 with its advisors available to visit parents and schools in the most remote locations. See **Who's Recruiting Now** for details.

Nurses will always find work, despite the ongoing consolidation of hospitals around the country. As a consequence of a strike by nurses earlier in 1997, they may initially find themselves being offered temporary contracts. Nurses who qualified outside of Ireland are required to sit an examination and should contact An Bord Altranais (http://www.nursing-board.ie) for more details.

Nursing continues to be an extremely popular option, particularly with female applicants, and more than 5,000 people competed for just 900 places in 1997. The traditional on-the-job training for nurses has been enhanced by a stronger academic element through association with third-level colleges. There are currently 17 schools of general nursing, each one of which is associated with a third-level college. There are also six psychiatric hospitals and two schools of mental handicap nursing, all of which are associated with colleges. The general nursing schools and associated colleges are:

• Adelaide Hospital, Dublin and Trinity College, Dublin

- Beaumont Hospital and Dublin City University

- Bon Secours Hospital, Cork and University College Cork

- Cork Voluntary Hospitals, Mercy Hospital, Cork and University College Cork

- James Connolly Memorial Hospital, Dublin and Dublin City University

- Letterkenny General Hospital, County Donegal and Letterkenny RTC

- Regional Hospital, Limerick and University of Limerick

- Mater Misericordiae Hospital Dublin and University College Dublin

- Meath Hospital, Dublin and Trinity College, Dublin

- Our Lady of Lourdes Hospital, Drogheda and Dundalk RTC

- Portiuncula Hospital, Mayo and University College Galway

- St James' Hospital Dublin and Trinity College, Dublin

- St. Vincent's Hospital Dublin and University College Dublin

- Sligo General Hospital and University College Galway

- University College Hospital Cork and University College Cork

- University College Hospital Galway and University College Galway

- Waterford Regional Hospital and Waterford Institute of Technology

Teachers should benefit from additional funding in education. European language skills and computer expertise will help, though it should be noted that the academic standards required for third level have rocketed. Anecdotal evidence suggests that a PhD is required for any permanent teaching post in certain of the RTCs and above, though persistence has been known to pay off.

Anyone seeking employment in this sector should ensure that they network extensively in advance of positions being advertised and look for opportunities to publish work if they can.

Accountants, too, have reason to be pleased. Following less buoyant times in the early 1990s, when the "Big Six" accountancy firms let go a number of young, newly qualified accountants both in Ireland and the UK, young accountants can now pick and choose. However, a recent newspaper report suggests that this is the case for those in their 20s or early 30s only, quoting the Institute of Chartered Accountants in Ireland as saying the cut-off age is 34, due to a perception among recruiters that older accountants may not be willing to move to a junior or less-well paid position.

Meanwhile, the **legal profession** has less reason to rejoice, due to the high number of solicitors without work. Despite abundant media coverage about lawyers' earnings, particularly in the wake of various tribunals in the past couple of years, the Incorporated Law Society has warned that there are far too many lawyers for the available jobs. Those hoping for a windfall from divorce cases will have to wait a little longer, as relatively few divorce applications have been made since it became an option on 27 February 1997. Some reports attribute the slow uptake to the cost — around £2,000 a time is quoted — and suggest that, having waited for so long already, many will hold out a little longer until they can afford it more easily.

The **charity sector**, whilst not booming, continues to maintain a significant presence in Ireland, despite competition from the National Lottery for people's spare cash. The 10 largest charities take in over IR£80 million per annum, 43 per cent of which comes from bequests and direct public donations. This sector is likely to win media coverage following pressure from the charities themselves for regulatory legislation. The 10 largest charities are: Concern, St. Vincent de Paul, Trocaire, Cerebral Palsy Ireland, Goal, People in Need, Irish Cancer Society, Oxfam, ISPCC and Barnardo's.

Tourism has not enjoyed a great 1997, with various reasons being given. Whether the disappointing weather, problems in Northern Ireland or Bord Fáilte's decision to dispense with the shamrock in marketing Ireland abroad in 1997 are to blame, the numbers are thought to be slightly down in 1997 from the £1.45 billion generated in 1996, the fifth successive year of growth.

Duty-free shopping, or more specifically, the European Commission's plans to abolish it, is a current talking point. An industry that supports 140,000 jobs within the EU and sources some 80 per cent of its products from EU manufacturers, duty-free shopping accounts for some 40 per cent of Aer Rianta's profits. Apart from the huge job losses that its abolition would cause, analysts point out that airport management companies will simply make up the financial losses by charging more for other items, such as airline service charges and car parking. It will be interesting to see whether the counter-argument that duty-free shopping facilitates the free movement of people within the EU by offering lower travel costs will prevail in the end.

Higher disposable incomes, more women in the workforce, more single/two-person households, greater commuting and work/leisure-related travel are the factors contributing to the medium-term growth in the **food service industry**, according to a report produced by Newfocus Ltd. on behalf of An Bord Bia and the IBEC/CBI Business Development Programme.

The report, *The Irish Food Service Market — An All-Island Profile*, details a market with significant growth potential, founded on underlying social and lifestyle patterns, which add weight to the belief that the growth of dining out is a long-term trend. The food service market is valued at approximately £1.6 billion north and south and represents 3 per cent of the combined GDP of both the Republic of Ireland and Northern Ireland.

Recruitment for the **Civil Service, Garda Síochána** and the **Armed Forces** is administered by the Civil Service Commission. Opportunities in all of these areas are heavily oversubscribed. However, the screening process is designed to be as fair as possible, so it is worth applying.

In May 1997, the Minister for Justice announced the recruitment of an additional 1,000 gardaí before the year 2000. At the same time, changes in the required educational requirements were announced and the two new Leaving Certificate programmes — Leaving Certificate Applied and Leaving Certificate Vocational — will now be accepted for entry. For the first time, foundation level English and Maths are also acceptable. Although there are ten times as many applications as there are places, a new selection process, which includes a written test and an interview, means that all applicants should have an equal chance.

Although just over eight per cent of gardaí are female, the number of women applying is on the increase. The range of skills training open to gardaí has also expanded. New recruits will have the opportunity to learn French and German, will receive training in broadcasting skills to enable them to promote new road safety programmes on local radio and, although there are currently no plans to train garda pilots, a lucky few may end up working on board the new garda helicopter which is part of the Garda/Air Corps Support Unit established to carry out surveillance. The surveillance equipment includes the latest thermal imaging technology, which works by tracking body heat and makes it possible to track suspects in dense wooded areas from the air.

The defence forces take on cadets, apprentices and recruits. Cadetships are scare and in high demand. There were just 46 places in 1997 — 24 in the army, two in the Equitation School, 10 in the Air Corps and 10 in the Navy.

Politics attracted more attention than many sectors in 1997 thanks to the General Election, which threw up many surprises with seat losses — notably among women — including at ministerial level, and a high number of first-time winners.

Teaching English as a foreign language is worth some £150 million a year to Ireland. The Marketing English in Ireland Co-operative represents 42 schools, mostly in Dublin. Some schools are purpose-built, others are part of a larger enterprise such as Dublin City University. In addition, Berlitz is known globally for its language teaching and is planning to make cultural orientation courses available in 1998. If you have fluency in another language, together with experience in teaching English, then these schools are a potential source of employment.

OUTLOOK FOR THE FUTURE

By any standards, Ireland's economy continues to experience exceptionally strong growth, and with the average rate of increase in GNP over the last three years at a phenomenal seven per cent, positive forecasts for the future appear well-founded. European credit-rating agency IBCA has recently confirmed Ireland's long-term foreign currency rating of AA+, pointing to rapid growth, low inflation, a substantial surplus on the balance of payments, fiscal restraint and a reliable supply of skilled labour as reasons for the high rating.

Up to September 1997, IDA-supported companies were creating more than 1,100 jobs a month and this looks set to continue. Many of these jobs were announced between two-and-a-half years and six months previously. The Department of Finance is forecasting a 45,000 overall increase in jobs in the 1997 calendar year, following a 50,000 increase in 1996. Its forecast is for a further increase of 37,000 in 1998 and 32,000 in 1999.

The Government recently announced a single rate of corporation tax of 12.5 per cent for all companies. The new tax regime will become effective from the beginning of the year 2001 for companies availing of the 10 per cent manufacturing rate of corporation tax, and from the year 2006 for all other companies including IFSC companies.

Even greater links between industry and education are being encouraged. Examples such as the National Microelectronics Research Centre (which is affiliated to University College, Cork, and serves the international semiconductor industry in such key areas as IC design, R&D and testing) and the excellent partnership between the Department of Education, various private companies in the international services sector and the post leaving certificate (PLC) colleges in devising a new two-year training course for the telemarketing sector (which will accommodate 690 students in its first year alone) will become more prevalent. As education and training are recognised as the key areas to be nurtured to ensure that Ireland protects its economic gains of the past decade, expect to see a lot more attention focused on strengthening already strong links, as representatives from education, industry and government establish sustained programmes of investment in training to prevent missed job opportunities.

The Irish Trade Board is expanding its traditional role (providing support services and financial incentives to Irish companies) by dedicating more than half of its resources to building partnerships with procurement teams in overseas multinational companies, with the aim of winning IR£2 billion worth of orders. In September 1997, the Irish Trade Board launched a new *Irish Sourcing Guide* containing economic summary sheets and profiles of potential suppliers, drawn from a database of more than 1,000 Irish companies. Irish exports totalled IR£30 billion in 1996 and are on target for a second successive year of 9 per cent growth.

As the economy continues to prosper, decentralisation of industry to regional locations will certainly be more pronounced. The civil service started this trend more than 10 years ago, and it is now reflected across many sectors. An industry that did not really exist in Ireland 10 years ago — the teleservices sector — will play an important role in this. Nobody should be surprised if, within two or three years, small telecentres are being built and filled in many corners of rural Ireland. At the current rate of progress, in a year's time Ennis's forays into technology will have been matched by many new initiatives. The latest proposal is an ambitious IR£1.6 billion plan to transform the Docklands area of Dublin into a vibrant new community with up to 40,000 new jobs created and an extra 25,000 people making their homes there. It too will have a major technological theme — its Technopole technology park will be located on the so-called Poolbeg Peninsula.

Chapter 2

How to Find a Job

Despite the healthy number of jobs available, accessing the labour market can be frustrating if you are not already in the country. Although there is quite a bit of detail available on the Internet, being remotely located from Ireland can make it difficult to know whether you are seeing the full picture. This chapter provides a guide through the maze and, combined with the details in the next chapter of leading companies recruiting now and throughout 1998, hopefully will lead you well down the path to finding a job.

YOUR CURRICULUM VITAE

Normally life is too busy to allow much time to reflect on the way our lives and careers are progressing and whether their direction is the one we want. Since you will probably need a new source of income once you move to Ireland, this could be a good opportunity to evaluate how you would like to make a living. It is worth giving this a lot of thought since, whatever you decide, your preparation will form the basis of your job search in Ireland.

Some commentators maintain that the best approach to finding a new job or changing career direction or location is to imagine that you are making a documentary of your own life (or even imagine you had to write your own obituary!). What were the highlights for you personally, what did you enjoy the most, what have you learned and what should you highlight to interest others in buying your services to gain some of what you have to offer? Using this approach will help you to focus on the type of work you enjoy and, more importantly, will highlight what transferable skills you have.

Having noted what your skills, experience and achievements are, the next thing you need to do is tailor your application to suit the Irish market; in other words, get your Curriculum Vitae (CV) into shape. There are significant differences in what is expected between different countries. For example, in Germany, a *Lebenslauf* is literally the story of the applicant's life, while in the US a résumé is a one-page summary of key points. A résumé-style CV is fine in Ireland too; lengthy scripts are definitely out.

The purpose of your CV is to sell yourself to the reader in order to get an interview, so you will need to change it, depending on the position on offer. Usually, the first person to receive your CV will be a Human Resources (Personnel) professional. That is, if you are lucky! Many companies, particularly large multinationals, use scanning technology to read your CV and then search for key words. In either case, the simpler you make the task for the reader, the better chance you have of getting their attention. Some key points to remember are:

- **Format**: Although not all companies use optical scanning technology to read and correctly categorise your CV, many do, so it is best to prepare for that. You should use standard-size paper, clearly printed and not folded — use staples or binding. Avoid using bold type, different fonts, italics, graphics or more than one column, and list telephone numbers on a separate line. It may not look as nice as a dressed up CV; however, use of these systems means that your details are easily accessible for future vacancies as well.

- **Content**: Keep it short — three pages absolute maximum. You want to give the reader key, relevant information, not bore them or keep them guessing. Start with your personal details. Do not include your martial status or details about your family. Irish recruiters do like to see your date of birth, although you probably will not be asked this at interview. Include an Irish contact address or telephone number if you can. Personal details should only take a few lines. Put your current or most recent job first and list the previous jobs in reverse chronological order. Be brief but informative.

- **Language**: Use key words to describe your experience. There is no need to use full sentences; however, do use action words. Examples are: *achieved, analysed, budgeted, built, co-ordinated, created, designed, developed, established, formulated, generated, highlighted, increased, initiated, joined, led, motivated, negotiated, organised, planned, recommended, saved, sold, trained, utilised, vitalised, wrote*. Words that imply teamwork are a must: *collaborated, contributed, group, participated, project, team, worked with*. While it is not the most important point, do try to keep your syntax and spelling similar to that used in Ireland.

FINDING WHERE THE JOBS ARE

Once your CV is ready, the next step is to check out available opportunities and to advertise your availability. Unlike in some other countries — for example, the US, where the job market is regionalised — the best recruiters in Ireland take a long-term view and realise that it makes sense to spread an awareness of their opportunities as widely as possible. Accordingly, even if you see details of an opportunity that does not apply to you now, follow up with your details for possible subsequent openings. Recruiters can maintain a much healthier cost-per-hire figure by following up on speculative applications, and they do so consistently.

JOB ADVERTISEMENTS

Job opportunities are advertised in *The Irish Times* Business Supplement every Friday (available on the Internet on http://www.irish-times.com), *The Irish Independent* every Thursday and in *The Sunday Independent*. *The Sunday Business Post* is also an excellent guide to what is happening in industry in Ireland and can provide valuable leads for the job search. The IE Professional (see below) is also well worth consideration and is becoming increasingly popular with employers. *Job News* is a weekly publication. Try local newspapers if you have someone to send them to you.

THE INTERNET

There are several Irish job advertisement services on the Internet, the principal ones being The Appointments Page and the IE Professional. All of the services carry details of job vacancies with a variety of employers, with no charge to the applicant. The Appointments Page offers an additional free service to jobseekers. You can create a skills profile based on a series of prompts (name, e-mail address, core skills, experience) which then enables you to search for matching vacancies. Employers only receive your details if you contact them directly.

In addition to the websites of the companies listed in **Who's Recruiting Now**, and employment specialists listed later in this chapter, the following sites are worth a visit:

- The Appointments Page: http://tap.gtc.ie/tap
- IE Professional and Irish Emigrant: E-mail iepro@iol.ie for details
- http://www.topjobs.ie
- http://www.jobfinder.ie
- http://www.exp.ie

AGENCIES

Bear in mind that a significant volume of recruitment is carried out using employment agencies, and it is essential that you find out which of these best caters for your particular skills set, meet them when you are next home and then keep in regular contact. Agencies charge the employer a percentage of the successful candidate's first year's salary. There is no fee for the applicant. You do not need to contact every agency. Meet as many as you can (you should send your CV first) and then decide which ones can sell you best. Keep in touch with your agencies regularly to remind them of your availability. Remember to check that the agency has a policy of contacting you prior to submitting your application to client companies.

EXECUTIVE SEARCH COMPANIES

These are not recruitment agencies, but charge a retainer fee to client companies to carry out the search and selection process, mainly of executives. Although they do occasionally advertise on behalf of clients, executive search companies tend to place more emphasis on getting to know their applicants and sourcing from an existing pool. Being put forward by a good executive search company is effectively a personal recommendation. Increasingly, the executive search firms are becoming involved in start-up situations, particularly Merc Partners and John Harty & Associates, so it is worth submitting your details. Professionals such as engineers and accountants aspiring to move into a managerial role should certainly contact these companies.

NETWORKING

Pyramid selling your availability to work can be effective. You should make anyone you know who may be able to help you aware that you are looking for a job in Ireland. You should not think of this as primarily a way of asking people for jobs, but as a means of identifying those who can provide information about the job market. These contacts need not be in the same industry sector or profession as you. The important thing is that they think of you when they come across opportunities that might suit you.

You should not hesitate to contact department heads or the human resources department of companies in which you are interested and ask for a 15-minute information interview. This is a way of obtaining an overview of future recruitment plans, and there is a good chance you will be remembered when a suitable vacancy does arise.

SPECULATIVE APPLICATION

It is well worth writing speculatively to companies which you know are expanding. Details of many with opportunities in 1998 are contained in the chapter **Who's Recruiting Now**. In addition, you should review trade journals and business publications, the business sections of the major papers (listed in Chapter 17, **Irish Culture**; many are on-line) and directories such as Kompass. You might also consider placing an advertisement in the classified section of *The Irish Times*.

FÁS/JOB CLUBS

You should register with your local FÁS office, as employers regularly use its free service to source employees. If you need assistance with interview skills/CV preparation, FÁS may also be able to help or will refer you to Obair, where trained staff work with you on your job search, or a job club, where participants meet weekly over a period of about six weeks to obtain training and motivate each other in finding employment.

Jobcare in Dublin actually send a team of recruiters to every household in the inner city and other areas of high unemployment and invite unemployed people to come to their open days. They run four-week long courses that aim to equip participants with the necessary job hunting skills. You do not have to have been long-term unemployed to be included, and Jobcare are interested in hearing from anyone who they may be able to help secure employment. Their success rate of 85 per cent speaks for itself.

HIGH SKILLS POOL AND EURES

Both of these initiatives are also supported by FÁS. The High Skills Pool aims to establish links with Irish graduates and professionals working overseas and to keep them up-to-date with business developments in Ireland. The High Skills Pool Jobs Fair at Christmas is a must for those considering a return to Ireland and generally takes place on 29 and 30 December in Dublin.

EURES, the European Employment Service, offers Irish people working in Europe the opportunity to access jobs throughout the EU.

RESPONSES

Most companies will respond to acknowledge your application fairly quickly. Do not be deterred if you receive a standardised reply. Follow up by telephone or e-mail and try to find a named contact. Unless you get an outright rejection, it is well worth keeping in contact with potential employers.

VOLUNTARY SECTOR

If you do not want to enter paid employment, but would like to work, there are literally dozens of organisations that need your help. Try within your local community, where various groups often advertise details of when they meet and the help they are seeking. Otherwise, *Hey You! A Guide to Voluntary Work Opportunities* (Wolfhound Press, currently out of print — try libraries) lists 94 voluntary organisations, the kind of help needed and the work you would be expected to do.

BUSINESS ETIQUETTE

For someone who has never worked in Ireland before or is returning after some time abroad, it can be useful to be aware of cultural differences in the way business is transacted. Some examples are:

- **Greetings**: Generally, business people in Ireland use first names from the initial meeting. Say your full name when introduced and always shake hands. The custom of shaking hands with regular colleagues is not really an Irish habit; however, in companies with a lot of other European staff, this does happen.

- **Titles**: If you are writing to someone, always take the time to check their title, for example, Mr or Ms (Miss is for pre-teens and Mrs for married women over 45), Dr, Prof., and so on. Irish women often retain their own surname when they marry, so it is best to continue to use it in addressing them until you are asked to do otherwise.

- **Formality**: Irish business practices often appear informal. For example, it is not unusual for people to turn up late for appointments or meetings and to behave very informally, right from the first meeting. However, to avoid making a faux pas, the best advice is for you to turn up on time and be friendly but businesslike. It is a common complaint of those who have contact professionally and socially with overseas nationals living in Ireland that, while appearing very outgoing — and socially, that is very true — Irish people are reluctant to voice their true concerns and complaints. This is usually a matter of politeness, and is something you will get used to in time. The better you get to know people, the less of an issue this will be.

Useful Contacts

Employment Agencies
Many of these companies have offices in addition to those listed, or may cover the whole country from one office. Check their websites for more information. The companies' specialisations (if any) are included in brackets after the address.

- Alfred Marks, 45 Grafton Street, Dublin 2. Tel: (01) 677 8348. Fax: (01) 677 8973.

- Atlas Sales, 14/15 St Andrew Street, Dublin 2. Tel: (01) 677 6477. Fax: (01) 677 6972. E-mail: atlas@iol.ie.

- Best Personnel, 5 Railway Road, Dalkey, County Dublin. Tel: (01) 235 0233. Fax: (01) 284 8433. (office staff).

- Butler Carolan, 3 Fitzwilliam Place, Dublin 2. Tel: (01) 676 2080. Fax: (01) 661 1026. (sales).

- Careers Register, 9 Anglesea Street, Dublin 2. Tel: (01) 679 8900. Fax: (01) 679 1970. E-mail: careers@iol.ie. (accountancy and financial).

- CMI Technical Recruitment, 43 Fitzwilliam Square, Dublin 2. Tel: (01) 676 5722. Fax: (01) 676 5774. E-mail: cmitechr@indigo.ie. (design and construction).

- Collins McNicholas Ltd., 3 Devon Place, The Crescent, Galway. Tel: (091) 585 358. Fax: (091) 581 758.

- Computer Placement, 83 Merrion Square, Dublin 2. Tel: (01) 614 6000. Fax: (01) 614 6011. E-mail: cpl@iol.ie. Website: http://www.cpl.ie.

- CSR Computer Staff, 27 Herbert Place, Dublin 2. Tel: (01) 662 0055 Fax: (01) 676 9953. Website: http://www.exp.ie/csr.html.

- Elan Computing, 70 Grafton Street, Dublin 2. Tel: (01) 670 5070 Fax: (01) 670 5080. E-mail: info@elaneire.demon.co.uk. Website: http://www.elan.co.uk.

- Engineering Appointments, 36 College Green, Dublin 2. Tel: (01) 609 8811. Fax: (01) 671 1615. E-mail: robert.ferrie@ppg.ie.

- Excel Recruitment, Limerick. Tel: (061) 410399 Fax: (061) 414128 E-mail: excelrecruitment.ie.

- Executive Connections, 1 The Mews, Merrion Place, Dublin 2. Tel: (01) 661 8740. Fax: (01) 661 8741. E-mail: info@executive-connections.ie. (financial and office).

- Firstaff, 85/86 Grafton Street, Dublin 2. Tel: (01) 679 7766. E-mail: Firstaff@iol.ie. Website: http://www.exp.ie/fstaff.html.

- Global Recruitment, Global House, Michael Street, Limerick. Tel: (061) 417263. (catering).

- Griffin Personnel, 11 Hume Street, Dublin 2. Tel: (01) 662 1548. Fax: (01) 661 8489. (office staff).

- Hays Montrose, 6 Dawson Street, Dublin 2. Tel: (01) 670 4844. Fax: (01) 670 4738. (construction/property).

- Headhunt, 68 Harcourt Street, Dublin 2. Tel: (01) 478 0222. Fax: (01) 478 1663.

- Henessey Recruitment, 47 O'Connell Street, Limerick. Tel: (061) 315511. E-mail: hrecruit@iol.ie.

- HRM Engineering, 2 Argyle Square, Morehampton Road, Dublin 4. Tel: (01) 667 1266. Fax: (01) 667 1276. E-mail: declan@hrm.ie.

- ICDS Recruitment consultants, 24 Upper Fitzwilliam Street, Dublin 2. Tel: (01) 676 1737. Fax: (01) 676 2079. E-mail: icds@iol.ie. (engineering).

- The IFSC Panel, 107 Lower Baggot Street, Dublin 2. Tel: (01) 661 4772. Fax: (01) 61 4959. (financial).

- IRC, 11 Ely Place, Dublin. Tel: (01) 6610644. Fax: (01) 6610648.

- JDR Recruitment, Executive House, National Technological Park, Limerick. Tel: (061) 332000. Fax: (061) 330322. E-mail: JDR@iol.ie.

- Kenny-Whelan Engineering, Rossdale House, Bishopstown, Cork. Tel: (021) 346100. Fax: (021) 346122. E-mail: kenny.whelan@indigo.ie.

- Key Personnel, 33 Dame Street, Dublin 2. Tel: (01) 671 4000. Fax: (01) 671 4244. (programmers and engineers).

- Marlborough, Marlborough House, 11–13 Tara Street, Dublin 2. Tel: (01) 677 7521. Fax: (01) 677 7546. E-mail: marlborough @iol.ie. Website: http://www.iol.ie/resource/margroup.

- Mary B. Cremin, 39 Fitzwilliam Place, Dublin 2. Tel: (01) 662 3000. Fax: (01) 662 8662. (secretarial).

- NRC, Dublin. Tel: (01) 676644. Fax: (01) 676 8662. E-mail: jobs@nrc.ie.

- The Recruitment Business, 27 Lower Mount Street, Dublin 2. Tel: (01) 676 3335. Fax: 676 3357. (financial).

- Richmond Recruitment Ltd., Rear Merchants House, Merchants Quay, Dublin 8. Tel: (01) 679 6266. Fax: (01) 679 6442. E-mail: richmond@indigo.ie.

- Rigney Dolphin Recruitment, 16 Parnell Street, Waterford. Tel: (051) 879312. Fax: (051) 852152.

- Skills Group, Skillbase House, 1 Lower Hatch Street, Dublin 2. Tel: (01) 662 3055. Fax: (01) 662 3063. E-mail: plager@skillbase.ie. Website: http://www.skillbase.ie. (Start-ups, all areas).

- Techstaff, 52 Pembroke Road, Dublin 4. Tel: (01) 667 2525. Website: http://www.exp.ie/techstaff.html.

Executive Search Consultancies

- Ernst & Young, Ernst & Young Building, Harcourt Centre, Harcourt Street, Dublin 2. Tel: (01) 475 0555. Fax: (01) 475 0599.

- GMB & Associates, MS House, Strand Road, Bray, County Wicklow. Tel: (01) 286 7692. Fax: (01) 286 1833.

- John Harty & Associates, Harbour House, Lock Quay, Limerick. Tel: (061) 414533. Fax: (061) 414128. E-mail: jharty@john-harty-associates.ie.

- KPMG, 1 Stokes Place, St Stephen's Green, Dublin 2. Tel: (01) 708 1000. Fax: (01) 708 1122. Website: http://www.kpmg.ie.

- Merc Partners, 12 Richview Office Park, Clonskeagh, Dublin 14 Tel: (01) 283 0144. Fax: (01) 283 0550. E-mail: postmaster @merc.ie. Website: http://www.merc.ie.

- Orion Executive Search, 121 Lower Baggot Street, Dublin 2. Tel: (01) 676 4755.

- Sean McHale and Associates, 63 Fitzwilliam Square, Dublin 2. Tel: (01) 661 8088. Fax: (01) 661 1987.

Others

- FÁS — Training & Employment Authority, 27–33 Upper Baggot Street, Dublin 2. Tel: (01) 668 5777.

- High Skills Pool, The Powerhouse, Pigeon House Harbour, Dublin 4. Tel: (01) 668 7155. Fax: (01) 668 7945.

- Jobcare Ltd., 28a Pearse Street, Dublin 2. Tel: 677 3897.

Professional Organisations

- Association of Chartered Certified Accountants, 9 Leeson Park, Dublin 6. Tel: (01) 491 0466.

- The Bar Council, Law Library, Four Courts, Dublin 2. Tel: (01) 804 5000.

- Incorporated Law Society of Ireland, Blackhall Place, Dublin 7. Tel: (01) 671 0711.

- Institute of Chartered Accountants in Ireland, 87 Pembroke Road, Dublin 4. Tel: (01) 668 0400.

- Institute of Engineers of Ireland, 22 Clyde Road, Dublin 4. Tel: (01) 668 4341. Fax: (01) 668 5508.

- Institute of Personnel and Development, 7–8 Upper Mount Street, Dublin 2. Tel: (01) 676 6655. Fax: (01) 676 7229. E-mail: ipd@iol.ie.

- Irish Medical Organisation, 10 Fitzwilliam Place, Dublin 2. Tel: (01) 676 7273. Fax: (01) 661 2758. E-mail: imo@iol.ie.

- Royal Institute of the Architects of Ireland, 8 Merrion Square, Dublin 2. Tel: (01) 676 1703. Fax: (01) 661 0948. E-mail: info@riai.ie.

Chapter 3

Who's Recruiting Now

This chapter contains listings for a selection of companies who will be actively recruiting in 1998.

Accuris
Telecom software solutions

Merrion House, Merrion Road, Dublin 4. Tel: (01) 269 2322. Fax: (01) 260 0144. E-mail: jobs@accuris.ie. Internet: http://www.accuris.ie.

The brainchild of three strategic partners, Telecom Eireann, PTT Telecom of the Netherlands and Telia of Sweden, Accuris is a software development house delivering IT solutions in the telecommunications environment. Underlying all that we do is our team approach and our dedication to delivering quality products and services. With our combined skills in the different areas of business analysis, software engineering, and customer support, we strive to achieve excellence in everything we do. We have vacancies for exceptional software people. Successful candidates should possess a degree in Computer Science, Engineering or equivalent. Our salary package depends on the nature of the job and the candidate's experience. If you require more information on opportunities at Accuris, contact Maria O'Carroll, Human Resources Manager, at the above address.

ACRA CONTROL LTD.

Landscape House, Landscape Road, Dublin 14.
Tel: (01) 295 1264. Fax: (01) 295 1265.

Acra Control Ltd. is an indigenous Irish company engaged in the design and manufacture of leading edge data acquisition equipment. Our compact and rugged equipment is used by the automotive, aerospace and wind-energy industries in demanding and difficult applications such as crash-testing. We have ongoing requirements for technical personnel in the following areas:

- **Software Development** (C++ and OOD, hardware knowledge essential)

- **Hardware Development**

- **Test and Production Technicians.**

Please send detailed CVs to the above address.

---

amdahl

Balheary, Swords, County Dublin.
Tel: (01) 840 3001. Fax: (01) 840 7690.

Amdahl Ireland is one of the most dynamic companies operating in the IT sector in Ireland. Our policy is to develop our young workforce in a stimulating environment, where open communications create an excellent working culture. As part of our expansion programme, Amdahl will be recruiting for the following positions in 1998: 5 **software engineers**; 4 **support engineers**; 10 **system management consultants** and 10 **applications management consultants**. Experience essential, preferably with a qualification in appropriate areas to degree or diploma level. Amdahl are offering a competitive salary package, commensurate with experience. Please send detailed CV to the Human Resources Manager at the above address.

ANALOG DEVICES

Raheen Industrial Estate, Limerick. Tel: (061) 229011. Fax: (061) 302263. E-mail: liz.frawley@analog.com. Internet: http://www.analog.com.

Analog Devices designs, manufactures and markets a wide range of high performance linear, mixed-signal and digital integrated circuits. The Limerick plant was established in 1976, with both design and manufacturing facilities. In 1998, we will be recruiting: **Graduate Engineers and Technicians**, together with experienced engineers in the areas of **IC design, test development, design evaluation, applications, marketing, process and equipment maintenance**. A degree in electrical/electronic or computer engineering and relevant experience in IC development or manufacture are required for the technical positions. Analog Devices offers competitive salaries and a valuable benefits package, including a bi-annual bonus plan based on company profitability.

THE APPOINTMENTS PAGE

Internet: http://tap.gtc.ie/tap. E-mail: tapadmin@tap.gtc.ie. Tel: (091) 758366. Fax: (091) 755635.

The Appointments Page offers an unequalled FREE service to people looking for work in Ireland. Once you have registered a keyword-based skill profile through a form from your web browser, you can: search for jobs on-line; receive e-mails detailing new jobs entered on the site; contact job providers directly from the site. It also allows job providers to contact you anonymously. (Your skill profile is password protected and confidential, with none of your personal contact details being published.) Currently, there are over 5,000 people registered with The Appointments Page, with hundreds of jobs advertised monthly. All areas are catered for, including: Computers; Engineering; Sales/Marketing; Accountancy/Finance; Graphic Design/Publishing Media.

BANK OF IRELAND SECURITIES SERVICES

1 Harbourmaster Place, IFSC, Dublin 1.
Tel: (01) 605 4529. Fax: (01) 670 1380. Andrew.Blair@BOI.ie.

BOISS is the largest provider of investment administration and custodial services in Dublin and is committed to providing staff with excellent development and career opportunities. We would like to hear from people with experience in the **Global Custody/Mutual Funds Administration** area, specifically in **Settlements, Valuations, Fund Accounting, Shareholder Servicing, Corporate Actions** and **Dividends**. Minimum requirement is a third-level business-related qualification. Salary is negotiable, commensurate with experience; there is also a comprehensive package of banking benefits.

♣ Bankers Trust
Architects of Value

BT Trustee Company (Irl.) Ltd./BT Fund Managers Ltd. (80 Harcourt Street, Dublin 2. Tel: (01) 790 2400. Fax: (01) 790 2410). Activities: provision of **Custody; Fund Administration;** and **Trustee Services for Offshore Funds**. (HR Officer: Karen Coveney).
BT Services (Ireland) Ltd., (Abbey Court, Irish Life Centre, Lower Abbey Street, Dublin 1. Tel: (01) 805 1000. Fax (01) 805 1198). Activities: **Money Transfer; Customer Service; Letters of Credit;** and **Loans Administration**. (HR Officer: Yvonne McGuinness).

Both offices now employ 190 people in total, and we are one of the market leaders in our businesses. We recruit people with enthusiasm and dedication; people who strive to make things happen; people who want to learn and develop. As we are a continually growing business, there is an ongoing need for experienced people in the above areas, as well as more junior candidates who are PC literate. We provide excellent remuneration packages designed to attract and retain the best candidates. If you feel you have these qualities and wish to join one of the largest US banks, please send a copy of your CV to either **Karen** or **Yvonne**.

BROADCOM EIREANN RESEARCH

Kestrel House, Clanwilliam Place, Dublin 2.
Tel: (01) 604 6000. Fax: (01) 676 1532.
Internet: http://www.Broadcom.ie/jobs/jobsopp.html.

Broadcom are a telecommunications research consultancy company that specialise in network management and advanced telecommunications services. Broadcom is a joint venture between
Ericsson, Telecom Éireann and Trinity College. We are actively recruiting self-motivated individuals interested in a career in research and consultancy. You will need a computer science degree
and/or some telecommunications experience, preferably in an
operators management environment, management systems ven-
dor or systems integration. Technology is dynamic and ever-
evolving and we are seeking people interested in the following
areas: Use of **Object-oriented technologies** including analysis and
design; **Object Relational Databases**; **Workflows**; **Process-driven
approach** to IT systems; **Object Modelling Techniques**; **CORBA**;
JAVA; and **C++**. Please forward your CV to: Carmel O'Brien

CITIBANK

Fleming House, Fleming Place, Dublin 4.
Tel: (01) 614 4000. Fax: (01) 614 4061.

Citibank is one of the leading companies in the Financial Services
sector. We are establishing our new Global Services Centre in
Dublin and are expecting to recruit up to 400 staff in 1998. We will
be looking for staff to work in a wide variety of areas, ranging
from Processors through to Customer Services Representatives
and Managers. We are interested in people from diverse back-
grounds who are seeking opportunities in Banking. Language
skills would be a major bonus for certain positions. Salary levels
vary, depending on the position applied for and level of experience. Please send detailed CVs to Moira Lynam (Tel: 614 3712) at
the above address.

CREATIVE

Creative Labs (Ireland) Ltd., Ballycoolin Business Park, Blanchardstown, Dublin 15.
Tel: (01) 820 6444. Fax: (01) 820 9891. E-mail: recruit@creative.ie. Internet: http://www.creativelabs.com.

Creative Labs is the world's leading provider of advanced multimedia solutions for PCs. Our Sound Blaster technology has been accepted as the global standard platform for PCs. Creative Labs actively recruits energetic and enthusiastic individuals who seek to work in a challenging, dynamic and fast-paced environment. The main opportunities will be in the areas of Technical Support — Call Centre (language skills required, no experience necessary) and Operations and Localisation (candidates should possess relevant experience and qualifications in their area of expertise). Contact the Human Resources department at the above address.

TELECOM

Esat Telecom, The Malthouse, Grand Canal Quay, Dublin 2.
Tel: (01) 602 6325. Fax: (01) 670 4616.

An example of motivation and innovation.

$$E = mc^2$$

As simple as it seems, the theory of relativity was realised through years of hard work, motivation and innovative thinking — principles Esat Telecom thrives on. Thanks to the driving ambition of our team, we are the future of business communications in Ireland. As such, we are always looking for individuals who have what it takes to take us further. For us, the future is full of opportunities — it can also be an opportunity for you. Call us today.

EXECUTIVE CONNECTIONS LTD.

Recruitment Consultants, No. 1 The Mews, Merrion Place.
Tel: (01) 661 8740. Fax: (01) 661 8741.
E-mail: info@executive-connections.ie.
Internet: http://executive-connections.ie.

YOU CAN TRUST AN EXPERT WHO UNDERSTANDS
THE ESSENTIAL ELEMENTS OF HUMAN RESOURCING

With the establishment of the International Financial Services
Centre and the introduction of many multicultural, multinational
and multilingual businesses to Ireland, Executive Connections
have adapted to cater for the resultant demands for qualified personnel. Should you be seeking a move or wish to recruit within
the Banking and Finance sector — call the experts now!

129 Blanchardstown Centre, Dublin 15. Fax: (01) 822 2156

Formative Fun retail outlets offer a wide range of top quality educational games, books, toys and CDs for children of all ages and
abilities in an informal environment, where children can play
whilst parents consult trained advisors. Following the highly successful launch of our first centre in Dublin in 1996, we have ambitious plans to expand in 1998. We are interested in hearing from
enthusiastic potential franchisees in any part of Ireland. You will
need a commitment to education, the ability to develop long-term
working relationships with the Formative Fun customer base, and
of course a strong desire to succeed in your own enterprise. To
find out more, please write to us outlining your background and
explaining how you believe your particular skills and experience
match our needs.

FORWARD EDUCATION AND TRAINING

PO Box 90, Naas, Co. Kildare.

Forward Education and Training is a new company which, from early 1998, will be offering a variety of learning related products. We will have two main areas of business: the supply of educational products directly to homes in all parts of Ireland, and the provision of training in interviewing techniques. We are looking for people interested in working with us part-time in one of the following positions: **Educational Product Advisors** — some experience in education either as a teacher or parent, a good understanding of the Irish primary school curriculum and excellent communication skills will be an advantage; **Trainers** — you will need extensive Human Resources interviewing experience and excellent presentation skills. A psychology background would be an advantage. If you have relevant experience in these areas, please contact us at the above address.

GRIMES & CO.

PO Box 5821, Dublin 4. Tel: (01) 667 56277. Fax: (01) 667 5629.
E-mail: grimesco@iol.ie.
Grimes & Co. is Ireland's new mail order catalogue for fresh, contemporary, design-led houseware and gift items. We are a small but rapidly growing company with big plans within this booming industry. Currently we are expanding into the UK, and throughout Europe via our new website. Periodically, we will be recruiting personable and reliable **telephone sales staff, packing and shipping personnel**, and other administrative people to join us in our exciting venture. If you are interested in any of the above positions, please send us your CV or call to find out more about Grimes & Co.

Hertz Europe Service Centre Ltd., Swords Business Park, Swords, County Dublin. Tel: (01) 813 3524

Hertz is the No. 1 vehicle rental company in the world. It is the largest and longest established with more vehicles (500,000), more locations (over 5,400) and more customers (approximately 25 million annual rentals) than any of its rivals. Hertz are delighted to be in Ireland as a significant employer in the teleservices industry. In order to sustain and enhance the strong growth we have experienced since our commencement in September 1996, we are continually seeking bright energetic individuals with excellent interpersonal skills to join our team. We offer excellent working conditions, competitive remuneration packages and a progressive career. If you are interested in learning more, please contact the Human Resources Department at the above address.

KAO Infosystems Ltd., Carrisbrook House, Pembroke Road, Ballsbridge, Dublin 4. Tel: (01) 405 6200. Fax: (01) 457 6814. E-mail: ppender@kao.ie

KAO Corporation is committed to a global approach to business, employing 15,000 people worldwide, with an annual turnover in excess of $8 billion. KAO Infosystems is the largest CD-ROM manufacturer in Ireland. It provides a variety of turnkey services and also operates a state of the art Fulfilment Services Centre in Ballsbridge. We would like to hear from people with exceptional skills and motivation to work in the following areas: **Software Analysts/Developers; Hardware Technicians; Customer Program Managers; Project Co-ordinators; Schedulers; Buyer Planners; Injection Moulding/Printing Technicians; Telemarketing Customer Service Representative (Multilingual)**. If you are interested in any of the above positions, please send us your CV or call to find out more about a career at KAO Infosystems (Ire.) Ltd.

THE KILDARE HOTEL AND COUNTRY CLUB

Straffan, County Kildare. Tel: (01) 601 7200. Fax: (01) 601 7299. E-mail: hotel@kclub.ie. Internet: http://www.kclub.ie.

The Kildare Hotel and Country Club, Ireland's only Automobile Association 5 red star hotel, is seeking high calibre staff with some experience to fill the following challenging positions: accommodation personnel, chefs, waiting staff, barpersons, reception staff, golf stewards and graduates. You will need to demonstrate excellent communication skills and ideally have some relevant experience in an environment where quality is of paramount importance. Training is provided. Please write to the Personnel Manager at the above address, outlining how your skills and experience match our needs.

LUCENT TECHNOLOGIES

Corke Abbey, Bray, County Wicklow.
Tel: (01) 204 2000. Fax: (01) 282 2864.

At Lucent we're designing and building a whole world of communications solutions. From the telephone on your desk, to the video conferencing systems that link you to the world, from the microchips that power your computer to the infrastructure behind the world's top communications service providers, we have the products that meet your needs, however large or small. Lucent Technologies will be recruiting for the following positions in 1998: **software engineers, software test engineers, development engineers, systems administrators** and **PC technicians.** Successful candidates will have at least two years' experience working in an IT environment. A degree-level qualification in Science, Engineering or similar is a must. Salary rates are very competitive. Please send detailed CV to the Human Resources Manager.

MANAGED SOLUTIONS CORPORATION

32 Upper Mount Street, Dublin 2.

At Managed Solutions Corporation, we are creating the next generation of software products for the international life and bancassurance markets. We will have the following opportunities in 1998 for dynamic team players who wish to be part of our continued success: **Application Developers** (C++ and Visual Basic); **Systems Application Designers**; **Automated Test Designers/Developers**; Technical Designers/Developers; Implementation and Integration Consultants; and Project/Account/ Sales Managers. Interested applicants should send their CV and covering letter, quoting Reference Number WL1, to: Laura Byrne, Human Resources Department.

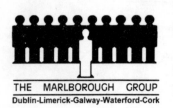

THE   MARLBOROUGH   GROUP
Dublin-Limerick-Galway-Waterford-Cork

The Marlborough Group, Marlborough House, 11–13 Tara Street, Dublin 2. Tel: (01) 677 7521. Fax : (01) 677 7546. E-mail: marlborough@iol.ie. Internet: http://www.iol.ie/resource/margroup.

The Marlborough Group is Ireland's largest and most successful recruitment company. Employing over 70 people across its five regional offices, The Marlborough Group has experienced phenomenal growth. The key to The Marlborough Group's success is its commitment to providing a fast, professional, quality driven service to its customers, which allows us to tailor personnel solutions for each company's individual needs. The Marlborough Group has five dedicated divisions: Marlborough Technical; Marlborough Computing; Marlborough Commercial; Marlborough Secretarial; Marlborough Contracts. Whether you are looking for the perfect job or the perfect person for the job, The Marlborough Group can supply the complete solution.

MEMEC IRELAND LTD.

Gardner House, Bank Place, Limerick.
Tel: (061) 411842. Fax: (061) 411888. E-mail: memec@iol.ie

With high technology semiconductor sales of some $20 million, Memec are probably the largest stocking representative in Ireland. Our group, Raab Karcher Electronics, now has the third largest semiconductor sales in the world which, along with our policy of small autonomous units, gives us the flexibility and focus that our customers and suppliers need, coupled with the necessary financial strength to invest for the future. Our franchise line up is based upon high technology niche products and includes Xilinx, Xicor, Cirrus, UMC and Mitel Semiconductor. As the next phase of our expansion, we are adding staff to our Product Marketing Group in Limerick and also are seeking an Area Sales Manager based around Dublin. If you would like to know more about us, please contact Brian McHarg, Managing Director.

MICROSOFT WPG IRELAND

South County Business Park, Leopardstown, Dublin 18.
Tel: (01) 295 5333. Fax: (01) 2958355.
E-mail: irljobs@microsoft.com.

Microsoft is the world's number one software company. Our Dublin localisation centre provides an excellent working atmosphere in state-of-the-art facilities. If you know our products and have a passion for technology, we would like to hear from you. As part of our recruitment programme, we have a continuous requirement for quality staff in the following areas: **Software Testers; Software Engineers; Program Managers;** and **Localisation Co-ordinators.** We offer a comprehensive remuneration package. Candidates should have a degree or certificate in computer science. Language skills an advantage. Teamwork skills a must. We welcome applications from international candidates or those with international work experience. Please e-mail your CV to us.

MOOG LTD.
Ringaskiddy, Co. Cork, Ireland.
E-mail: hhaussmann.ireland@moog.com

Founded in 1951, Moog Inc. is a Multinational Corporation based in Buffalo, New York State, USA. We have grown to become a world leader in high-reliability motion control systems, with over 3,000 employees worldwide. We have operating units in most of the developed countries of the world and are continuing to re-engineer our business on a more global business model. Our Cork facility is our prime base for electronics design and manufacturing. Our philosophy is simple — belief in our employees. It's a philosophy that demands and rewards maximum effort, integrity and responsibility from every individual. Please send your detailed CVs to: Helga Haussmann, Human Resources Manager.

NATIONAL ASSOCIATION FOR DEAF PEOPLE
35 North Frederick Street, Dublin 1.
Tel: (01) 872 3800. Fax: (01) 872 3816.

The National Association for Deaf People, together with the Irish Hard of Hearing Association, is organising a one-year part-time course leading to a qualification to teach lipreading to adults with late onset hearing loss. The course aims to provide the student teacher with a broad grounding in the skills and understanding required to help and teach adults with acquired deafness to enhance their communication; to provide them with information and support; and to make effective referrals to other specialists and organisations. Student teachers must have confidence, a clear speaking voice, an interest in people with hearing problems, and a Leaving Certificate or equivalent. Teaching experience in Adult Education is considered an advantage. Applications are welcome from people with a hearing impairment. For further information contact: Brigid Haugh MacSweeney, Course Director.

N**⊘**RTEL
Mervue Industrial Estate, Galway. Tel: (091) 733556. Fax: (091) 733264.

Nortel is the market leader in total communications solutions, integrating telecommunications and computer system technology. Our campus in Galway (celebrating its twenty-fifth anniversary in 1998) employs 800 people in the development, manufacturing and supply of communication equipment products. We are currently recruiting qualified people for positions in the following areas: **Hardware or Software Development; Hardware or Software Support; Configuration and/or Test Engineering; Call Centre Consulting and/or Call Centre Product Management; Internet/Multimedia Applications; Localisation; Product Line Management; Finance;** and **Marketing**. If you are interested in any of these positions and you have relevant experience in the telecommunications and/or IT industries, please send your CV or call us.

JOHN SISK & SON LTD.

Wilton Works, Naas Road, Clondalkin, Dublin 22.
Tel: (01) 409 1500. Fax: (01) 409 1550. E-mail: info@sisk.ie

John Sisk & Son Ltd. is Ireland's leading construction and civil engineering group, with turnover in excess of £250 million, working for both domestic and international clients in all sectors. In 1998 we will be recruiting for the following positions: **Contract Managers – General Foremen – Civil Engineers – Services Co-ordinators – Graduate Quantity Surveyors**. A minimum of three years on-site experience with medium–large construction companies is required as well as the appropriate qualifications, e.g. Civil Engineering Degree – Trade – Mechanical & Electrical Engineering Services Qualifications – A.R.I.C.S. (or equivalent). We are offering a superior salary package, commensurate with experience and qualifications. Please send detailed CV to the Managing Director at the above address.

TELLABS LTD.

Shannon Industrial Estate, County Clare.
Tel: (061) 703000. Fax: (061) 703333.
E-mail: hrdept@tellabs.ie. Internet: http://www.tellabs.ie.

Tellabs is an exciting, innovative and profitable company specialising in Telecommunications Design and Manufacture, with a heavy involvement in ATM technology. We will be recruiting for the following positions in 1998: 30 **software engineers**; 6 **project leaders**; 5 **hardware engineers**; **system engineers**; and **technical support engineers**. Applicants must possess a minimum of a degree in electronic/computer engineering or computer science, with at least two or three years experience working in a development environment, preferably with a knowledge of telecommunications or data communications. Tellabs are offering a very attractive and competitive compensation and benefits package. Please send detailed CV to M. Coughlan or telephone (061) 703368.

Chapter 4

Salaries and Benefits

Executive Compensation

According to the consulting firm Inbucon, over the period 1966 to 1996, executive salaries have tended to outstrip inflation. They have been generally linked to the Consumer Price Index (CPI) and enhanced by individual merit awards.

During 1996 increases were running at an overall average of 5 per cent for basic gross salary, whereas inflation was just 1.5 per cent for the same period. This trend is unlikely to change in the near future.

Compared to their counterparts 30 years ago, Irish executives are much better off. Inbucon's 1996 salary survey shows that the average salaries of a financial controller and a purchasing manager are 2,000 per cent higher than in 1966 and that of a marketing manager is 1,500 per cent higher. During the same period, the CPI increased by nearly 1,000 per cent. As a result, real living standards of the average executive have improved significantly.

A number of factors have contributed to changes in working life in Ireland, not only in monetary terms, but in the very nature of work. The revolution in information technology has had a catalytic effect in changing organisational structures, vastly improving telecommunications and positioning Ireland as the software capital of Europe.

The effects have been that, while compensation packages have increased, so has the need for increased flexibility. For many, the portfolio approach to work forecast by Charles Handy in *The Age of Unreason* has become a reality.

Flatter organisational structures with huge emphasis on team-work and the ability to acquire a range of skills and competencies is reflected in pay, as is greater competitiveness with its resultant reorganisations. Some companies offer financially attractive five-year contracts, in the belief that a good performer would need a new challenge by then anyway. There is a noticeable generational difference in how people react to this. People in their 20s and 30s hardly expect to stay with the same employer for more than a couple of years and view their peers who do not move in a negative light. Although it has been an obvious trend for a number of years, people a mere decade older are often visibly shocked at this. Despite its demise, the "job for life" remains the ambition of some.

There is evidence of a steady increase in the numbers of female managers in the workforce, which in turn has played its part in creating more flexible work environments. While corporate success stills translates into long hours for many, some organisations are leading the way with flexible working arrangements, with excellent results. AIB, for example, has introduced a working-by-choice programme for all staff up to assistant manager level, which allows employees of either gender to pro-rate their contracts to fit in with family commitments.

Ireland's success in attracting sustained overseas investment means that new types of jobs are becoming available. Examples include fund managers for the IFSC, customer service managers for the plethora of international services firms and quality assurance managers for the world's leading health care, pharmaceutical and technology firms that have all established a presence here. The impact of these start-ups can be seen by looking at the best paying industries. Whereas 30 years ago executives in the chemicals industry and mining topped the list, the best paid executives today are in financial services, followed by the chemicals, health care and pharmaceutical sectors. With IDA forecasts that health care and pharmaceutical expansions will provide most of the employment growth in Ireland over the next few years, these trends are likely to continue. A combination of the Millennium bug and a global shortage of software engineers and programmers will ensure that this sector also will always be well paid.

Linking Pay to Performance

According to Inbucon, survey findings have shown that performance-related rewards have grown in popularity; more and more companies are linking a percentage of salary increase to individual performance. In addition, there has been significant growth in performance-related incentive packages, which take the form of share ownership, profit share schemes or performance-related cash bonuses. For companies offering incentive schemes in 1996, bonus schemes were the most popular, followed by profit share and share options.

In the companies surveyed, 57.3 per cent of executives received profit-related bonuses in 1996, with an average value of 19.4 per cent of basic salary. Incentive schemes are no longer the preserve of top level management, although managing directors still receive the highest portion, with 67 per cent receiving incentives worth on average 24.5 per cent of their basic salary. Meanwhile, at middle management levels, some 52 per cent of executives receive a bonus, worth on average 14 per cent of their basic salary.

In the majority of current schemes, the bonus earned is based on both company and individual performance criteria. Clearly, fair compensation packages are essential in retaining staff, so both individual employees and their employers select and agree performance criteria, quantify the targets and measure the results, which quantifies the amount awarded. Generally, bonus payments are paid annually; however, experts report a trend developing in longer-term schemes where bonus is based on achievements over three years or more.

Inbucon's figures for 1997 indicate that 18.3 per cent of Irish executives enjoy profit-sharing schemes, while the number of managing directors entitled to participate is 16 per cent — significant increases over 1996. The figures for share options schemes are 12 per cent and 21.5 per cent respectively.

Although it appears that performance-related pay is here to stay, the IMI points out that this could clash with the successful introduction of teamwork, since performance-related pay assesses and rewards the individual's performance and not that of the team. The IMI instead recommends flexible compensation pro-grammes that can have a positive impact on individual and or-ganisational performance and provide a powerful lever for or-ganisational change.

The debate on performance-related pay gained extensive cov-erage earlier in 1997 when the pay saga involving a former Chief Executive of Bord na Mona resulted in a radical review of public sector pay as it applies to commercial semi-state bodies. The Buckley Report recommended the removal of the ceiling placed on the remuneration of chief executives of these organisations, concluding that otherwise they would fail to attract the necessary expertise for the top level jobs. The Report recommended stronger links between pay and performance with a greater focus on re-sults, although, bearing in mind ongoing outrage in the UK over top management compensation packages, it also sets out clear guidelines for setting amounts. With both the Voluntary Health Insurance Board (VHI) and Electricity Supply Board (ESB) facing a dilemma regarding adequate compensation for their chief execu-tives in relation to similar jobs in the private sector, it is expected that the current Government will implement the Buckley Report in the December 1997 Budget.

Non-executive Pay

Although the question continues to attract attention, there is still no statutory minimum wage in Ireland, except for some tradition-ally poorly paid sectors such as contract cleaning. Instead, wage levels are determined through collective agreements. Since 1971, collective bargaining has moved from centralised national agree-ments (1970–81) to enterprise level bargaining (1982–86) and since 1987, back to national bargaining. The three national wage agreements since 1987 have contributed to maintaining low levels of price and wage inflation. The Programme for National Recovery (1987–90) provided for pay increases of 2.5 per cent per year; the Programme for Economic and Social Progress (PESP, 1991–93) for increases between 3 and 4 per cent per year; and the Programme for Competitiveness and Work (PCW, 1994–97) for increases of between 2 and 2.5 per cent.

The current national agreement, Partnership 2000, covers a range of measures relating to Ireland's economic and social development. For example, it contains a commitment to promoting industrial peace and to developing further the partnership between employers and employees and their representatives, where applicable. On pay and taxation, under Partnership 2000, the Government agreed to make £1 billion available for all tax measures covered by the agreement over its 39-month duration. The first instalment was included in the 1997 budget. The effect on the personal tax changes and the actual pay terms on take-home pay will mean real increases for employees. IBEC maintains that, for those on the average industrial wage, after-tax income will increase by up to 14 per cent.

The pay terms over the 39 months are as follows:

First 12 months	2.5%
Second 12 months	2.25%
Next 9 months	1.5%
Last 6 months	1%

Provision is also included for local level negotiations within certain timeframes and for companies which cannot meet the proposed increased wage costs.

Setting Salary Levels

The task of analysing jobs and establishing their relative worth is an industry in itself and is highly complex. Compensation and benefits experts collect data from a broad range of industry sectors and companies of different sizes and benchmark the information to determine current levels of pay. This analysis is based on fact, and an important element of it is identifying trends so that companies can keep up to date with the market. According to experts, the primary factors influencing levels of remuneration are:

- The nature of the job itself

- The level or rank of accountability of the job within the organisation

- The size of the organisation measured by sales turnover and number of employees.

A critical factor in analysing pay is comparing like with like. It is worth remembering that a small indigenous company is unlikely to be able to match the pay scales of a long-established multinational. The best advice is to weigh up all the factors that matter to you in a job and compare how each company measures in your opinion (see Chapter 2, **How to Find a Job**).

Research shows that regional location makes little difference to executive pay packages; however, there are variations between the sectors. The following ranking shows how different industry sectors are ranked:

Basic Salary Differentials by Industry Group	
Industrial Group	*Average Basic Salary as % of All Industries*
Financial services	142
Chemical and allied industries	115
Pharmaceuticals and health care	108
Telecommunications	107
Timber and wooden furniture	107
Haulage, transport, aviation and communications	107
Food, drink and tobacco	106
Medical devices	104

Industrial Group	Average Basic Salary as % of All Industries
Public administration	102
Oil and gas exploration	102
Construction, bricks and cement	101
Other manufacturing	99
Computer industry	97
Agriculture, forestry and fishing	94
Motor vehicles and parts	92
Hotel and catering	91
Plastics	89
Textiles, rubber and leather	88
Instrument engineering	88
Printing and publishing	86
Electrical and electronic engineering	85
Mechanical and other engineering	83
Metal manufacturing	83
Manufacturing of paper and paper products	79
Wholesale and retail distribution	75
Glass and pottery	66
Other services	65

Source: Inbucon

SALARY EXAMPLES

Executive Salaries

The data given in this section is taken from two professionally compiled salary surveys, one by Inbucon and one by the Irish Management Institute (IMI). Both relate to data for 1996; however, where appropriate, figures have been adjusted for 1997. Inbucon's survey includes the survey responses of 182 companies, while the IMI's includes those of 166. IMI has found the following results in its *sectoral* analysis:

Health Care and Pharmaceuticals

Information on the salaries of 497 individual managers from 21 companies, with an average of 24 managers and supervisors per company, is reflected here.

Department	Position	IR£
	Chief Executive	77,075–106,295
Finance and Accounting	Function Head	38,938–63,073
	Middle Manager	28,311–38,875
	Front Line Manager	18,930–27,154
Production/ Manufacturing	Function Head	43,100–58,600
	Middle Manager	27,100–41,864
	Front Line Manager	19,300–28,000
Manufacturing/ Engineering/ Maintenance	Function Head	47,550–61,973
	Middle Manager	27,700–34,600
	Front Line Manager	17,900–28,837
Logistics	Function Head	29,660–52,512
	Middle Manager	26,800–34,200
	Front Line Manager	18,300–26,000
Marketing/Sales Home and Export	Function Head	46,600–49,000
	Middle Manager	28,875–36,000
	Front Line Manager	—
Human Resources	Function Head	28,125–55,338
	Middle Manager	23,170–32,538
	Front Line Manager	20,500
General Administration	Function Head	30,500–45,300
	Middle Manager	30,373–43,800
	Front Line Manager	14,000–19,800
All Functions	Function Head	41,500–56,525
	Middle Manager	27,300–38,050
	Front Line Manager	19,300–28,000

Computers and Electronics Manufacturing		
The data from 18 companies with an average of 32 managers per company are included in this section. Data was provided on the salaries of 560 individual managers.		
Department	**Position**	**IR£**
	Chief Executive	68,650–102,000
Finance and Accounting	Function Head	40,350–63,200
	Middle Manager	28,623–34,650
	Front Line Manager	21,000–30,300
Production/ Manufacturing	Function Head	37,000–60,600
	Middle Manager	30,000–37,000
	Front Line Manager	19,900–30,100
Manufacturing/ Engineering/ Maintenance	Function Head	44,218–52,000
	Middle Manager	39,900
	Front Line Manager	20,900
Logistics	Function Head	40,840–50,200
	Middle Manager	29,700–40,200
	Front Line Manager	24,463–30,100
Marketing/Sales Home and Export	Function Head	48,500
	Middle Manager	32,500–35,400
	Front Line Manager	20,900
Human Resources	Function Head	33,375–57,000
	Middle Manager	25,900–41,000
	Front Line Manager	29,700–35,103
Information Technology	Function Head	48,701–56,200
	Middle Manager	32,000
	Front Line Manager	30,350–31,500
General Administration	Function Head	46,100
	Middle Manager	31,850–42,200
	Front Line Manager	31,200
All Functions	Function Head	41,000–57,000
	Middle Manager	31,410–39,900
	Front Line Manager	25,950–30,100

Banking, Insurance, Professional and Scientific Services Sector
Nineteen companies with an average of 39 managers each took part in this section of the survey. Data was supplied on the salaries of 747 individual managers.

Department	Position	IR£
	Chief Executive	75,300–150,000
Finance/ Accounting	Function Head	45,000
	Middle Manager	38,500–39,733
	Front Line Manager	21,514–29,500
Production/ Manufacturing	Function Head	33,000–60,000
	Middle Manager	—
	Front Line Manager	24,000
Marketing/Sales Home and Export	Function Head	42,900–57,424
	Middle Manager	30,400–41,200
	Front Line Manager	26,200
Human Resources	Function Head	41,150–71,063
	Middle Manager	33,925–42,778
	Front Line Manager	—
General Administration	Function Head	40,388–62,150
	Middle Manager	35,000–44,262
	Front Line Manager	23,958–27,246
All Functions	Function Head	45,000–57,600
	Middle Manager	28,500–40,772
	Front Line Manager	22,760–27,246

Field Sales Force

The IMI surveys the earnings of field sales people separately, as their compensation tends to be structured differently. In IMI's 1996 survey of 91 companies, 34 had between one and 10 sales people in the field, while more than 20 per cent had over 30 field sales people.

In 70 per cent of the companies surveyed, the top earning sales person earned between £20,000 and £40,000 in 1996, while in 1995 half the companies surveyed said that average earnings were between £20,000 and £30,000. More than two-thirds of those surveyed indicated that their lowest earners in 1996 grossed about £20,000.

Not all companies pay a commission or bonus. However, of those which do, 20 per cent paid a commission whilst 10 per cent paid a bonus. Of the companies surveyed, 87 per cent supplied a company car, and just under half supplied a car telephone. All of those surveyed cover expenses; in the case of two-thirds of the companies, overnight expenses were limited to between £26 and £50 per night, whilst per diem expenses (lunch and evening meal) were mainly in the range of £21–£30.

Executive Salaries — Some Examples by Size of Company

We now compare some of the best salaries (excluding chief executive/managing director) by rank and function based on *size of organisation.*

Best Paid Positions ranked in order	Average Base Salary (IR£)	Average Total Remuneration
Fewer than 50 Employees		
Marketing	28,093	30,620
Sales	23,671	27,138
Technical	24,541	25,828
50–99 Employees		
Marketing	33,461	37,097
Finance	31,756	34,538
Technical	32,739	34,297
100–249 Employees		
Marketing	37,422	38,980
Finance	36,836	39,601
Technical	32,172	34,000
250–499 Employees		
Marketing	39,127	44,836
Finance	39,105	46,759
Technical	37,869	41,878
Over 500 Employees		
Marketing	40,184	42,880
Finance	36,420	37,935
Technical	34,141	35,866

Bear in mind that these are *average* salaries (not to be confused with approximate) across the range of ranks and matching salaries in each function. For example, in the finance function of companies with over 500 employees, 25 people were included. The average total compensation among the seven least well paid was £23,417, whilst the three best paid averaged £109,388 in total remuneration.

Computer Programmers/Software Engineers

Inbucon also analyses salary data *by job* within organisations defined by size and turnover. The following information relates to specified information technology jobs by size of company:

- Head of Information Technology (also DP Manager/IT Manager): most senior line executive responsible for all data processing activities in the company.

- IT Project Leader/Manager: responsible for undertaking business reviews of current and future IT requirements, making strategic and operational recommendations and implementing them.

- Computer Operations Manager (DP Administration or Operations Manager): responsible for the processing and scheduling of all centrally processed company data.

- Systems Development Manager: responsible for the overall development of IT programmes and systems, ensuring conformity with overall company strategy.

- Systems Analyst: executive responsible for the design and/or development of computer solutions to user requirements.

- Analyst Programmer: implements and supports range of business applications.

- Other IT executives: all those not specified above who perform IT tasks for the business unit e.g. Database Administrator, Communications Manager, Network Administrator.

Best Paid Positions ranked in order	Average Base Salary (IR£)	Average Total Remuneration
Fewer than 50 Employees		
Head of IT	' 36,467	38,507
Systems Analyst	25,825	27,259
Analyst Programmer	20,367	20,641
Other IT executives	20,488	21,626
50–99 Employees		
Head of IT	34,786	37,290
Computer Operations Manager	27,622	28,311
Other IT executives	21,538	24,200
100–249 Employees		
Head of IT	43, 586	50,225
Computer Operations Manager	29,916	30,731
Analyst Programmer	20,350	23,410
250–499 Employees		
Head of IT	47,218	50,891
Computer Operations Manager	36,943	38,682
Systems Development Manager	30,458	31,217
Systems Analyst	29,819	30,419
Analyst Programmer	25,657	26,284
Other IT executives	20,771	21,380
Over 500 Employees		
Head of IT	43,284	45,078
IT Project Leader	40,927	42,074
Computer Operations Manager	36,513	38,763
Systems Analyst	25,436	26,381

Again, it must be stressed that these are *average* salaries.

NON-EXECUTIVE SALARIES

The amount of professionally compiled salary analysis is vast and companies whose main business is to compile and analyse compensation data produce books of salary surveys and analysis every year. You should be aware that your employer will want to ensure that they remain competitive and pay fairly and will in all likelihood use the scientific analysis explained above, while making a clear distinction regarding the specific job description.

However, it is also interesting to review surveys compiled by other organisations whose main business lies in other related areas. The main data, summarised in Appendix 1, is extracted from a survey conducted by the Marlborough Group. If the salary for the employment category that interests you is not included in the above examples, check this list which is based on commonly used job titles.

BENEFITS

The rate of personal taxation in Ireland is high, especially when considered with PRSI (social security) rates. This can make employee rewards expensive. Yet, employee motivation is a key factor in the retention of employees and the success of a business. Employers therefore endeavour to offer a tax-efficient and attractive range of benefits.

Mercers Ltd. reports a trend away from considering pay and conditions in a similar manner for all employees and towards allowing employees a degree of choice in designing their own benefit packages by offering flexible ("flex") benefits programmes. Gateway 2000, Xilinx and Sun are among the companies adopting this approach. The trend is attributed to a number of factors: a change in demographics with more women in the workforce, more single parent families and two working spouses who often have duplicated benefits packages; better value for money; enhanced employee perception of their package; and, hardly surprisingly with the number of multinationals established here, influence from the USA, where research shows that almost 40 per cent of companies now operate flex benefits plans.

A wide range of benefits fit into flex programmes; for example:

- Pension

- Holidays

- Life Cover

- Share Plans

- Disability Insurance

- Serious Illness

- Cars

- Medical Funds

- VHI/BUPA cover

- Medical Check-ups

- Cash.

Understanding Flex Benefits

Flex programmes can be structured in one of three different ways:

1. **The Core Plus Plan**: This approach works well where employers want to provide a flexible benefits programme to all of their workforce. It provides a minimum level of core benefits that the employer will want all employees to have — for example, some level of pension and death-in-service benefit. The employee may also be entitled to extra credits with which to purchase extra benefits tailored to suit their individual needs.

2. **The Modular Approach**: In this type of plan, modules of specified benefits are targeted at specific categories of employees.

3. **Full Flexibility**: With this structure, the finance available for benefits can be used as chosen by the individual, subject to Revenue restrictions.

Pension Schemes

Most companies in Ireland operate a pension scheme to provide an income after retirement which is greater than that provided by the State. In addition to the employee's pension, such schemes typically include provision for ill health, early/later retirement, death-in-service and a spouse/dependant's pension. The cost of such schemes to the company typically lies between 10 per cent and 20 per cent of employees' pay, depending upon whether employees contribute towards the scheme or whether it is funded entirely by the employer's contributions.

Over 95 per cent of companies have established pension schemes. Of these schemes, 76.4 per cent are defined benefit and 23.6 per cent are defined contribution.

The maximum pension approved by the Revenue Commissioners is two-thirds of final salary. A typical scheme would provide 1/60th of final salary for each year of service with the company. Thus, an employee would need to stay with the same company for 40 years to reach the full pension entitlement.

There are, however, arrangements whereby employees can make additional voluntary contributions (AVCs) to a scheme to achieve full pension in a shorter period, or similarly a company can choose to pay much higher contributions on behalf of an executive in the form of a "Top Hat" pension, thereby shortening the period of service needed to reach full pension entitlement. In recent years, smaller and newly established companies have adopted defined contributions plans (where the contribution to be made by the employer is defined in advance). However, the majority of medium- to large-sized companies in Ireland with long established pension schemes continue to operate on a defined benefit basis (where the pension available to a member on retirement is defined in advance). Even in companies with defined benefit schemes, new members are likely to be invited to join new defined contribution schemes.

It should be noted that the definition of eligible salary is different for defined benefit and defined contribution pension schemes. In defined contribution schemes, a percentage of your total base salary is contributed by the employer; with defined benefit schemes, your "pensionable" salary means your salary after a portion has been offset in respect of the State pension.

There are differences in the extent to which, as a pension scheme member, you can influence the value of your eventual pension. Investment decisions for defined benefit schemes are made by the pension trustees, whereas with defined contribution schemes, each member makes an individual choice between cash and managed funds and their pension operates like a pension bank account.

Contributory plans are plans (for both defined contribution and defined benefit schemes) in which covered employees make contributions up to a personal limit of 15 per cent of earnings. Although the majority of defined benefit schemes were non-contributory in the past, the expansion in the range and extent of benefits provided has caused the introduction of employee contributions. The average value of employee contributions has remained around 5 to 7.5 per cent. Given the tax advantages of AVCs (additional voluntary contributions — that is, more than your employer requires you to contribute), it is surprising that this figure is not higher. This may be due, in part, to a lack of comprehension among pension plan members about the potential benefits. Women in particular should check how their pension will be impacted if they take a career break.

There are several tax advantages to making pension contributions. The first advantage is that you get full rate income tax relief on your contributions, so if you pay your highest rate of tax at 26 per cent, you get a refund of 26 pence in every pound; if you pay your highest rate at 48 per cent, then you get 48 pence in every pound. Accordingly, a £1,000 pension contribution will cost the 26 per cent taxpayer £740 and the 48 per cent taxpayer £520. An additional advantage is that employer pension contributions are a non-taxable benefit, unlike cars for example, on which you are taxed for benefit-in-kind. You will also not have to pay tax on the growth of funds you have invested in your pension. Finally, you will have the option to take a cash lump sum from your pension on retirement. After that, your actual pension income will be taxed in the same way as any other income.

An employee's contribution can be voluntary, but increasingly tends to be compulsory. The breakdown of pension scheme types for 1996 in the companies Inbucon surveyed was:

- 26.9 per cent are voluntary (contributory or non-contributory)

- 51.9 per cent are compulsory contributory

- 21.2 per cent are compulsory non-contributory.

A total of 54.9 per cent of companies adjusted their benefits in 1996 to make provision for early retirement. The age at which the early retirement option can be taken is normally 50 or 55 years.

Pensions for Self-employed

It is reported that as few as one in four self-employed people contribute to a pension scheme, which is somewhat alarming. Organisations representing the interests of the self-employed have provided an added option for the self-employed by launching their own schemes. Both the Irish Small and Medium Enterprises Association (ISME) and the Small Firm's Association (SFA) now offer schemes, a move which some analysts credit with providing the impetus to life assurance companies to reduce their initial charges on pension plans and start presenting material more easily understood by the layperson.

Company Cars

Probably the most significant change in the executive remuneration package in the past few years has been the decline of the company car as a benefit. This is largely due to the changes in the taxation system; many companies are now reviewing their car schemes and offering cash alternatives instead.

Company cars are treated as benefits-in-kind by the Revenue Commissioners. In April 1992, the benefit-in-kind scale charges were increased by 50 per cent and the tax base increased from 20 per cent to 30 per cent of the original market value of the car. This major increase left many employees questioning the value of their cars as a perk. However, in 1996, 45.2 per cent of executives overall still received a company car, down from 53.9 per cent in 1991. The IMI recommends that, where an executive has a company car and is liable for benefit-in-kind taxation, consideration should be given to replacing an expensive company car with two cheaper cars. For example, if a £36,000 car was to be replaced with a £22,000 company car (which would cover a range of 2-litre choices) and a £14,000 car to be used by the spouse of the executive, there would be no additional benefit-in-kind charge on the employee, who would now have their entire motoring costs paid. Furthermore, the company's own tax position is improved because none of the expenses of running the £14,000 car are disallowed and the proportion of the running expenses of the more expensive car (£8,000/£22,000) is lower.

In most cases where a car is supplied, the company also meets the cost of tax, insurance, repairs, service and fuel. Where employees are not eligible for either a car allowance or a company car, most companies pay a mileage rate when your car is used for company business. Employees in this position should check that their insurance policy covers business use.

Annual Leave

Although 20 days annual leave is not yet legally required, in practice most medium and large companies already give this. Further, many employers provide additional paid annual leave to reward length of service.

Private Health Insurance

The kinds of health care available are described in Chapter 14. Private health insurance is a popular benefit in Ireland. A 1997 survey of 194 employers by Mercer found that:

- 133 (69 per cent) contribute towards the cost of employees' health insurance.

- Of the 133 companies which pay health insurance premiums:

    ◊ 65 per cent pay for all employees

    ◊ 17 per cent pay for management only

    ◊ 18 per cent exclude hourly paid staff only

- 80 per cent of these companies pay all the cost of the specified plan, while 20 per cent require employees to contribute.

Life Cover

Many employers provide life cover from the employment start date, up to 2.5 times base salary. This is not an automatic benefit; you should check with your employer what cover is available.

Employee Share Plans

Employee Share Plans, provided they are approved by the Revenue Commissioners, are a tax-efficient way of receiving a part of your reward. Under an approved plan, employees are given the right to convert a "profit sharing bonus" into shares in their company or its parent. Employees may also contribute a percentage of their base salary towards the purchase of shares. The shares are held in trust for a minimum of two years, after which they can be sold but are subject to income tax. Shares held for three years are free of income tax. There are no signs that Ireland will follow the lead of the UK in introducing legislation which negatively impacts employee share plans, as happened there in 1997. Quite the contrary, these plans are very popular in Ireland, and some companies offer them to employees at all levels.

Disability Benefits

Most employers provide a short-term disability benefit of up to 100 per cent for up to six months, less any State benefit. Long-term disability cover varies, and companies are increasingly looking at providing critical illness cover instead. You should read your employer's company handbook and benefits information carefully for further details.

Relocation Expenses

An employer may make certain relocation payments to an employee free of tax if they ask the employee to move or, if in order to take up a position, an employee has to move home. The kinds of expenses that may be reimbursed are legal fees, stamp duty, removal costs and subsistence. Reasonable expenses are allowable and they must be vouched. If you receive relocation benefits, you should ask about whether they are taxable and, if they are, who will pay the tax. If you are moving from another country, you might ask for the assistance of a tax specialist as part of your package.

Employee Assistance Programmes (EAP)

An Employee Assistance Programme (EAP) is a form of assistance provided (generally free of charge, although some services may be charged for) to provide advice and counselling on a range of issues that cause concern or stress to employees. These programmes are being offered by more companies, particularly larger ones. To be of most benefit to employees, an EAP should be run by external experts with the qualifications and training to assess and counsel people in need. A contact telephone number should be available to employees and the employer should receive reports showing the number of enquiries, the categories they fall into and any recommendations that might benefit them. The employer should never be told who contacted the service.

At the Employee Assistance Programme Conference held in Dublin in September 1997, experts contended that there has been a rapid increase in illegal drug use in Ireland since 1979 and that in the early 1990s more than 2,000 people a year sought help from treatment clinics. Among other statistics given was that the effect of drug abuse in the workplace was a two-and-a-half-fold increase in absenteeism and a tenfold increase in sick leave. The cost to business of addiction to legal drugs is also increasing. Experts at the conference estimated that up to 22,000 people in Ireland are at risk of becoming tranquilliser-dependent, whilst there are 95,000 alcohol dependants and over 750,000 nicotine-dependants. While experts stress the need for managers to combat stress in the workplace, the likelihood is that the availability of EAPs will increase.

USEFUL CONTACTS

- Inbucon Ireland, International Business Consultants,
  63 Fitzwilliam Square, Dublin 2. Tel: (01) 661 8088.
  Fax: (01) 661 1987.

- Irish Management Institute, Sandyford Road, Dublin 16.
  Tel: (01) 295 6911. Fax: (01) 295 5150. E-mail: carrollb@imi.ie.

- Irish Small and Medium Enterprises Association (ISME),
  32 Kildare Street, Dublin 2. Tel: (01) 662 2755.

- Mercer Ltd., Actuaries and Consultants, St James House,
  Adelaide Road, Dublin 2. Tel: (01) 478 2866. Fax: (01) 478 2297.

- Small Firms Association, 84 Lower Baggot Street, Dublin 2.
  Tel: (01) 660 1011.

Chapter 5

Your Rights as an Employee

Legislation can be heavy going, and the following pages aim to provide only an overview of employee rights. The area of employee rights is one that can give rise to misunderstanding. Misperceptions of rights are not uncommon, and given the necessarily complex nature of legislation, this is hardly surprising. A common and inaccurate belief is that legislation can vary greatly. For example, some countries specify that maximum length of a probationary period (just two months in the Netherlands, compared to up to a year in Ireland), whether sick leave is payable and how salary increases are determined.

This degree of specification can have a major impact on working conditions. For example, the very lengthy sick leave allowable in the Netherlands has simply meant that it has become extremely difficult to become a permanent employee; instead, temporary contracts have become the norm. Some of the European legislation may seem incredible to those used to working in the US, where employment-at-will prevails in many states, and four weeks' annual holidays is a reward you work towards after years of service. Overall, employee legislation in Ireland is reasonable and fair to both the employer and employee. Indeed, there is a strong attraction to many companies investing here. From an employee perspective, it is important to gain an understanding of what your rights are, but also to understand that it is pointless wishing that they mirrored exactly those in your current or former country of residence. It goes without saying that, if in doubt, you should check with your employer or a legal professional.

CONTRACTS OF EMPLOYMENT (TERMS OF EMPLOYMENT (INFORMATION) ACT 1994; UNFAIR DISMISSALS ACTS 1977–1993)

Anyone who works for an employer for a regular wage automatically has a contract of employment, whether written or not. Employers are legally obliged to provide all new employees with a written statement of terms and conditions governing their employment within two months of commencing employment. An existing employee must also be given a written statement within two months, if requested. This applies to any person:

- Working under a contract of employment or apprenticeship for more than eight hours per week and whose employment is expected to exceed one month's duration

- Employed through an employment agency (the party who pays the wages is deemed to be the employer).

Employees should therefore be given a contract of employment that contains the following:

- Full name of employer and employee

- Address of employer and principal place of business

- Place of work, or if there is no fixed place, a statement that the employee is required to work at various places

- Job title or nature of work

- Commencement date

- For temporary contracts, the duration of the contract

- The method of calculation of remuneration

- Payment intervals

- Hours of work/overtime requirements

- Holidays/paid leave

- Sick pay/pensions (if any)

- Notice periods.

Employers may specify other conditions, as appropriate.

Employers are required by the Unfair Dismissals Acts 1977–1993 to give notice in writing to each employee of the procedure which the employer will observe before and for the purpose of dismissing the employee. This must be given within 28 days of entering into a contract of employment, and is usually specified in the company handbook.

Fixed Term Contracts .

A special contract is required where a person is employed for a fixed term or for a specified purpose. To exclude application of the Unfair Dismissal Acts, a contract must be written and signed by both parties, specifying dates of commencement and ending of contract, or in the case of a specified purpose contract, specifying the type of job the person is required to work on until its completion, and specifically excluding the provisions of the Acts.

Employers should note that the use of successive contracts of employment in order to avoid the impact of the Acts are made ineffective by the anti-abuse provisions of the 1993 Act.

Probation

A contract of employment should state, where relevant, the length of a probationary period and management's discretion to extend (normally 3–6 months) or to terminate employment. The Unfair Dismissals Acts will normally apply only after an employee has 12 months service, with two exceptions: dismissals related to trade union activity and maternity/pregnancy. In both cases, the employee is covered from the first day of employment.

PAYMENT OF WAGES (PAYMENT OF WAGES ACT 1991)

While there is no general minimum wage legislation in place, in certain sectors legal minimum rates have been set down through Joint Labour Committees (JLCs), set up by the Labour Court. Employment Regulation Orders are also made by the Labour Court on the basis of proposals submitted by the JLCs.

The categories that JLCs cover include agricultural workers, grocery assistants, contract cleaners, hairdressers in Dublin and Cork, law clerks, and hotel and catering workers in certain areas.

The Payment of Wages Act 1991 provides that every employee has the right to a readily negotiable mode of wage payment. The list of modes provided in the Act include payment by cheque, credit transfer, cash, postal/money order and bank draft. The vast majority of Irish companies pay by credit transfer. The Act obliges employers to give each employee with every wage envelope a written statement of gross wages, itemising each deduction separately.

Deductions may not be made from wages unless required by law (e.g. PAYE or PRSI), provided for in the contract of employment (e.g. pension contributions, breakages or till shortages) or when termination occurs (and the paid holidays already taken exceed the paid holiday entitlement on the date of termination) or made with the written consent of the employee (e.g. VHI/BUPA payment or trade union subscriptions).

HOLIDAYS (HOLIDAYS (EMPLOYEES) ACTS 1973–1991)

General requirements:

• Timing of leave decided by the employer

• Leave must be taken in leave year or within six months following

• Holiday pay must be paid in advance

• If employment is terminated, any outstanding leave must be paid for by the employer.

Where pay is calculated wholly by reference to time, holiday pay is the same as pay for normal working hours in the week immediately preceding leave. Where pay varies in relation to work done, holiday pay is the average weekly payment for normal working hours in the 13 weeks ending on the day immediately preceding the leave.

- **Full-time employees**: at the time of writing, legal minimum is 3 working weeks (15 working days) annual leave. This is to increase to 4 working weeks (20 days) by April 1999. In practice, many companies already give their employees 20 days holidays.

- **Part-time employees**: Regular part-timers — i.e. those working at least six hours per week — are entitled to six hours paid holidays for every 100 hours worked, and proportionately less for periods of less than 100 hours.

- **Public holidays**: There are currently nine public holidays as follows:

  ◊ New Year's Day (1 January)

  ◊ St Patrick's Day (17 March)

  ◊ Easter Monday

  ◊ First Monday in May (May Day)

  ◊ First Monday in June

  ◊ First Monday in August

  ◊ Last Monday in October

  ◊ Christmas Day (25 December)

  ◊ St Stephen's Day (26 December).

Good Friday is not a public holiday. For public holidays, full-time employees have the following entitlement, as the employer may decide:

- Paid day off on the day or

- Paid day off within the month or

- An extra day's pay.

Where full-time employees would not normally work a full day on a public holiday, they are nevertheless entitled to a full day's pay.

Regular part-timers who normally work on the day of the public holiday should be paid their normal day's pay. Regular part-timers who would not normally work on a day on which a public holiday falls, should be paid pro rata for the day by dividing the number of hours that they work by the number of days in a normal working week, which is five.

MINIMUM NOTICE (MINIMUM NOTICE AND TERMS OF EMPLOYMENT ACTS 1973–1991)

Employees (except those who work fewer than 8 hours per week and with less than 13 weeks service) are entitled to notice prior to termination of employment.

Employee Entitlements

Continuous Service of Employee	Minimum Notice
More than 13 weeks and less than 2 years:	1 week
2 to 5 years:	2 weeks
5 to 10 years:	4 weeks
10 to 15 years:	6 weeks
15 years or more:	8 weeks

Note that your employer may require you to give longer notice, so you should pay careful attention to what is agreed.

Employer Entitlements

Employer entitlements are: One week's notice from an employee who has been in employment for 13 weeks or more, regardless of the length of service, unless the contract states otherwise. It is important therefore that in appointing staff to senior positions, the employer specifies the required notice period, e.g. one month, three months, etc.

Waiver of Notice/Payment in Lieu

The employer/employee may waive right to notice or accept payment in lieu. Employees may be summarily dismissed without notice for serious misconduct.

MATERNITY LEAVE
(MATERNITY PROTECTION OF EMPLOYEES ACT 1994)

This Act covers:

- Right to maternity leave for a minimum of 14 weeks (a Social Welfare payment will be paid during this leave. There is no obligation on the employer to make any payment)

- Right to additional unpaid maternity leave of up to 4 weeks

- Right to time off for ante and post natal appointments without loss of pay

- Right to return to work

- Right to health and safety leave, where the employee is at risk due to the nature of her work, and where a temporary adjustment of working conditions is not technically or objectively feasible

- Right of an employed father to leave if the mother dies within 14 weeks of the birth

- Right not be dismissed for any pregnancy-related reason

- Entitlement to benefits is subject to certain notification procedures

- Notice of intention to take maternity leave, notice of intention to take additional maternity leave and notice of intention to return to work must all be given in writing.

ADOPTIVE LEAVE (ADOPTIVE LEAVE ACT 1995)

An adopting mother or sole male adopter who is in employment is entitled to:

- A minimum of 10 consecutive weeks of adoptive leave from work from beginning of the day of placement of the child. Social Welfare payment will be paid during such leave. There is no obligation on the employer to make a payment.

- Up to 4 weeks additional adoptive leave, which may be taken before adoptive leave in the case of a foreign adoption.

Notification

You must give adequate notice in writing of intention to take leave. The minimum notice is four weeks before the expected placement of the child, and certification of placement must be given to the employer as soon as is reasonably practicable. Notice of additional adoptive leave must be given in writing at least four weeks before your intention to take additional leave. You must also give at least four weeks before the date on which you intend to return to work after adoptive leave or additional leave.

DISCIPLINARY PROCEDURE (UNFAIR DISMISSALS ACTS 1977–1993)

A disciplinary procedure dealing with general misconduct should contain the following steps:

1. Counselling

2. Verbal warning

3. First written warning

4. Final written warning/suspension

5. Dismissal.

Through stages 2–5, employees should be advised of their right to representation. Employees should be given an opportunity to state their case and, where appropriate, the right to appeal. The disciplinary procedure may be set aside in cases of very serious misconduct, but an employer has a duty to fully investigate all cases.

UNFAIR DISMISSAL (UNFAIR DISMISSALS ACTS 1977–1993)

The Unfair Dismissals Acts enable employees to claim unfair dismissal. The Acts require that within 28 days of commencement of employment, an employee must be advised of the procedures that will be used for dismissal.

The Acts do not apply to employees:

- With less than one year continuous service (unless dismissed for pregnancy, exercising maternity leave rights, or trade union activity)

- Who work less than eight hours per week

- Who have reached "normal retirement" age or 66 years

- Statutory apprentices (during first six months of apprenticeship and one month after completion of apprenticeship).

Every dismissal of an employee will be presumed to have been unfair unless the employer can show substantial grounds justifying the dismissal.

Unfair Grounds for Dismissal

A dismissal is deemed automatically unfair, unless the employer proves otherwise, for the following: trade union membership/activity, religious/political opinions, taking legal proceedings against one's employer, race or colour, pregnancy of employee, exercising statutory maternity leave rights, and age.

Fair Grounds for Dismissal

A dismissal is deemed not unfair if it arises principally from: capacity, competence/qualifications, conduct, regulation or statute, redundancy, expiry of fixed term or specified purpose contract.

Fair Procedures

The law has laid down certain general principles which must be adhered to if dismissals are to be justified. These are the principles of natural justice which essentially establish fair procedures as being central to all unfair dismissal cases.

Strict adherence to procedures now carries equal weight to the act or actions which led to the dismissal. The requirements of procedural fairness that are of particular importance in dismissal cases include the following: the right to know the reasons for the proposed dismissal; the right to reply to those reasons and to have that reply and any other arguments or submissions listened to and evaluated before the decision to dismiss is taken; the right to be represented by an appropriate person so that the right to reply is real; the right to an impartial hearing.

Remedies to unfair dismissal are: re-instatement, re-engagement, or compensation (up to a maximum of 104 weeks' remuneration).

REDUNDANCY (REDUNDANCY PAYMENTS ACTS 1967–1991; PROTECTION OF EMPLOYMENT ACT 1977)

Selection for redundancy should be on the following bases:

- As agreed between company/union
- As established through custom and practice in the employment concerned
- In the absence of either of the above, an objectively fair criterion.

An employer must pay redundant employees a lump sum if they are aged between 16 and 66, have 104 weeks continuous service, work more than 8 hours per week and are in employment which is insurable for all benefits under the Social Welfare Act.

The lump sum is calculated as follows:

- One week's pay plus
- One/two week's remuneration for each year of continuous employment under the age of 41 plus

- One week's pay for each year of continuous employment over the age of 41 years

- Any earnings above £300 per week are disregarded (£15,600 per annum).

The procedure is as follows:

- Written notice to the employee on form RP1 at least two weeks before the date of dismissal

- A longer period of notice may be required under the Minimum Notice and Terms of Employment Acts 1973 and 1991 or by the employee's contract of employment

- The employee must receive their lump sum and redundancy certificate (form RP2) no later than the date when redundancy commences

- The employee should be given reasonable time off to look for work during the final two weeks of notice

- An employee laid off for periods of longer than four consecutive weeks or six broken weeks within 13 weeks may be entitled to claim redundancy

- An employer normally qualifies for 60 per cent rebate of any statutory redundancy payment made.

Collective Redundancies

A collective redundancy is one where the proportion of the employees to be made redundant is at least:

- Five employees out of a total of 21–49

- Ten employees out of a total 50–99

- Ten per cent of a total 100–299

- At least thirty of a total of 300 or more.

In a collective redundancy, 30 days before the first redundancy takes place, an employer must notify the Minister for Enterprise and Employment and provide basic information concerning the redundancies, and notify/consult employee representatives.

GRIEVANCE PROCEDURE (INDUSTRIAL RELATIONS ACT 1990)

An important element in the relationship between a company and its employees is a provision for handling any grievances or disputes that may arise. This agreement is usually included in the company handbook.

HEALTH AND SAFETY (SAFETY IN INDUSTRY ACTS 1955–1980; SAFETY, HEALTH AND WELFARE AT WORK ACT 1989; GENERAL APPLICATION REGULATIONS 1993)

There is a legal requirement to protect the safety, health and welfare of all persons at work.

Employer's duties include the provision of a safe place of work, a safe system of work, a safe means of access to and exit from the workplace, safe machinery and equipment, protective clothing and necessary training and supervision. In addition, employers/self-employed persons must also prepare a Safety Statement that must be brought to the attention of all persons affected by it.

Employees have a duty to take reasonable care for their own health and safety and that of others, to co-operate with their employers in complying with safety requirements, to use protective clothing and equipment and to report without delay any defects in the workplace which may involve danger and of which they are aware.

The 1989 Act allows for an *employees' safety representative* with certain powers to make representations to the employer, carry out safety inspections and obtain information from the employer.

OTHER REGULATIONS

Jury Service (Jury Act 1976)

Every citizen between 18 and 70 years who is on the register of Dáil Elections is eligible for jury service. An employee on jury service is treated as employed during the period — i.e. will receive normal pay.

Sick Pay/Pensions

There is no legislation at present that requires an employer to pay any employee who is absent on sick leave. Similarly, there is no legal obligation on an employer to provide a pension scheme for employees. You should refer to your Employee Handbook for details of relevant policies.

If an employee is certified by a doctor as being sick on a certain day during their annual leave period, that day is considered as sick leave, not annual leave.

Young Persons

The Protection of Young Persons Act 1977 legislates for the protection of workers under the age of 18.

Equality

(Anti-Discrimination Pay Act 1974; Employment Equality Act 1977; Pensions Act 1990)

Disputes under these Acts are dealt with by Equality Officers of the Labour Relations Commission.

Men and women employed by the same or an associated employer on like work in the same place are generally entitled to the same remuneration. Remuneration includes basic pay, bonuses, shift premiums/overtime payments, sick pay, pension schemes and other benefits.

Discrimination on grounds of sex or marital status is prohibited in terms of access to employment/training, or experience and promotion, or conditions of employment. If fewer or no members of one sex have been engaged in a particular job, the employer may lawfully provide special/additional training facilities for members of that sex.

Job advertisements should clearly state that the job is open to both men and women, except where the sex of the employee is an occupational qualification. Discriminatory questions should not be asked at interviews. An employee who takes an action against an employer for unequal treatment cannot be dismissed for this reason.

INDUSTRIAL RELATIONS
(INDUSTRIAL RELATIONS ACTS 1946–1990)

Trade Union Membership

This right is guaranteed to employees under the Irish Constitution. In practice, trade union membership has declined over the past few years, although where they do represent employees, they can play an important role.

Industrial Action

The Industrial Relations Act 1990 provides legal protection for those engaging in industrial action in order to further a trade dispute.

- **Secret ballots**: Trade Unions must have a provision in their rulebooks to hold secret ballots before taking industrial action. At least one week's notice must be given. Failure to do so will result in loss of legal immunity.

- **Picketing**: Subject to compliance with the above procedures, peaceful picketing at the place of work or, where it is not practicable, at the approaches to where an employer works or carries on a business is lawful. Secondary picketing is lawful only if the picketers have a "reasonable belief" that the employer in question "directly assisted" the employer who is party to the dispute for the purpose of frustrating the industrial action.

One-person disputes involving an individual employee will only be protected by legal immunity if an agreed procedure for resolving individual grievances, including dismissal, has been exhausted.

- **Injunctions**: If balloting and notice requirements have been complied with, the right of an employer to obtain injunctions to stop industrial action is curtailed by the 1990 Act.

EUROPEAN DIRECTIVE ON THE ORGANISATION OF WORKING TIME

This legislation covers minimum periods of daily rest, weekly rest, annual leave, breaks, maximum weekly working time, together with certain aspects of night work, shift work and pattern of work.

Definitions

- **Working time**: Any period during which the worker is working at the employer's disposal and carrying out their activities or duties.

- **Rest period**: Any period which is not working time.

- **Night time**: Any period of not less than seven hours and which must include the period between midnight and 5.00 a.m.

Rest Periods

- **Daily rest**: Every worker will be entitled to a minimum daily rest period of 11 consecutive hours per 24-hour period. There must be a break if the working day is longer than six hours.

- **Weekly rest**: Every worker will be entitled to a minimum uninterrupted rest period of 24 hours per seven-day period. This may be averaged over a reference period of up to 14 days. This 24-hour period has to be added to an 11-hour daily rest period, giving a total rest period of 35 hours. However, if objective technical or work organisational conditions justify it, only the minimum period of 24 hours need to be given.

Maximum Weekly Working Time

The Directive extends Member States' obligations to ensure the protection of the safety and health of workers. Average weekly working time for each seven-day period including overtime must not exceed 48 hours. The average of 48 hours per seven-day period may be averaged over a reference period of up to 4 months. There is now an obligation to compensate employees involved in Sunday working.

Night Work

Normal hours of work for night workers may not exceed an average of eight hours in any 24-hour period. Where the work involves special hazards or heavy physical work, night workers may not work more than eight hours in any 24-hour period during which they perform night work. Night workers will be entitled to a free health assessment before being assigned to night work, and thereafter at regular intervals. Night workers suffering from health problems connected with the fact that they work at night may be transferred to day work where possible.

Night workers and shift workers must have safety and health protection appropriate to their work. They must also have equivalent facilities to other workers (day workers).

USEFUL CONTACTS

• The **Department of Enterprise, Trade and Employment**'s responsibilities include the formulation, review and monitoring of labour legislation and the administration of industrial relations and trade union law. Davitt House, 65A Adelaide Road, Dublin 2. Tel: (01) 661 4444. Fax: (01) 676 9047.

- **Employment Appeals Tribunal** determines matters of dispute arising under the following Acts: Redundancy Payments, Minimum Notice, Maternity Protection, Adoptive Leave, Unfair Dismissals, Protection of Employees (Employers' Insolvency), Worker Protection (Regular Part-time Employees), Payment of Wages and Terms of Employment (Information). Davitt House, 65A, Adelaide Road, Dublin 2. Tel: (01) 676 5861. Fax: (01) 676 9047.

- The **Labour Relations Commission (LRC)** is generally responsible for the promotion of good industrial relations through the provision of a range of services designed to help prevent and resolve disputes. The LRC has responsibility for the following services: conciliation, equality officer, rights commissioner, Joint Labour Committees/Joint Industrial Councils. The LRC can be contacted at: Tom Johnson House, Haddington Road, Dublin 4. Tel: (01) 660 9662. Fax: (01) 668 5069.

- The **Conciliation Service** deals with disputes concerning pay/conditions of employment involving groups of workers. Unresolved disputes may, with the agreement of the LRC, be referred to the Labour Court. (Address as above)

- **Rights Commissioners** deal mainly with disputes concerning individual grievances. They issue a recommendation, which is not binding. Recommendations may be appealed to the Labour Court, whose decision is binding. The Rights Commissioners can be contacted at: Tom Johnson House, Haddington Road, Dublin 4. Tel: (01) 660 9662. Fax: (01) 668 5069.

- The **Labour Court** deals with disputes on appeal from Rights Commissioners or after failure to resolve matters at conciliation. LC recommendations are binding only in certain circumstances. Tom Johnson House, Haddington Road, Dublin 4. Tel: (01) 660 8444. Fax: (01) 660 8437.

- **Employer-Labour Conference** is a national forum for the review and discussion of developments and problems in industrial relations, pay determination and related matters. Davitt House, 65A Adelaide Road, Dublin 2. Tel: (01) 676 4884.

- **The Irish Congress of Trade Unions (ICTU)** is the central authority for the trade union movement in Ireland. There are 68 unions affiliated to the Congress, some of which operate in Northern Ireland. Membership of the affiliated unions in the Republic of Ireland is in excess of 450,000, with the two big general unions, SIPTU and ATGWU, representing about 45 per cent of total affiliated membership. 19 Raglan Road, Ballsbridge, Dublin 4. Tel: (01) 668 0641. Fax: (01) 660 9027.

- **Irish Business and Employers Confederation (IBEC)** represents business and employers in all matters relating to industrial relations, labour and social affairs. In addition, IBEC represents industry on all matters of trade, economics, finance, taxation, planning and development. It has over 3,700 member companies, while the Small Firms Association, for businesses with fewer than 50 employees, has 1,600. Both are located at Confederation House, 84/86 Lower Baggot Street, Dublin 2. Tel: (01) 660 1011. Fax: (01) 660 1717.

- **Health and Safety Authority** is representative of workers, employers and the government and is responsible for the administration of occupational health and safety legislation. Temple Court, Hogan Place, Grand Canal Street, Dublin 2. Tel: (01) 662 0400. Fax: (01) 662 0417.

- **Citizens' Information Centres (CICs).** There are more than 80 centres around the country providing a free and confidential information service to the public on a range of services, entitlements and citizens' rights. These centres are registered with the National Social Service Board, 71 Lower Leeson Street, Dublin 2. Tel: (01) 661 6422. Fax: (01) 676 4908.

Chapter 6

Interview Techniques

Ever felt misunderstood at interview or that you didn't get a fair chance to sell yourself? Not any more, for the latest trend in interviewing is: "Talk to me! That is, about yourself, in depth, for at least ten minutes, starting now".

Even in a job market where skills are in high demand, employers generally invest considerable time and effort in selecting the right employees. The required technical skills are almost taken for granted — though you will be asked for a lot of detail about these. The cost of a mismatched hire can be high with time wasted on training and, at times, ill feeling on either or both sides.

Employers are looking for strong evidence of interpersonal skills and the ability to work as part of a team and will usually not sacrifice these requirements, even if they are short-staffed. These are crucial qualities, particularly as many "promotional" opportunities now represent a chance to broaden your skills and experience in a team environment rather than an upwards move.

The first thing to remember is that interviewing is a *two-way* process. You should be evaluating how the interviewing company suits your particular personality and career goals. Typically, you will be interviewed at least twice, by individuals or a panel. It is critical to be well prepared. Good sources of information are Internet websites, trade journals and, of course, current or former employees. If you are approached by an applicant to give information about a current or former employer, be aware of the confidentiality of your information — most contracts restrict the disclosure of company-specific information, even after you have left.

For company information, try the business section of your local library, or the Central Business Library, ILAC Centre, Dublin 1.

Most companies are concerned with how you will interact with others, and you will be expected to provide specific examples. A general sales pitch will not suffice. In addition to proving that you are a team player, you will be expected to answer questions, with examples, that illustrate your ability to plan and organise work, lead and motivate peers and subordinates, adapt quickly and creatively to changing circumstances, use sound negotiating skills, communicate well at different levels and represent your company's corporate image.

Interviewers adopt many different styles, some more structured than others. You are likely to encounter all of these in some format in your quest for a job. To get the best results from your job search, it is important to equip yourself with as much information about these processes as possible so that you understand what the hiring company is trying to achieve at interview.

Leading organisational psychologist and founder of Behavioral Technology™ Inc., Dr Paul Green, who has spent more than 25 years conducting interviews and researching interviewing techniques, classifies the different kinds of interviewing into four categories: gut feeling, trait, conversational and behavioural. So, how do they differ?

GUT FEELING INTERVIEWS

This is an unstructured interview with little or no reference to job requirements, where the interviewer relies on their gut feeling or intuition and on whether or not they like you. Gut feeling interviewers tend to subscribe to "pet theories". For example, they might ask you questions about what type of sports you have played, because they believe that playing contact sports builds competitiveness. An interviewer who relies on their instincts about you will often be looking for your similarities to themselves. If they are someone who has had to fight their way to the top, they might ask you if you are confrontational (by which *they* mean assertive and able to influence), perceiving this as positive assertiveness, whereas the trait interviewer may take a different view.

This example illustrates how the arbitrary nature of unstructured interviews can disadvantage the candidate. Another disadvantage of unstructured interviews is that the interviewer can form an opinion in the first few minutes and then spend the remaining time justifying their gut reaction. Needless to say, lawyers advise against this kind of interviewing, as it leaves itself open to bias against some groups.

TRAIT INTERVIEWS

Trait interviews are person-related and may or not be structured and you will be asked questions that relate more to your personal characteristics than your job skills, sometimes without reference to the kind of work to be done. This is where you are most likely to be asked your most positive and negative traits. A typical question would be: "What are your three greatest strengths and weaknesses/areas for development?" You should prepare for this question by identifying a list of your positive characteristics; for example, "I enjoy working on projects with other people". When you cite your negative traits, do so in a positive light, for example: "It bothers me when others do not pull their weight in meeting a deadline." Then follow up with a specific example of a time you put this particular positive trait into practice.

Although experts acknowledge that trait interviews, if combined with personality tests and carried out by well-trained interviewers, can produce accurate results, the pitfall from the candidate's perspective is that a trait (characteristic) can become a label that reflects an impression rather than actual information. For example, one well-known stereotype is to classify an assertive, confident male as "decisive", a similar female as "bossy". Classifying an everyday task such as cooking as something that women do has the reverse effect; a person who thinks this way may consider men who like cooking to be feeble. The downside for the interviewer is that a practised candidate can perform well at interview and give all the right answers without having to give specific examples from their past actions.

CONVERSATIONAL INTERVIEWS

This approach is an unstructured interview focusing mainly on job experience and job skills. There is no prepared list of questions and the conversation will usually flow naturally from one topic to another, similar to a social situation. Although this may seem likely a friendly chat, the conversational interviewer is using rapport rather than structure to gain information. The intention is to make you feel comfortable, and therefore perhaps more likely to reveal information that you may otherwise have felt reluctant to mention.

It is absolutely fine for you to behave informally in this situation; however, maintain your professionalism and give plenty of examples about yourself and your colleagues, rather than using generalisations. It would be a mistake to treat this kind of interview as easier than others, although it may seem this way. A good conversational interviewer is using a clever technique to get you to open up. Provided you are aware of the technique and have prepared (as outlined in the following pages), you can turn this to your own advantage by leading the conversation yourself through the examples and topics that you introduce to illustrate your own skills. As with all interviews, you cannot control the questions, but you can control the content.

BEHAVIOURAL-BASED INTERVIEWING

Several developments have contributed to a change in approach to interviewing in the past 15 years. In the late 1970s, industrial psychologists in the US began questioning the effectiveness of typical employment interviews, and their research concluded that the predictive power of these interviews was little more effective than randomly selecting CVs to hire people. At the same time, more attention was being paid to the cost of hiring the wrong person — a figure put at two to four times that person's annual salary by some experts. As organisations began to flatten, more emphasis was being placed on interpersonal skills. The ability to function as part of a team, or indeed to work alone or to be capable of completely changing work type, and sometimes even career, gathered credence as critical skills. The challenge is not to source employees who are all things to all people, but to use scientific methods to put the right person in the right job.

As a result of extensive research, psychologists concluded that only structured, behavioural-based interviews could accurately select the right candidates.

Behavioural-based interviewing is based on the premise that the best indicator of future performance is past performance and that the best way to elicit this information is by asking a set of predetermined and objective questions that relate to the job being interviewed for.

Understanding How It Works

Trained behavioural interviewers usually develop the questions by analysing the available job and deciding what skills and personal characteristics are needed. Whereas trait (characteristics) interviews look within the individual to *understand* why people behave as they do, Behavioral Technology™ interviewing is based on the concept that anything a person does can be observed and measured, and that examples of past behaviour can be used to *predict*, rather than understand behaviour. Given that not many interviewers are qualified psychologists — and in any event interviews are not long enough to analyse someone — it appears logical that this is a safer approach to selection. The behavioural interviewer's questions should prompt answers that give the information needed to determine whether the candidate has those skills and characteristics. If you are unable to answer (for example, if you have no experience relevant to the question on which you can draw), this is not considered a negative and the interviewer simply poses the question from a different approach.

An interview using Behavioral Technology™ techniques will entail questions that are designed to prompt answers giving specific examples which illustrate certain skills, also known as competencies. This approach is based on research, and properly trained interviewers effectively become interview technicians, selecting from a structured set of open questions devised by psychologists for each skill, writing down descriptive notes about what the candidate says (unlike in some other interview types where the interviewer notes their own impressions, or worse, nothing at all) and measuring your responses against a guide for evaluating the evidence of behaviour that you supply in your reply.

For example, imagine you are an experienced language teacher applying for a position as a translator, of which you have little commercial experience. However, you have brought work with you that shows you have the necessary written and comprehension skills, together with the ability to understand complicated technical subjects. Translators work to tight deadlines, set by themselves in conjunction with clients. The interviewer is looking for evidence of your *skills in setting goals*:

> Question: "In a busy working environment of this kind, we have to *prioritise our work* to ensure that commitments to clients are met. Tell me about an important time when you set goals successfully in a work situation."

Having written down what you have said, in analysing your answer, a trained behavioural interviewer may ask another question, following on from what you have said to look for evidence that you have used *initiative in organising work* (a separate skill), including the use of available resources.

What happens when the client has no choice but to bring the deadline forward? This happens to translators frequently and the interviewer will need to know what *coping skills* you have displayed in the past to predict how you may act in the future.

> Question: "Tell me about a time when you had to cope with a highly pressurised situation at work?"

In analysing your answer, the interviewer will look for evidence in what you said of your skill in adapting to the situation in a constructive and positive way.

Remember, companies do not need every potential employee to want to rule the world. While you should use high profile examples if you actually have this experience, simple, practical, well illustrated, everyday examples are exactly what the interviewer needs in order to see how you normally behave and to predict how you might behave in the future.

SUCCEEDING AT INTERVIEW

Although you will not know in advance the kind of style your interviewer will adopt, you can greatly enhance your chances of success by thorough preparation. Having made a list of your different skills using the sample questions above, you need to structure your answers. Preparing for a behavioural-based interview should equip you for any interview. Your golden rule should be to back up whatever you say with examples of when you used specific skills. The SHARE technique is an excellent guide for preparing your examples in a way that will best illustrate your skills and experience. A SHARE answer provides specific information on the situation, hindrances, actions, results and evaluation.

- **S**ituation: Begin by describing the situation in which you were operating.

- **H**indrances: Describe any constraints or hindrances to your actions.

- **A**ctions: Explain exactly what you did.

- **R**esults: Describe the results that can be attributed to your actions.

- **E**valuation: Summarise the evaluation with a positive example of your skill.

Reproduced with the kind permission of Behavioral Technology™.

Now make a list of about 20 answers relating to the skills detailed below using this technique. You may surprise yourself at how skilled you are. Having prepared in this way will leave you feeling much more confident on the day.

WHAT TO PREPARE

As you cannot expect to predict exactly which company uses which technique, the best approach is to prepare thorough answers of a range of job- and skills-based questions that you can use at every interview, using real examples.

Using the SHARE technique described above, in preparation for interview, ask yourself and be prepared to answer the following questions. These examples highlight some of the skills that interviewers look for. The skills required for every job differ, so try putting yourself in the interviewer's position and try to think of questions you might pose relating to your particular job to gain evidence of each of the listed skills.

- **Confirm details on your CV**: why you made certain choices at different times, such as choice of education, job, why you are moving/returning to Ireland. This is an opportunity to show that you are someone who can think things through. Without appearing to be an extreme planner, be ready to illustrate how you used reasonable and logical thinking when making decisions that have had an impact on your life.

- **Interpersonal skills:** give simple, everyday examples to illustrate that you can build different kinds of relationships with other people and that you are aware of their feelings and opinions. Think of examples that show your flexibility in interacting with others. The importance of these skills cannot be stressed enough.

- **Describe situations where you had to deal with stress**: questions may be posed about meeting a deadline, dealing with an angry person, dealing with conflict where the conflict concerns you. The interviewer is looking for evidence of your *coping* skills.

- **Ability to cope with change**: give an example where you had to deal with the unexpected at work. Think carefully about this; you could cite an example where you had to resolve not to do something because of changing circumstances. Here, evidence of your skills in dealing with and tolerating unclear and unstructured situations is required.

- **Acting decisively**: be ready to describe situations where you have had to act *quickly*, make unpopular decisions, put contingency plans into place, keep to decisions.

- **Decision-making/problem-solving:** this is not the same skill as being decisive, where the speed with which you take action is a skill. Here the interviewer is looking for your ability to understand issues and use reason and good judgement. As you think of your examples, consider to what extent emotion guided your decision. If you have examples of where you have displayed *creativity* in solving problems, use them. Listen carefully to the questions. If the interviewer asks you about having to *accept an unpopular decision*, they are looking for a different skill, such as the ability to accept company culture.

- **Verbal and written communication**: two distinct skills important for all jobs, particularly those involving leadership. The interviewer is seeking evidence that you possess listening skills, can speak and write clearly, and can influence others. Think of examples in both positive and negative situations. The question may be phrased in a number of different ways, depending on the context. For example, be aware that if you are asked about having to be *assertive*, it is worth thinking of times when you succeed in being *tactfully* so when you select an example.

- You may be asked if you ever had to *follow a set of written instructions*. Be careful on this one. It is surprising how many candidates reply "no", although they may have just completed written aptitude tests with instructions on how to complete each part.

- **Leading and Motivating**: think of examples where you had a motivating effect on others. It could be in any situation, not just work. This skill is desired in employees of all levels, not just managers, and your answer merits good preparation. This is also a good opportunity to include examples of when you have recognised the contributions of colleagues and others, which is evidence of motivational ability in itself. Remember too that competition can motivate, so the interviewer is not looking for examples that emphasise purely soft skills. If you are interviewing for a leadership position, the interviewer is probably also looking for evidence of your ability to evaluate objectively.

- **Following the party line**: be ready to describe situations where you had to follow, implement or explain company policies and procedures. Every job and company has routine, established procedures. Nobody will hire someone who wants to reinvent the wheel every time. Equally, as a leader you will be called on to implement *with conviction* decisions you do not agree with, as though they were your own. Try to think of some real everyday examples in your response to this question. Another related skill is your ability to *understand the corporate and organisational culture* and recognise where and when you can use this to achieve goals. For example, you may have found that before making an important presentation, it helped to talk individually and informally to your audience in advance to individually gain their support.

- **Alertness**. Think of examples where you were prepared and alert in a normal daily working environment. Although quick thinking is part of this skill, it is not the same as being decisive. Being alert is proactive, displaying decisiveness reactive. The interviewer is looking for examples of how alert you are. This is a question that you would particularly expect to be asked in a manufacturing environment, where changes in the physical surroundings where machinery is being used can have a major impact. However, your examples need not be high level. For example, you are responsible for ensuring that your team's weekly overtime hours are communicated to payroll and notice that your neighbouring team leader is absent through illnesses and, without being asked, take steps to ensure that their team gets paid.

- **Solving problems using analysis**: give examples of when you had to make an informed decision based on a range of possible solutions. This question will not be asked for every job, but many positions do involve the use of analytical tools to some extent. Think of any examples that involve using maths at any level.

- **Setting goals and objectives**: for yourself and others, prioritising workload, time management. Evidence of initiative and logic should feature in your response.

- **Planning work:** a valid question for many jobs. Everyone has examples of organising and if you have better examples from your life outside work, then use them. This point is often brought home when, after much agonising, teamwork is introduced in companies, only to find that many of the members of the production teams already held managerial responsibilities in their sports and leisure activities.

- **Showing commitment**: think of examples where you had to work extra hours or give up leisure time because you were committed to achieving something, or perhaps stuck with something boring until it was complete. You should not limit your examples to work situations. Remember that working long hours every day may raise questions about your organisational ability.

- **Team-building**: evidence is being sought of your ability to work with other people in a way that builds morale and contributes to the team/group meeting its goals. This is one of the most important skills required in jobs in Ireland. Give real examples of where you contributed to planning and meeting group goals, were able to step back and allow someone else complete a desirable task or be the spokesperson, even if you wanted to yourself. This is a good opportunity to illustrate that you have learned new skills.

Remember, these are not trick questions. There is no right or wrong answer. The interviewer is trying to predict how you might act in similar situations in the future by asking you to decide how you have acted in the past.

ASSESSMENT CENTRES

Assessment centres are used in particular types of selection, such as graduate recruits to accountancy firms or major banks. One global bank with a world-wide processing centre in Dublin requires all applicants to attend an assessment centre that includes group interviews, simulation (role play) interviews and individual meetings. Other selection tools employed may include psychological testing, language testing, group problem-solving exercises and individual written exercises.

Briefly, these involve:

- **Group interviews**: the point here is to carry out initial selection. The group is given a topic to discuss and the ensuing discussion is then observed. This type of exercise is really only appropriate where very strong interpersonal skills are important — for example, airlines and customer service centres would use this method. The key to success here is moderation. Speak clearly but not constantly, acknowledge others in the group and use examples from your own experience to substantiate what you say.

- **Psychological tests** (also known as occupational or psychometric tests) are designed and developed by occupational psychologists and are accompanied by detailed manuals on how to interpret the results. Abilities in areas such as numeracy are commonly tested. With personality tests, there are no right or wrong answers, as they are designed to present a profile of the individual. The Institute of Personnel and Development recommends that tests should not be used as the sole basis for decision-making and that test administrators should ensure that candidates have information about receiving feedback.

- **Aptitude testing**: used frequently in the international services sector, particularly to test language ability. Native speakers should expect to be asked to take the same tests as non-native speakers.

DEALING WITH QUESTIONS YOU WOULD PREFER NOT TO ANSWER

As the law currently stands in Ireland, employers must not discriminate on grounds of an individual's sex or marital status, either in advertising for employees, or when interviewing and hiring them. Should the Employment Equality Bill eventually be passed into law, these grounds would be extended to prohibit discrimination on the further grounds of religion, age, race, disability, family status, sexual orientation and membership of the travelling community.

This Bill, while passed by the Oireachtas (the legislature), has been referred by the President to the Supreme Court to test its constitutionality. The Supreme Court found the Bill to be unconstitutional in relation to three areas.

Meanwhile, most employers know the kind of questions to avoid, particularly among the big multinationals. However, although the Small Firms Association and other business groups provide good guidelines, not all employers can be expected to have the same level of understanding in this area.

There are a number of ways of dealing with an objectionable question. It depends on how much you want the job and how inappropriate the question is. The least preferable approach is to make an issue on the spot. Equally, it is interesting to observe how a candidate can inadvertently put the interviewer in a position where any response they give could be interpreted as discriminatory. For example, a female returning to the workforce may start to talk about her children and the arrangements she plans to make for their care. There is simply no suitable response. In this case, the well-trained interviewer does not show that they have registered that they have heard the comment, does not give any kind of reaction and simply moves on to the next question. It may be the smartest strategy for candidates as well: you do not have to accept the job, but it is nice to have the choice.

QUESTIONS YOU COULD ASK

- Why has the vacancy arisen?

- Company/department goals for the next quarter/year?

- Plans for expansions into new markets?

- Most successful product and why?

- Company culture — for example, formal, informal, hierarchical or team-based?

- Is training provided? If you have certain skills that can be passed on to others, will you get that opportunity?

- Do employees meet socially?

- Company's links with the community e.g. sponsoring charities, providing work placements for the unemployed, etc.?

THINGS TO WATCH

Be aware of your choice of language: talk about leading rather than supervising, do not miss any opportunity to show how you facilitated teamwork and give credit to colleagues at all levels. Bearing in mind that humour differs according to culture, avoid any tendency to be sarcastic.

Much is written about observing and trying to read the body language of those you meet. To do this could distract you from what you are at the interview to achieve: to listen to the company's job requirements, illustrate how your skills and experience match these and get a job. You should ignore advice about mirroring other people's body language and instead, without placing undue importance on it, be conscious that your own is professional. For example, sit or stand up straight, focus on the person you are talking to and avoid gesturing.

Never criticise a former employer at an interview, even if the interviewer gives you an obvious opening. You do not have to like them, but they could be a customer in the future. Also, this kind of criticism reflects badly on the speaker.

Finally, Ireland is a very small marketplace and you will constantly encounter people with whom you find you have acquaintances in common. It is useful to bear this in mind in all your professional dealings.

FOLLOWING UP ON YOUR INTERVIEW

Interviewers tend to be busy, and as a way of ensuring that you get called to the next round of selection or get a job, invest a few minutes in writing a thank you letter within a day or two. This should be succinct. If you have something important that you forget to mention, telephone instead. Here is a sample thank you letter:

Dear

I am writing to thank you very much for your time yesterday. I enjoyed meeting with you and hearing about the (position) and the plans that (company name) has for the future.

Having reviewed the points we discussed, I believe my particular skills and experience closely match your requirements and would welcome an opportunity to discuss this role further.

Yours sincerely,

If you receive an offer, it is likely to be conditional on passing a medical examination and the receipt of satisfactory references. On the subject of medicals, recent reports suggest that an increasing number of Irish-based companies are having employees tested for drug abuse, both before and during employment. If you receive an employment offer, the best approach is not to resign from an existing job until you have a written offer and are sure these points have been satisfactorily covered. Keep to the existing notice period committed to in your existing job.

If you receive a rejection, move on to the next application. Some companies will provide feedback, and behavioural interviewers are generally trained to do so constructively. However, while it is useful to receive this, it is not worth pursuing relentlessly. Employment rejections are not personal slights and it is important to remember that they are not cause for complaint unless you have been treated in a way that may be discriminatory. Occasionally, unsuccessful applicants take it out on the interviewer and vent their anger in writing. Unless you have grounds for discrimination, this serves only to reinforce the validity of your rejection in the first place. A better tactic is to telephone the person involved, thank them for their time and ask them to think of you if they come across another opportunity that might suit you. This means that instead of forgetting you, the interviewer will be left with a positive impression of you and, particularly if their job involves a lot of recruitment, is likely to consider you again later.

BACK TO THE BEGINNING

Now that you are familiar with the technical and interpersonal skills sought in the Irish market, and have used the guidelines in *How to Find a Job* to produce a relevant CV and sent it to the right people and places, you should be ready for interview. There are certain ways to find out what kind of interview awaits you. Ensure that you find out the name and job title of everyone you are to meet. If you simply ask the person arranging the interview what the roles of these people are, you will usually obtain clues to the kinds of things that are important to them (for example, someone at head of function level may be a candidate for an internal promotion). Ask too how much time you should allow — this will provide some indication of the type of interview.

However, it need not be all guesswork. Many companies using behavioural techniques will also tend to be team-based or moving towards that structure. Some well-known examples are Guinness, Intel, Hewlett-Packard and Motorola. Meanwhile, in the international services sector, UPS is trying out a computer-based aptitude test that will test your skills in customer service by taking you through an hour of (at times exasperating) scenarios. Citibank favour assessment-centre style interviewing while one of the call centres recently introduced an innovative pre-recorded telephone interview which basically allows you to leave your CV verbally while cleverly checking some of the necessary skills.

Chapter 7

Setting Up in Business

Once looked down upon, enterprise is now fashionable in Ireland. Although hard figures are difficult to come by, it is estimated that there are some 160,000 small and medium-sized businesses in Ireland (measured by the EU definition, all but a handful of Irish companies are SMEs) and that this number is growing by 10 per cent annually. Small business has been a major contributor to employment growth in the past decade, with 130,000 jobs created in this sector in the past two years alone, and a further 100,000 projected by the millennium.

STATE SUPPORT FOR ENTERPRISE

State support for enterprise is well resourced though fragmented across a range of agencies, boards and other bodies whose roles and activities often appear not to be co-ordinated — indeed, sometimes even in competition with one another.

Primary responsibility for enterprise lies with the Department of Enterprise, Trade and Employment, (Small Business and Services Division, Davitt House, Adelaide Road, Dublin 4. Tel: (01) 661 4444). Policy is set by Forfás (Wilton Park House, Wilton Place, Dublin 2. Tel: (01) 668 8444) whose two executive arms, IDA Ireland and Forbairt (both at Wilton Place), provide support for incoming and indigenous industry respectively. Support is focused on manufacturing industry and internationally traded services. With only a few exceptions, principally tourism, services do not benefit from State support, though there are indications that this may be changing.

In the west and mid-west, Údarás na Gaeltachta (Na Forbacha, Galway, Tel: (091) 503100, Fax: (091) 503101, E-mail: eolas @udaras.ie) and Shannon Development (Town Centre, Shannon, County Clare, Tel: (061) 361555, Fax: (061) 361903, E-mail: info@Shannon-Dev.ie) provide on a regional basis the services and support offered nationally by Forbairt, as well as services targeted at local needs.

Also reporting to the Department of Enterprise, Trade and Employment are City and County Enterprise Boards, Area Partnership Companies, Business Innovation Centres and State agencies, including An Bord Tráchtála (The Irish Trade Board, Merrion Hall, Sandymount, Dublin 4, Tel: (01) 269 5011, Fax: (01) 269 5820). Other State agencies that report to different Government departments include:

- An Bord Bia (food), Clanwilliam Court, Lower Mount Street, Dublin 2. Tel: (01) 668 5155. Fax: (01) 668 7521.

- Bord Fáilte (tourism), Baggot Street Bridge, Dublin 2. Tel: (01) 676 5871. Fax: (01) 676 4764.

- Bord Iascaigh Mhara (fisheries and aquaculture), Crofton Road, Dun Laoghaire, County Dublin. Tel: (01) 284 1544. Fax: (01) 284 1123.

- FÁS (the training and employment authority) 27–33 Lower Baggot Street, Dublin 2. Tel: (01) 668 5777. Fax: (01) 668 3691.

More information can be found in "Innovation Ireland: A Directory of State Assistance for Industrial Innovation", published by Forfás.

CITY AND COUNTY ENTERPRISE BOARDS

The City and County Enterprise Boards (CEBs), of which there are 35 (addresses from the Small Business and Services Division, Department of Employment), are the first-line source of support for entrepreneurs. CEBs provide grant-aid, advice and assistance to start-up and existing businesses that employ or expect to employ fewer than 10 people. Above the ten-person threshold, enquiries are referred to Forbairt.

Although each CEB operates autonomously in meeting the needs of its catchment area, in practice they tend to offer similar packages of feasibility study grants, employment or capital expenditure grants (one or other, not both), training and general advice. CEBs do not normally consider proposals involving grant support in excess of £50,000 or projects with investment costs in excess of £100,000.

AREA PARTNERSHIP COMPANIES

The Area Partnership Companies (APCs) were established as a means of alleviating unemployment in black spots (addresses from Area Development Management Limited, Holbrook House, Holles Street, Dublin 2. Tel: (01) 661 3611. Fax: (01) 661 0411). APCs work at local level to generate more jobs through sustainable enterprises and through the promotion of local economic projects and initiatives. Because the needs of areas served by APCs differ, and because each APC is autonomous in deciding how to meet those needs, even where a common problem is addressed, the approach taken can be dramatically different.

ENTERPRISE LINK

This is a "one-stop shop" service operated by Forbairt on a low cost telephone number — 1850-353333 — that will guide you to the appropriate State agency to meet your needs. Very knowledgeable on enterprise matters generally.

OTHER SOURCES OF ASSISTANCE

Other organisations that assist the potential entrepreneur in starting up and/or developing their business include:

- **Bolton Trust:** Runs the Powerhouse, which rents office space and has a full-time Enterprise Development Manager to advise and work with companies. (The Powerhouse, Pigeon House

Harbour, Ringsend, Dublin 4. Tel: (01) 668 7155. Fax: (01) 668 7945).

- **Business Incubation Centres**: Offer entrepreneurs rented workspace and other assistance at the Richmond Business Campus, North Brunswick Street, Dublin 7, and Ossory Business Park, Ossory Road, Dublin 3. Tel: (01) 807 2400. Fax: (01) 872 6252. E-mail: Richmond@iol.ie.

- **Business Innovation Centres**: Six BICs — Dublin, Cork, Galway, Limerick, Waterford and Derry — provide a multi-disciplinary approach to the development of technology-based and innovative projects. (Dublin: The Tower, IDA Enterprise Centre, Pearse Street, Dublin 2. Tel: (01) 671 3111. Fax: (01) 671 3330.)

- **Central Statistics Office**: Another source of information. (Skehan Road, Mahon, Cork. Tel: (021) 359000. Fax: (021) 359090. E-mail: information@cso.ie.)

- **European Information Centres**: in An Bord Tráchtála offices in Dublin, Cork, Galway, Limerick, Sligo and Waterford.

- **First Step**: Provides seed funding (up to 50 per cent, with matching funds usually required) for projects or people with no security. (Jefferson House, Eglinton Road, Donnybrook, Dublin 4. Tel: (01) 260 0988. Fax: (01) 260 09890.)

- **Food Product Development Centre**: Services include sensory assessment, ingredient sources and testing, shelf-life, market research, packaging, labelling and concept-testing and advice on recipe development and design and marketing of new food products. (Dublin School of Catering, Cathal Brugha Street, Dublin 1. Tel: (01) 874 6058. Fax: (01) 874 8572.)

- **Irish Small and Medium Enterprises Association**: Represents the concerns of owner-managed businesses to government and provides its members with group schemes offering significant savings on insurance, etc. (17 Kildare Street, Dublin 2. Tel: (01) 662 2755. Fax: (01) 661 2157.)

- **Liffey Trust**: Assists start-up businesses with preparation of business plans, feasibility studies and grant applications, advice on raising finance and setting up accounting/control systems, and combined marketing of products. (117–126 Upper Sheriff Street, Dublin 1. Tel: (01) 836 4651. Fax: (01) 836 4818.)

- **National Food Centre**: Provides research, consultancy and training, product and process development and analytical services for the food industry (except milk products, for which the National Dairy Products Centre at Moorepark, Fermoy, Co. Cork is responsible). (Dunisea, Castleknock, Dublin 15. Tel: (01) 838 3222. Fax: (01) 838 3684.)

- **National Microelectronics Application Centre**: Services include design, simulation, evaluation, fabrication, education and consultancy. (University College, Lee Maltings, Prospect Row, Cork. Tel: (021) 904092. Fax: (021) 270271.)

- **Project Development Centre**: Offers enterprise training to high-potential companies in the form of hands-on projects. (17 Herbert Street, Dublin 2. Tel: (01) 661 1910/676 7175. Fax: (01) 661 1973.)

- **Small Firms Association**: Acts as a distinctive voice on behalf of the small business community and advises, assists and informs its members on a range of issues. (Confederation House, 84–86 Lower Baggot Street, Dublin 2. Tel: (01) 660 1011. Fax: (01) 677 7823.)

- **Telework Ireland**: Represents teleworkers and micro-enterprises. Members are provided with a comprehensive *Teleworking Handbook*, *Teleworker Magazine* and an indirect membership of the Small Firms Association. (7 Clones Road, Monaghan. Tel: (047) 72069. Fax: (047) 72070. E-mail: carroll@connect.ie.)

More information can be found in *Enterprise Ireland: A Directory of Sources of Assistance for Entrepreneurs and Small Business Owners* (Oak Tree Press, £9.95).

START-UP STEPS

Leaving aside the question of your business idea, the steps involved in starting a business in Ireland are as follows:

- **Decide on a legal structure**: Sole trader, partnership, limited company or co-operative.

- **Register your business name** (if not trading as a limited company, or if trading under a name different from that of the limited company): Use Form RN1B, available from the Companies Office, Parnell House, 14 Parnell Square, Dublin 1. Tel: (01) 804 5200. Fax: (01) 804 5222.

- **Register for taxes**: Use Form TR1 (sole trader/partnerships) or TR2 (limited companies) to register for income/corporation tax, VAT and as an employer. The Revenue Commissioners publish a free *Starting in Business* guide, which won an award for design in the 1997 *Irish Independent* Communications in Business Awards. Contact your local tax office (see green section of telephone directory).

- **Write a business plan**: None of the State agencies, CEBs or banks will entertain a proposal for grant-aid or loan finance without a written business plan. For small start-ups, Ron Immink's *Planning for Success: A Business Plan Workbook for Start-ups* (Oak Tree Press, £7.99) is recommended.

- **Open a business bank account**: Essential for a limited company, but recommended even for sole traders, to keep your business and personal income and expenditure separate.

- **Raise finance**: see below.

Note that, unlike in many European countries, there is no requirement to register a new business with the local chamber of commerce — though membership can be a useful way of making contacts (addresses from Chambers of Commerce in Ireland, 22 Merrion Square, Dublin 2. Tel: (01) 661 2888. Fax: (01) 661 2811. E-mail: chambers@iol.ie).

For more information on setting up a new business in an Irish context, read *Starting a Business in Ireland* by Brian O'Kane (Oak Tree Press, £10.95).

RAISING FINANCE

It is important that you raise as much as you can from your own resources, since most Irish financiers work on a "matching funds" basis — that is, they will only invest the same amount as you are investing. Be creative and include as part of your investment some items that would have been available to the business in an informal way anyway. Your investment might now be made up of £3,000 cash and £10,000 equipment — which looks better than just £3,000 cash!

Sources of equity include:

- **ACT Venture Capital Limited**: A £50 million venture capital fund that invests between £300,000 and £5 million for the expansion of growing companies. Also operates an £8 million fund, jointly funded by ACT Venture Capital and Forbairt, to provide between £100,000 and £750,000 to Irish early stage SMEs. (Jefferson House, Eglinton Road, Donnybrook, Dublin 4. Tel: (01) 260 0966. Fax: (01) 260 0538. E-mail: infor@actvc.ie.)

- **Bank of Ireland Entrepreneurs Fund**: A £10 million early stage fund focusing on the technology and food sectors, investing £100,000 to £500,000. The fund managers, Delta Partners, have the capacity to complete larger transactions through other funds under its management. (Bank of Ireland Enterprise Support Unit, Head Office, Lower Baggot Street, Dublin 2. Tel: (01) 661 5933. Fax: (01) 767 3493.)

- **Business Expansion Scheme (BES)**: A form of venture capital, intended to help small businesses to obtain additional capital. Fund-raising companies must be incorporated and resident in Ireland, must not be quoted on the Stock Exchange (other than on the Developing Companies Market), and must be engaged in a qualifying trade. It is up to the business to find potential investors and, when it does so, to obtain approval of the arrangement from the Revenue Commissioners. Usually, businesses that want to raise finance in this way go through a broker or accountant who sponsors the share issue. (Business Expansion Scheme, Direct Taxes Administration Branch, Office of the Revenue Commissioners, Dublin Castle, Dublin 2. Tel: (01) 679 2777. Fax: (01) 671 0012.)

- **Business Innovation Centres** (see above): These operate an Investor Register Service, matching businesses seeking funds with individuals or companies looking for investment opportunities. Dublin BIC also manages the Dublin Seed Capital Fund which invests between £25,000 and £100,000.

- **Business Innovation Fund**: An independent seed capital fund that provides seed capital (£25,000 to £75,000) for start-up and early-stage businesses, in return for a minority share. Projects should have fewer than 10 people employed, an annual turnover of less than £75,000, potential to grow significantly in the future, pre-investment issued fully-paid-up share capital of less than £1.15 million and previous risk capital of no more than £40,000. (Molyneux House, 67–69 Bride Street, Dublin 8. Tel: (01) 475 3305. Fax: (01) 475 2044.)

- **Shannon Development**: Operates a seed capital fund (£2,000 to £5,000), early stage financing (£20,000 to £200,000) and a Tourism Enterprise Fund (up to £50,000).

- **The Smurfit Job Creation Enterprise Fund**: Invests between £100,000 and £500,000 as a minority equity stake in selected new or expanding Irish companies that can demonstrate sustainable job-creation potential (at least 10 jobs). (94 St Stephen's Green, Dublin 2. Tel: (01) 478 4091. Fax: (01) 475 2362.)

Sources of loan finance include:

- **AIB Bank Enterprise Development Bureau**: AIB's focal point for start-up and expanding businesses, both in manufacturing and service industries. It administers AIB Bank's £40 million

Enterprise Loan Scheme, aimed at export-oriented and import-substitution businesses with significant job-retention or creation prospects. (Bankcentre, Ballsbridge, Dublin 4. Tel: (01) 660 0311. Fax: (01) 668 2009.)

- **Bank of Ireland Enterprise Support Unit**: has a £50 million fund available, combining hands-on support, no personal guarantees required, full range of lending products, AA lending rate and a normal lending range £20,000 to £150,000. Also has a new Entrepreneurs Fund (see above). Bank of Ireland's start-up package exempts entrepreneurs from most bank charges and fees in the first year of operation.

- **Credit Unions**: increasingly willing to assist members to start businesses, especially co-operatives. (Irish League of Credit Unions, Lower Mount Street, Dublin 2. Tel: (01) 490 8911. Fax: (01) 490 4448.)

- **Forbairt Fund**: Operated by AIB, Bank of Ireland and Ulster Bank, this provides £60 million of EU-subsidised loan capital.

- **ICC Bank**: Facilities include short, medium and long-term loans. Tends towards short-term finance, though its long-term loans continue to offer a longer repayment period than the commercial banks. The Eurofix facility aims to take the volatility out of borrowing in the run-up to EMU, while ICC's Supplier Payline provides working capital. (Head Office: 72/74 Harcourt Street, Dublin 2. Tel: (01) 475 5700. Fax: (01) 671 7797.)

- **National Irish Bank**: NIB's New Enterprise Loan Fund supports the creation and development of small and medium-sized businesses with employment potential, by way of loans of between £15,000 and £75,000. No personal guarantees are required. Access to this scheme is through any of NIB's branches or the specialist regional offices. (Head Office: 7/8 Wilton Terrace, Dublin 2. Tel: (01) 678 5066. Fax: (01) 678 5949.)

- **TSB Bank**: Though geared primarily towards the personal banking market, TSB is rapidly growing in the small business sector and offers current account facilities, overdrafts and loans to business customers. (Head Office: 114 Grafton Street, Dublin 2. Tel: (01) 679 8133. Fax: (01) 671 1239.)

- **Ulster Bank**: Has at least one trained Small Business Advisor at each Ulster Bank Branch. The Ulster Bank Enterprise Loan Scheme comprises repayments spread over 10 years, standard commercial AA rates, repayment "holidays" where appropriate and no personal guarantee or mortgage on the family home required. In addition, the SME Loan scheme provides loans at Prime Rate and free banking for the first year of trading (50 per cent off in years two and three). (Small Business Section, 33 College Green, Dublin 2. Tel: (01) 677 7623. Fax: (01) 702 5875.)

You should not be asked for — and you should not give lightly — a personal guarantee for borrowings, though Ireland's risk-averse lenders will invariably require security for all but the smallest borrowings.

Part Two

LIVING IN IRELAND

Chapter 8

Moving to Ireland

As anyone who has relocated will testify, the better you plan your move, the easier it will be. It is worth contacting the Irish Embassy in your current country of residence for any further assistance you may need. For a list of Irish Embassies abroad, look up http://www.irlgov.ie. This chapter deals with some of the key points you need to consider.

TRAVELLING TO IRELAND

By Air

You can get to Ireland by air or sea from the US, Canada, Britain, or Europe. Ireland's national airline, Aer Lingus, operates services from nine airports in Britain and nine major cities in Europe, many of which are also serviced by Ryanair. Frequency is high, so you can choose a flight any day of the week. Ireland has nine airports, but the principal ones for international arrivals are Dublin, Cork in the south and Shannon in the west. Sample flying times are London–Dublin, around one hour; New York–Dublin, just over five hours; Rome–Dublin, around three hours. Within Ireland, flights are available from Dublin to Cork, Shannon, Galway, Knock, Sligo and Kerry.

Direct flights to Ireland from the USA are:

Airline	Gateway	Destination
Aer Lingus	Boston	Shannon, Dublin
	Chicago	Shannon, Dublin
	New York	Shannon, Dublin, Belfast
	Newark, NJ	Shannon, Dublin

Airline	Gateway	Destination
Aeroflot	Chicago	Shannon
	Miami	Shannon
	Washington, DC	Shannon
Delta Air Lines	Atlanta	Shannon, Dublin
	New York	Shannon, Dublin

Aer Lingus, Air Inter, Alitalia, Iberia, Lufthansa, Ryanair, Sabena, SAS, TAP all fly from Europe to Ireland.

By Sea

Ireland is linked to Britain and Europe by regular ferry services on a number of routes. All have drive-on/drive-off facilities. There are between one and six sailings in each direction per day, depending on the route and time of the year.

Services operate between Scotland and Northern Ireland and between Wales and the Republic of Ireland. New high-speed "superferries" make the crossing between Holyhead and Dublin or Dun Laoghaire in about an hour-and-a-half. Services from Fishguard and Pembroke operate to Rosslare and there is a service between Swansea and Cork.

Ferries also operate from France to Rosslare and Cork, and because Ireland is a member of the Eurail network, your fare on these services is included in the price of a Eurail pass.

Full details on any of these services can be obtained from travel agents or by visiting Bord Fáilte's website at http://www. irelandtravel.ie.

IMMIGRATION/WORK PERMITS

Irish and EU nationals and their spouses have the right to work in Ireland. Any person born in Ireland is considered Irish, as is anyone whose parents were born here. You may also be able to claim Irish citizenship if you can prove that one of your grandparents was born here. Irish citizens do not need immigration paperwork to work here.

EU nationals do not need a work permit; however, they do need to apply at their local Garda (Police) station for a resident's permit if they plan to stay more than three months.

If you are not an EU or EEA national, or married to one, then you need a work permit to work in Ireland. A work permit will only be issued if the Minister for Enterprise, Trade and Employment is satisfied that all reasonable steps have been taken to recruit a suitably qualified person who already has the right to work here. Applications must be made by employers in advance of the person's arrival to Work Permits Section, Department of Enterprise, Trade and Employment, Room 105, Davitt House, Adelaide Road, Dublin 2.

CUSTOMS AND EXCISE

If you are moving to Ireland from within the EU, you can import tax-free any belongings which you have owned prior to relocation. If you are importing a car or other vehicle, you must be able to show that you have used it for at least six months before relocating. You can import this property up to one year before or one year after you take up residence here, and there are no restrictions on disposing of these belongings after you move.

If you are relocating from outside the EU, you can import, free of duty, any property that you can show you owned and used for at least six months prior to taking up residence. You can import property from six months before and up to one year after relocating, but you cannot dispose of it (for example by selling) within the first year.

Further information can be obtained from the Office of the Revenue Commissioners, Dublin Castle, Dublin 2. Tel: (01) 679 2777.

Revenue Charges on Cars

Vehicle Registration Tax (VRT) is payable on the first registration of new and secondhand vehicles at a rate of 23.2 per cent for cars up to 2,500 cc, and 29.25 per cent on cars over 2,500 cc — again, on the estimated value of the car in Ireland. VRT must be paid within one working day of importation. However, you may be exempt if you are moving within the EU and can show that you bought the car privately, and that VAT was originally paid on it. **Value Added Tax (VAT)** is currently payable on new vehicles at 21 per cent and is assessed on the value of the vehicle for Customs purposes, as increased by the amount of customs and excise duties payable. Further information can be obtained from the Office of the Revenue Commissioners, Dublin Castle, or from your local Vehicle Registration Office.

Procedure

You need to declare the importation of your vehicle at the time of importation and pay the appropriate charges. You will also need to complete a customs entry form if the vehicle is coming from outside the EU. More information about the actual import charges can be obtained from the Office of the Revenue Commissioners, Dublin Castle, or from your local Vehicle Registration Office.

SHIPPING YOUR BELONGINGS

What to Bring and What Not to Bring?

This is where it really pays off to have made an exploratory trip in advance to see for yourself what is on offer and to think about which of your possessions you might like to bring with you. While it probably does not make sense to take all your belongings with you, you should investigate the cost of shipping, as it may make financial sense to ship many of your high quality items. You need to bear in mind that house sizes are probably different to where you currently live and that not all electrical goods can be used here. Mains electricity is supplied at 220 Volts (50 cycles per second). Plugs are flat with three pins. You need an adapter to convert to the correct plug size and a transformer is needed to convert American appliances (except for dual-voltage equipment, which only need an adapter). Certain appliances, such as electrical clocks, will not work even with a transformer. Cordless telephones may not work, video formats may be different, and televisions that do work will still be of limited use, because broadcasting standards differ from country to country.

When choosing a shipping company, make sure it is one with a good reputation. You should go through their written conditions in detail, including their loss and damage cover. You must insure your shipment and, as with selecting a shipping company, it is worth shopping around for the best value in insurance, though this is not always the least expensive. Obviously you need to take into account how long the shipment will take, what you need straight away and what you can discard before you leave. If you are travelling with children, it is a good idea to bring some of their favourite toys with you, rather than leaving everything to a surface shipment.

To determine what clothes to take with you, remember that the coldest months are January and February, with mean daily air temperatures of four to seven degrees Celsius. The warmest months are July and August with mean temperatures of 14 to 16 degrees Celsius and the sunniest are May and June, averaging five to seven hours of sunshine per day. It also rains all year round!

You should write a checklist of all the things you need to do before you leave and start keeping a separate note of Irish contact details. For example, you may want to note that the Irish emergency number is 999. Calls to these services are free of charge. You ask the operator for the emergency service you require: Fire, Gardaí (Police), Ambulance, Boat and Coastal Rescue, Mountain and Cave rescue. When the emergency service answers, state the address or location at which help is needed.

Shipping Your Pet

Current quarantine rules require all pets, with the exception of those coming from the UK, to spend six months at a quarantine station approved by the Department of Agriculture's quarantine section. This can be contacted at Lissenhall Kennels, Swords, County Dublin, Tel: (01) 840 1776. Fees do not include transportation and vary. Quarantine for cats is £1,000 for six months and around £1,200 for an average-sized dog. In order to have the necessary paperwork on time, you should contact the Department as soon as possible, ideally at least four months before relocating. You will also be required to obtain an import licence. Some embassies may have the necessary forms; otherwise, write to the Department of Agriculture, Veterinary Division, Kildare Street, Dublin 2.

Relocation Companies

There are a number of relocation companies who can assist you with your move to Ireland. This is particularly helpful if you have not lived here for some time and are moving with children. The range of services varies and you can generally work out a tailor-made package to suit you. If you are contacting these companies from abroad, it is useful to know the time differences between your current country of residence and Ireland. From late March to October, Ireland is on GMT, i.e. five hours ahead of US Eastern time and one hour behind standard European time. From late October to March, Ireland is on GMT plus one hour, i.e. six hours ahead of US Eastern Time.

Ireland goes to daylight saving time two weeks ahead of the US, and to winter time one month later than the rest of continental Europe, so for most of September, Ireland and France are on the same time.

Relocation Companies

- Celtic Relocations, Fastnet, Castleknock, Carrigaline, Co. Cork Tel: (021) 373763. Fax: (021) 373386.

- Corporate Care, 27 Linden Avenue, Beaumont, Cork. Tel: (021) 294878.

- PHH Ireland, Merchants House, 27–30 Merchants Quay, Dublin 8. Tel: (01) 671 0022. Fax: (01) 671 0712.

- Relocation Services International Ltd., Clareville, Streamstown, Malahide, Co. Dublin. Tel. and Fax: (01) 845 4046 and at 28 Fortfield Park, Terenure, Dublin 6W. Tel. and Fax: (01) 490 3902.

Chapter 9

Adjusting to Life in a New Country

It is often said that forewarned is forearmed. This is certainly true when it comes to gathering details that will enable you to make informed decisions, about changing jobs, moving house, or in this case moving to a new country. And it is a new country. Many returning emigrants will find enormous changes, even if they have only been away for a couple of years. However, it would still appear different, even if Ireland had remained fixed in time, because the fact is that someone who has been away gaining new experiences in a different culture can hardly remain unchanged themselves. It follows that anyone moving to Ireland, regardless of whether it has already been home to them, will face a period of settling in. The transition to a new country and culture is too personal an experience for estimates on how long it takes for different types of people to settle to have any real meaning. Based on experience of working with over 600 people who moved, and a personal experience of living in four countries, I would say you should allow for about six months transition.

CULTURE SHOCK

To state the obvious, people from different cultures cannot be expected to be the same, which is why it takes some adjustment living somewhere new. Just think about the places you have visited on holiday and the comments that you may have made — for example, the Germans are organised, the Scandinavians detached and the Irish friendly. The nice thing about holidays is that if you don't like the way they "do it over there", it does not matter, because you can always leave and do not have to return. Indeed, when on holiday, you have a certain amount of choice about whether you want to interact with the locals at all.

Unless you are a psychologist, or your work involves people who relocate, or you have been lucky enough to avail of an orientation programme as part of an employer-organised move, you probably would never have had much reason to ponder cultural differences. It is more usual simply to stereotype the differences. However, if you do think about it, we all share many similarities with other people from our own culture.

Experts define culture as the "collective programming of the mind" that distinguishes people in one category from those in another. If you think about it, this starts from birth. For example, in many Eastern cultures, children are born at home, while in Western ones, most births are in hospital. Then there is the question of how close the infant stays to its parents. In the UK, many babies sleep in separate rooms from their earliest days, whereas in Japan they stay close to their parents for the first couple of years and in many African cultures are carried around on their parents' backs while they work.

The area of childcare and working parents is another distinguishing factor. It is not an issue in many African and Indian cultures, where mothers are automatically the main care-providers and also work, so the baby is simply taken along. In Western cultures, work and childcare are perceived as totally separate. There is a movement towards recognising the unpaid work a mother does in the home and a higher incidence of men choosing to stay at home. It would be tempting to give endless examples tracing the programming of culture throughout life, but there is no need. You can see quite clearly how, from our earliest days, our environment defines who we are and instils in us our core beliefs. If you are an emigrant, you can probably see changes in yourself since you moved to your current country, whilst still retaining your core beliefs.

If you are a returning emigrant, it is probably those beliefs that are driving you to move home. For example, you may prefer the "safer" environment you grew up in, the approach to education etc. Add to this our natural inclination to believe that our own culture is best — for example, the English perceive their own sang-froid in a positive light, the Germans pride themselves on their punctuality and organised approach to life, Americans value their ability to be direct and say what they mean, while to the Japanese the ability to function as part of a team is sacrosanct. It is clear why people experience culture shock when they encounter a new way of doing things.

Read through Chapter 17 on **Irish Culture** to identify some cultural characteristics that are typically Irish.

RECOGNISING THE STAGES OF CULTURE SHOCK

Once the initial euphoria of moving and renewing old friendships begins to wear off, you will soon experience small niggling difficulties with your new environment. You may mourn the amount of space you used to have, find the absence of numbered streets infuriating, wish for longer shopping hours and better weather, miss your friends, long for someone who will use the English language in the same way that you do, wonder how anything gets done with such an attitude to punctuality or that it is possible to arrive anywhere with so few signposts and, most of all, yearn for a time when arranging simple things like finding a good dry cleaners were so automatic that you didn't even have to spend time thinking of them.

Many of the stages that psychologists say people experience when they go through other life changes are also true of the culture shock experience. After the initial euphoria and then confusion, it is not uncommon for people to simply deny to themselves that anything unsettling is happening to them. This manifests itself by postponing what you think you should be doing — such as looking for a job — and days seem to get swallowed up in routine tasks that seem to take ages. It is not unusual for this to be followed by anxiety, frustration and loneliness caused by feeling different to and alienated from the environment around you. This gradually passes as you let go of your past experience and begin to adapt to your new environment.

WHO IT AFFECTS

People who move countries with the same company probably will suffer least from culture shock, as most multinationals have a "corporate" culture no matter where their parent company is located. Young children seem to settle fairly quickly, particularly if they soon meet new friends. Relocation can be tough for adolescents. Quite apart from leaving behind friends at an age where they are all-important, they may be entering a school system that is radically different from what they are used to. That the move to Ireland may have been for the good of their education is likely to be of little consolation to someone leaving a co-educational school with a casual dress code if they are to attend a single-sex school run by a religious order where the colour of the uniform pales into insignificance compared with being limited in what kind of shoes they can wear. However, the stress of relocation and culture shock is probably most acute for women working at home. In addition to the fact that their role means that they are responsible for most of the organisation and settling everyone else in, the cultural perception of what is still referred to as a "housewife" varies dramatically between countries, and even between locations within countries.

In Ireland, how women working at home are perceived depends on their generation. Many women now in their 50s and above would have had little choice about continuing to work once they married, due to the "marriage bar" that was in existence in the public service until the 1970s.

Women in their 20s and 30s who have children can opt to work or not. Neither option is considered inferior any longer. While some would justifiably argue that the cost of childcare, in the absence of any tax breaks, prohibits women from working, this is only one factor. Many women work without much net financial gain, while others simply opt for more family time.

Ireland still has some way to go as far as equality and women's rights are concerned, although it has made significant progress. Having had a female president for seven years, followed by a presidential election where the single male candidate only barely made it into an otherwise all-female race, plus the fact that many women choose to retain their own name when they marry, does not show the complete picture. Women still earn up to 20 per cent less than their male counterparts, according to the Employment Equality Agency. But perhaps the most telling example of the changing situation is that 40 per cent of all new businesses established in 1997 were set up by women.

REACTING TO SIGNIFICANT CHANGE

The impetus to move to Ireland may have been provided by a range of factors — from the desire to raise children in a similar environment to the one you grew up in, to spending more time with family or friends, or perhaps by a change in your circumstances abroad, such as the breakdown of a relationship or loss of your job. Bearing all of these possibilities in mind, it is worth briefly looking at the kind of reactions that people are known to experience when they encounter a significant loss. Although not everyone will experience ups and downs with relocating, things can go wrong. Anticipating how you might react to significant losses may help minimise the stress associated with dealing with more minor ones when relocating.

The most common reaction involves a degree of defensiveness, anger and other characteristics of a normal grieving process, combined with an obvious concern for pragmatic issues. In other words, you may be upset, but your main focus is on what you are going to do next. Sometimes people anticipate what is going to happen and do not try to change what they see as inevitable; however, do try to avoid confronting it.

When feelings of anger and hurt are especially strong, people may react with aggression and hostility, either by being argumentative and making threats or by becoming violent and losing control. Other people react by withdrawal and refusing to deal realistically with the situation facing them. This reaction can take several forms. An individual may react very quietly, even abnormally well and appear to have everything under control, only to become distraught or have their emotions explode suddenly some time later. Another reaction may be of disbelief or alternatively of simply wanting to escape from the situation, although sometimes people will then try to revisit the situation some time later.

You might give some thought to past experiences that have been "hot buttons" for you and how you reacted. You may find it proves helpful to establish a plan of action in advance for hitches with your move so that you can reduce the likelihood of stress.

MINIMISING CULTURE SHOCK

Realising in advance that experiencing some malaise while you adjust to a new country, even if it was formerly home, is perfectly normal and can only be a good thing. The next step is to address and minimise the unsettling effects of acclimatising. Here are some suggestions:

- Discuss how you feel with someone. If you can discuss what the problem is, it should help. The chances are you will meet people who have been in a similar situation.

- Find somewhere quiet to relax. Considering the amount of work that is involved in a move, the energy required to settle into a new area or to find a job, it is worth devoting time to just unwinding.

- Try thinking of how things were prior to the transition. This includes thinking about the good things that you would like to retain. If these are material things, try to find a substitute here.

- Take exercise and keep fit.

- Concentrate on positive aspects of your current situation. This includes trying to accept the aspects that are different. This may mean you decide to make some changes that you had not expected. For example, you may notice your speech and use of syntax becoming more like what is used here.

- Try to accept the reality of your situation, even it if means accepting that you simply do not like it. You are not under any obligation for your relocation to be a huge success.

- Imagine the worst possible scenario and how you would deal with it. It probably won't happen anyway, but thinking out what you would do will show you just how in control you really are.

- Try to avoid comparing the old with the new. This comes back to cultural differences again. If you are a returned emigrant, you may be a little disgruntled if people seem uninterested in your overseas experiences. Irish people quite like to complain about "the state of things" themselves; they also like hearing about other countries and what is available there. However, direct criticism of Ireland if you have just arrived/returned may not be so well received. Irish people's informal friendliness should not be mistaken for directness.

- Treat yourself and your family. If you are finding orientation to Ireland difficult, having a pleasant event to look forward to will help and you will have memories of the good things associated with relocation.

- Think about the reasons why you made the move and what you want to get out of it for yourself and your family. You may find that you are well on the way to achieving your goals.

- Create a support network. This will help minimise feelings of isolation and help you settle in. You could try contacting local groups — asking at the local church is a good place to start in Ireland, regardless of your personal religious affiliation. If you have children, meeting other parents through school events and committees is another avenue. Some local chambers of commerce organise "newcomers' clubs"; Cork City is an example.

• Don't feel compelled to deal with everything at once; take one decision at a time.

REVERSE CULTURE SHOCK

Having carved a successful life in another country, where you fitted in very well and adjusted to the local culture, the last place you expect to feel like a foreigner is home. Yet, this happens. Few returning emigrants are prepared for the anti-climax of returning home, which most of us tend to idealise while we are away. Holidays spent at home are good for keeping in touch with family and friends; however, they are usually too short to become involved in everyday life. The realisation of how much life has gone on in your absence can come as a surprise, particularly when you see significant changes in attitudes of people you expect to remain comfortably the same, such as your parents.

You will probably also find your lifestyle here is very different, both in terms of where you live and your social life. For example, if you met regularly with other Irish people when you were abroad, you may miss the kind of camaraderie that comes from being together overseas. Despite the fact that you feel so different once you return, there are certainly many parts of your overseas experience that you can put to good use here. Once again, just being aware in advance that there is such a thing as reverse culture shock will enable you to give it some thought in advance and try to minimise its impact on you.

Chapter 10

Finance and Taxation

365 Days to Go

Those of you coming to Ireland from outside Europe may be a little surprised at Ireland's preoccupation with the euro, the single European currency unit. However, with just 365 days to go from 1 January 1998 to one of the most significant steps in the history of the European Union, the information campaign launched in Ireland in December 1996 to educate the public on monetary union and the changeover to the euro is unlikely to slow down. On the contrary, euro information analysis has grown into an industry, with the daily newspapers packed with statistics and reviews and small firms around the country attending seminars on how to handle the dual pricing challenges that they will face, amongst other things, when the changeover begins. There are daily bulletins on how well placed Ireland is for entry to European Monetary Union. It seems we are well organised too. By the end of the first half of 1997, Ireland was one of only six countries to have published a national changeover plan for the introduction of the new currency.

On the 1 January 1999, some or all of the EU Member States will participate in an irreversible economic and monetary union. The countries to participate will be decided in early 1998. Economic experts, including former EU Commissioner and former Head of GATT, Peter Sutherland, are adamant that, despite its size, Ireland will be included in the first phase of economic and monetary union (EMU), provided it complies with the convergence criteria set out in the Maastricht Treaty (1993).

It is government policy that Ireland should qualify to participate in EMU from the beginning. Experts agree that Ireland is on
course for entry to EMU and has made excellent progress in recent years towards achieving the targets set out in the Maastricht
Treaty. The key areas include inflation, government debt, the public sector borrowing requirement deficit, interest rates and exchange rate stability.

Inflation has been reduced to one of the lowest rates in Europe,
running at 1 per cent by September 1997. The Treaty specifies that
Government debt is to be 60 per cent of GDP or approaching it at
a satisfactory rate. Ireland's government debt has fallen sharply as
a percentage of GDP, from 104 per cent in 1989, and is projected as
68 per cent for 1997. The Maastricht Treaty called for the public
sector borrowing requirement deficit to be no more than 3 per cent
of GDP by 1999, and the projection made for Ireland in the early
part of the year was for 1 per cent for 1997. The interest rate criteria have also been satisfied. Ireland is also maintaining the necessary exchange rate stability during the period in the lead-up to the
qualification for EMU and, despite the separate problem of a fall
in its value against sterling in August 1997, the Irish pound (punt)
is one of the strongest currencies in the ERM, leading to discussion about whether it should be revalued.

The coverage of EMU is such that you are likely to hear an up-
date of these figures when you visit your local pub. Since all Government departments and banks and other financial institutions
must be ready to transact their business in either currency from
the inception of EMU, this level of interest must be considered
healthy. A three-year changeover using both currencies is
planned, after which no more local currency will be issued, just
euro notes and coins. Given that the new millennium and all its
anticipated computer problems will fall in the middle of all of
this, we have much to look forward to. Without a trace of irony, it
must be said that Ireland can be expected to handle its duality of
currency well. Some 20 years after it was introduced, the metric
system is thriving in Ireland — alongside the imperial system it
was intended to replace!

BEFORE YOU LEAVE

Fascinating as EMU undoubtedly is, you will have some more immediate and simpler matters to address if you are planning a move to Ireland in 1998. Your move will seem less disconcerting if you can try to sort out your financial arrangements in advance. Although bank accounts can of course be set up within a couple of days, it is important to try to establish your bank account before you arrive in Ireland. The advantage of this is that you can then transfer funds from another country, hopefully in a cost effective manner, and travel with one less worry.

Credit rating is handled differently in Ireland compared to other countries and it is worth gathering as much information as you can about your financial status in your current country of residence and taking it with you. For example, you could ask your current bank for a letter of introduction.

It makes sense to maintain a financial status in your current country, at least for a while, as there are often small final bills that arrive and end up being disproportionately expensive if you have to exchange currency to settle them. Or you may want to continue certain subscriptions in that currency. If you are maintaining an overseas bank account in this way, be sure to let your bank know your plans. You may be eligible for tax relief on any interest (although in the UK, for example, the law on maintaining accounts has tightened up and your bank may advise you to open an off-shore account). At least ensure that the bank charges do not exceed the amounts going through.

If you are leaving a country where credit rating is very important, such as the US, and to which you may later return, it is worth enquiring from your bank or credit card company if it is legally possible to maintain a credit card rating whilst out of the country. Although it is not advocated without checking the legalities first, there are stories of people maintaining their credit cards by asking a friend to make small, regular purchases using it, and of course to pay the bill promptly. Credit cards that are invoiced in Europe will not show up in credit records in the US.

BANKING CHOICES

Retail banking has made considerable strides forward over the years. Most transactions will be reflected in your account the same day, while 24-hour banking (by telephone) is becoming standard, and in September 1997 Bank of Ireland introduced the first Internet banking service. Despite the high-tech advances, you can still expect to be known by someone in your local branch, even if mainly by telephone.

One way in which the Irish banking system differs to many others is the amount of authority accorded to individual branch managers. For example, if you have recently arrived here after a long absence and need an overdraft, the branch manager has the discretion to grant or deny it. This is in stark contrast to the United States, for example, where maintaining a credit rating is absolutely crucial. However, no system is easy to use if you do not understand how it works, and when dealing with money there is something especially reassuring about not having to make too many changes.

As a result of legislation to control the laundering of the proceeds of drugs activities, bank officials responsible for opening bank accounts are legally obliged to ask you for two forms of identification and proof of address. Sometimes this takes new customers by surprise; however, apart from this, banking here is fairly non-bureaucratic.

Since most people are paid through paypath — that is, directly into their bank accounts — there is usually little reason to visit your branch. Accordingly, proximity to where you live need not be your main consideration. If you already had a bank account in Ireland, no matter how long ago, it is probably easiest simply to continue banking there. Otherwise, ask family, employers or friends for a recommendation, or read through the literature from each and see which appeals to you most. Although you may be pleased to see banks from your current country of residence in operation here, many of these do not operate retail banking services. You need to consider the convenience of the bank you select

— how many branches they have, how widely you can use their ATM and other cards, and so on.

Your options are:

Banks

The banks are AIB Bank, Bank of Ireland (BoI), National Irish Bank, Ulster Bank, Trustees Savings Bank (TSB), ACCBank, ICCBank, Irish Permanent Bank. The first four are known as the Associated Banks because they operate a clearing system for all the other institutions. For further information on services, contact the addresses below. The number of branches that each has in the Republic of Ireland is noted after the telephone number.

- ACCBank, ACC House, Upper Hatch Street, Dublin 2. Tel: (01) 478 0644 (49 branches)

- AIB Bank Headquarters, Bankcentre, Ballsbridge, Dublin 4. Tel: (01) 660 0311 (327 branches)

- Bank of Ireland, Head Office, Lower Baggot Street, Dublin 2. Tel: (01) 661 5933 (300 branches)

- ICC Bank, 32 Harcourt Street, Dublin 2. Tel: (01) 475 5700 (5 branches)

- Irish Permanent Bank, 56/59 St Stephen's Green, Dublin 2. Tel: (01) 661 5577 (91 branches)

- National Irish Bank, Head Office, 7/8 Wilton Terrace, Dublin 2. Tel: (01) 678 5066 (60 branches)

- Trustee Savings Bank, Frederick House, South Frederick Street, Dublin 2. Tel: (01) 679 0444 (80 branches)

- Ulster Bank, 33 College Green, Dublin 2. Tel: (01) 677 7623 (114 branches).

Banks are generally open from 9.30 a.m. to 4.00 p.m. Monday, Tuesday, Wednesday and Friday and until 5.00 p.m. on Thursdays. In some towns, the late opening may be on another day.

Building Societies

Building societies, or more accurately mutual societies, are owned by their members (account holders). Building societies are offering a growing range of services and becoming more like banks. In fact, the Irish Permanent was a building society until it became a bank in 1994. ICS is part of the Bank of Ireland group. The signs are that First National will become a public company (bank) in 1998 or the first half of 1999. The change of status from building society to bank yields welcome windfalls in the form of free shares for members; however, anyone hoping to make a quick killing by becoming a member now should be aware of the conditions on length of membership needed to qualify.

Building societies are open from 9.30 a.m. to 5.30 p.m. and most open until 7.00 or 8.00 p.m. on at least one day per week. Some are open on Saturdays, particularly those located in major shopping centres.

- Educational Building Society (EBS), 30 Westmoreland Street, Dublin 2. Tel: (01) 677 5599 (50 branches)

- First National Building Society, Skehan House, Booterstown, Dublin. Tel: (01) 283 1801 (77 branches)

- ICS Building Society, Haddington Centre, Percy Place, Dublin 2. Tel: (01) 611 3000 (7 branches)

- Norwich Irish Building Society, 33/35 Nassau Street, Dublin 2. Tel: (01) 671 7181 (10 branches).

Credit Unions

Credit unions are non-profit-making, community-based co-operative organisations offering loans and savings facilities. Interest rates on loans are quite low, although the rate paid on savings can be as good as you might get in a bank. Credit unions also offer favourable rates on home insurance and operate group health insurance schemes. Opening times vary. All credit unions open on certain evenings and some on Saturday mornings. Banks deduct tax at source on interest on your savings, but credit unions are only required to notify the Revenue of your interest if it exceeds £500 per year. Otherwise, it is your own responsibility to do so. Irish League of Credit Unions (representative body), 33/41 Lower Mount Street, Dublin 2. Tel: (01) 490 8911. Fax: (01) 490 4448 (700 branches).

Post Offices

An Post is a semi-state organisation responsible for running the postal system and has a presence of some sort in most towns and villages around the country. In addition, post offices offer a range of savings and investment options. They also handle various social welfare payments, the sale of television licences and other matters. An Post's savings products are State-guaranteed, so they have an extra level of security.

Types of Accounts

There are numerous types of account available and when selecting one or more, you should look at the rates of interest payable, how easily you can access your money, whether the account is accessible using ATM or laser debit card and what the charges are. The main types of account are current (checking), loan and deposit (savings). Even within these, there are sub-categories — for example, AIB's cashsave account is a kind of current account, although you cannot overdraw or write cheques on it. There are also budgeting accounts to help spread out the cost of regular bills. You can open accounts in one name or jointly.

ATM

Many people access their cash using ATM (automated teller machine) cards. All the banks, most of the building societies, and now even the credit unions, issue ATM cards. Generally, they can also be used at ATMs other than those at a branch of the issuing institution. For example, the credit unions' new IQ card can be used at any AIB or BoI branch ATM.

Charges

Before selecting a bank, it is worth reviewing their charges. Not all
accounts carry charges; however, for those that do, you may be
charged for transactions (automated are invariably cheaper than
paper-based), overdraft approval, standing orders and other
items. You should always check your statements carefully and
query charges you are not sure of. Most institutions have conditions that exempt you from charges — these involve staying in
credit within specified guidelines. Certain groups are exempt for
some charges; for example, the over-55s can avail of certain foreign exchange facilities free of commission.

Credit/Charge Cards

All of the banks, most building societies and even one upmarket
department store offer credit cards. Visa and Mastercard (Access)
are the most common. American Express and Diners' Club charge
cards are also available. Interest rates are steep, with APRs ranging upwards from 21 per cent. The US credit card (MBNA) has
also become available through its UK office and at a very competitive rate. However, if you let the outstanding amount build
up, the rates become more punitive.

TAXATION

Taxation always stimulates debate and this is true in Ireland as
much as anywhere else. The Government is continually lobbied to
reduce tax rates, with some results. The unpopular residential
property tax, which mainly affected higher income earners living
in cities, was discontinued in 1996/97. Tax relief for covenants
was also restricted once third-level tuition fees were abolished.
However, not all courses are free and some tax relief remains in
place for approved courses. There have also been reductions in
the employer and employee rates of PRSI and, as this is seen as
essential for job creation, calls continue to be made for further reductions. The lower rate of income tax was reduced by one point
in the current tax year, 1997/98; however, although the positive
budgetary position for 1997 might allow for some adjustment, the

budget to be announced in December 1997 (most elements take effect in April 1998) is not expected to give away too much. Analysts cite two reasons for this. The first is that in the qualifying period for EMU, continued fiscal restraint is extremely important. The second concerns the likelihood that, after 1999, EU Structural Funds to Ireland will not be on the same scale as in recent years. This is a major concern, as the Structural Funds have been the key source of finance for most of the transforming infrastructural improvements that have taken place over the past number of years.

Understanding the System

The Irish tax year runs from 6 April to 5 April the following year. The current tax year is the 1997/98 tax year and began on 6 April 1997 and will end on 5 April 1998. The Budget for 1998/99 will be announced in the first week of December 1997. Most items will take effect from 6 April 1998, although some social welfare changes come into effect in June, and increases in duty on cigarettes, alcohol and fuel much sooner than April.

PRSI (Pay Related Social Insurance)

The vast majority of employees, full- and part-time, and self-employed people, pay PRSI. These contributions are paid into a special Social Insurance Fund to contribute towards the cost of social welfare benefits and pensions. The first £80 per week is exempt from PRSI, as are any contributions up to 15 per cent of your net relevant earnings that you pay into an occupational pension fund.

PRSI Contributions 1997/98

- **Employer:** If an employee is earning up to £260 per week (£13,520 per annum), then the employer pays 8.5 per cent. If the employee earns more than £260 per week, then the employer pays 12 per cent on the first £536 per week (£27,900 per annum) of their salary.

- **Employee**: The first £80 per week is exempt from PRSI. 4.5 per cent is payable on anything above £80 per week up to £446 per week (£23,200 per annum). This rate is not payable above £23,200 per annum. Additional levies (health contribution at 1.25 per cent and training and employment levy at 1 per cent) are also payable on your entire salary, unless you earn less than £10,250 per annum or hold a medical card, in which case you are exempt.

PAYE (Pay As You Earn) Income Tax System

If you are paid through an Irish payroll, you must pay PAYE and your employer is obliged to deduct it from your salary (unless your earnings are lower than the PAYE entry level — see below) and pay it to the Revenue Commissioners. The obligations on employers to make PAYE deductions are strict and employers have no discretion in the amount deducted. They can only act on information supplied on your tax-free allowance certificate. This information is also contained in your P45 when you leave your employer. It is your own responsibility to obtain a valid tax-free allowance (TFA) certificate. If you are new to Ireland or have not worked here since the start of the *current* tax year (i.e. this year since 6 April 1997) then you need to complete Form 12A, which is available from your employer or any tax office.

You do not have to pay income tax if your income is lower than the PAYE entry level. The entry level for a single person under age 65 is £4,000 per annum and £8,000 per annum for a married couple. In either instance, additional allowances are given for children: £450 for each of the first two children and £650 for each subsequent child. So a married couple with four children can earn up to £10,200 without becoming liable for income tax.

Income Tax (PAYE) Rates

Tax rates on taxable income (i.e. after you have deducted your allowances) are 26 per cent on the first £9,000 for a single person and on the first £19,800 for a married couple. The lower rate was

27 per cent up until the current tax year. 48 per cent tax is payable on the balance.

Income Tax Tables

The purpose of tax tables is to ensure that your tax liability is spread evenly over the year. The way in which tax tables work is that your level of taxable income for the year is anticipated (based on information supplied by you). All income is then taxed at your highest rate for the entire year. If the highest rate you pay is the standard rate, 26 per cent, then you will be taxed on Table A (single) or R (married). You will not need a table allowance. If your highest rate is 48 per cent, then the appropriate table is B (single) or S (married) and you will receive a table allowance, which is a compensating additional allowance that means you end up paying the exact same amount of tax that you would pay if your income was split and taxed at the two rates. It is unwise to stay on the 26 per cent rate when you know your income exceeds the limit; you could end up worse off at the end of the tax year and temporarily lose the benefit of having your tax payments spread equally over the year. There is a cut-off point about two months before the end of the tax year where the tax office cannot make any more changes until the next tax year.

Emergency Tax

If your new employer does not receive either a certificate of tax-free allowance from the tax office or a P45 from you, they are obliged to deduct tax on an emergency basis when paying your salary. Under this system, a temporary tax-free allowance is given for the first month of employment, after which tax deductions are increased progressively. If you are paid weekly, the temporary tax-free allowance is 1/52 of the single personal allowance (currently £2,900 per year); if paid monthly it is 1/12.

The following rates and allowances apply, regardless of how much you earn:

- Weeks 1–4: Tax-free allowance of £56 per week. Remainder taxed at 26 per cent.

- Weeks 5–8: No tax-free allowance. All taxed at 26 per cent.

- Week 9 onwards: No tax-free allowance. All taxed at 48 per cent.

Once details of your tax-free allowances are received by your employer, you will receive any rebate due in your next pay packet. However, you should be aware that, although you can receive the benefit of your full annual tax-free allowance even if you arrive after the start of the tax year — for example if you start working in July — this should not be taken for granted. A lot depends on how clearly you have completed your Form 12A. If you state that you intend to reside here, then you may get the full allowance. However, if you arrive in June and state your intention is to stay six months, then the tax office can only give you a "week or month one" allowance, i.e. not backdated to 6 April, but effective from a subsequent date. If you end up staying longer and believe you are owed a refund, you can then follow that up with the relevant tax office at the end of the tax year.

Important Documents

- Form 12A — you must complete this to obtain an RSI (Revenue and Social Insurance) number and tax-free allowance.

- P60 — given to you by your employer at the end of each tax year. Shows how much pay you have received from your employer, the PAYE tax and PRSI deductions.

- P45 — given to you by your employer when you leave employment. You need it to give to your new employer, claim social welfare and claim a refund of tax if unemployed.

Only one original copy of a P60 or P45 can legally be made. If either contains an error or is lost, the information is confirmed by letter to the Revenue by your employer. They are not permitted to reissue an original of either document.

ALLOWANCES AND DEDUCTIONS

Mortgage Interest Repayments

You can claim tax relief on interest on your mortgage repayments. The amount of tax relief on mortgage interest has gradually reduced and is likely to reduce further.

There are currently two categories of tax relief for mortgage interest repayments. The first applies to "first-time buyers", i.e. anyone who first claimed interest relief after 6 April 1993 (for 1997/98 tax year). The special relief for first time buyers applies only for five years from 1994/95. The relief thresholds are as follows:

1997/98	Maximum Tax Relief	
	First Time Buyer	*Other*
Single	£2,500	£1,900
Married	£5,000	£3,800
Widowed	£3,600	£2,780

If the interest for 1997/98 is less than £2,500, the first-time buyer will qualify for tax relief on the full amount of interest. Others receive an allowance of 80 per cent of the interest, less £100 for a single or widowed person and less £200 for a married couple. Therefore, a married couple paying mortgage interest in 1997/98 of £2,300 will receive tax relief of £1,640.

Tax relief on employee contributions to an occupational pension scheme is an important consideration for those who want to work in Ireland. These contributions are exempt from PRSI and PAYE deductions. Therefore, if you pay 48 per cent tax, each pound invested by you in your pension costs just 52 pence, whereas if you are on 26 per cent tax, each pound invested costs you 74 pence.

Tax relief is also available for rent paid on private rented accommodation. The maximum amounts of relief are £500 per year for a single person, £750 per year for a widowed person and £1,000 for a married couple. So a single person on the 26 per cent tax rate who avails of their full allowance will be better off by £130 per year.

Within specified time limits, certain urban renewal projects attract special tax status, following the introduction in the Finance Act 1994 of a second incentive scheme for designated areas and streets in Dublin, Cork and Galway. There are also tax incentives attached to investment in traditional seaside resorts.

Refer to the Personal PAYE Income Tax Tables listed in the Appendices.

Tax and Marriage

The method of handling taxation of married couples changed in 1994. Under current rules, both partners continue to be treated as two single people for tax purposes in the year of marriage. However, if the tax you pay as two single people in that year is greater than the tax that would be payable if taxed as a married couple, you can claim a refund of the difference. Any refund is due only from the date of marriage and will be calculated after the current tax year ends. A refund of tax would normally only arise in the year of marriage where you are on different tax tables. In this case, one of you can benefit from the unused lower tax rate of your spouse or from some of their unused allowances.

In subsequent years, you have the following choices:

Joint Assessment/Aggregation

This is usually the most favourable basis of assessment for a married couple. It is really the only option open to married couples where only one person is earning. It is automatically given by the tax office once you have advised them of your marriage, but you can elect for either of the other options.

Under joint assessment, the allowances and reliefs can be allocated between the spouses to suit their circumstances. For example, if only one spouse has taxable income, all transferable allowances will be given to that person. If both spouses have taxable income, they can decide which spouse is to be the "assessable spouse" and request the tax office to allocate the allowances and tax relief between them in whatever way they wish. PAYE and employment expenses are not transferable.

You should notify the tax office about who you decide is to be the assessable spouse. If you do not notify them, the Revenue will determine that, until further notice, the assessable spouse is the person with the highest income in the latest year for which details of both incomes are known (where the couple married in 1993/94 or later). Otherwise, it is the husband.

Joint assessment can also apply where one partner is employed and the other self-employed. In this case, one spouse pays tax under PAYE and the other pays tax under the self-assessment system. You can determine whether most of the tax should be paid under PAYE or in a lump sum on assessment. If you want to pay most of the tax under PAYE, then the tax-free allowances (except PAYE allowance, which is not available to proprietary directors and the self-employed) and employment expenses should be off-set against the self-assessment income, and vice versa.

Separate Assessment

Under Separate Assessment, your tax affairs are independent of those of your spouse; however, the amount of overall tax payable is the same. The following allowances are divided equally between you: Married Allowance, Age Allowance, Blind Allowance, Incapacitated Child Allowance. The balance of the allowances are given to each of you in proportion to the cost borne by you.

You will each be entitled to claim PAYE and expenses allowances. Any allowances, except PAYE and employment expenses, which are unused by one spouse are allowed to the other spouse. The allowances will not generally be adjusted until after the end of the tax year. Then, unused tax-free allowances, except PAYE and employment expenses, of one spouse can be transferred to the other. This is most likely to arise where one of you is liable at a different rate of tax to the other. If you think that this applies to you, you should contact the tax office for a review after the end of the tax year.

Assessment as a Single Person

Also referred to as separate treatment, this is not the same as separate assessment. Under assessment as a single person, each spouse is treated as a single person for tax purposes. Both spouses are taxed on their own income, get allowances and rate bands due to a single person, pay their own tax, complete their own Return of Income forms and claim their own allowances.

One spouse cannot claim relief for payments made by the other spouse and there is no right to transfer allowances or rate bands to each other. This kind of assessment can be financially unfavourable because you cannot transfer unused allowances and there can be a loss of some double allowances.

Take Home Pay at a Glance

Using the information in the tax tables provided in the Appendices and some worked examples later in this chapter, you can work out your potential take-home pay. In the immediate aftermath of

Changes in Private Sector Take-home Pay — Single Person				
Gross Annual Income	*1994/95*	*1995/96*	*1996/97*	*1997/98*
10,000	7,453	7,597	7,685	8,099
12,500	8,903	9,194	9,317	9,555
15,000	10,009	10,301	10,496	10,929
17,500	11,115	11,407	11,603	12,060
20,000	12,221	12,513	12,709	13,191
25,000	14,659	14,898	15,045	15,521
30,000	17,147	17,365	17,499	17,980
40,000	22,122	22,315	22,431	22,919
50,000	27,097	27,274	27,381	27,872
60,000	32,072	32,239	32,339	32,832
75,000	39,534	39,691	39,784	40,280
85,000	44,508	44,661	44,751	45,249
100,000	51,972	52,118	52,205	52,703

Changes in Private Sector Take-home Pay — Married Couple (one spouse working — includes child benefits)				
Gross Annual Income	*1994/95*	*1995/96*	*1996/97*	*1997/98*
10,000	8,567	8,906	9,250	9,647
12,500	10,198	10,481	10,708	11,019
15,000	11,830	12,112	12,339	12,701
17,500	13,461	13,744	13,971	14,382
20,000	15,092	15,373	15,602	16,063
25,000	17,989	18,545	18,967	19,493
30,000	20,477	21,012	21,421	22,260
40,000	25,452	25,962	26,353	27,199
50,000	30,427	30,921	31,303	32,152
60,000	35,402	35,888	36,261	37,112
75,000	42,864	43,338	43,706	44,560
85,000	47,838	48,308	48,673	49,529
100,000	55,302	55,765	56,127	56,983

the Budget, the newspapers, in conjunction with the big accountancy firms, provide very detailed analysis of its impact. The above tables are prepared by Craig Gardner/Price Waterhouse and show the approximate tax-home pay at different levels from 1994 to April 1998.

Comparing Net Take Home Pay in Other Countries

The following tables compare net take home pay in Ireland, the UK, the US, Canada, France and Germany. These figures are what you would have in Irish pounds equivalent in those countries after tax and social security are deducted.

The exchange rates used were those at October 1997. This makes a significant difference to the comparison. For example, in the case of the Irish/UK comparison, the Irish pound was weak in October. However, if the comparison had been made six months previously when the Irish pound and sterling were more or less on a par, the net Irish amounts shown here would be stronger.

After Tax Salary Comparison — Married, 2 Children			
Gross Salary	*£20,000*	*£35,000*	*£50,000*	*Plus Child Benefit for 2 Children*
	Net (IR£)	*Net (IR£)*	*Net (IR£)*	*Net (IR£)*
Ireland	15,353	24,015	31,444	720
UK	15,162	25,770	34,770	1,158
USA	16,579	26,866	35,945	None
Canada	14,877	23,455	30,678	1,017
France	15,560	26,382	36,438	921
Germany	15,022	23,228	32,704	1,956

After Tax Salary Comparison — Single Person	
Gross Salary	*£35,000*
	Net (IR£)
Ireland	20,445
UK	25,464
USA	23,172
Canada	22,636
France	22,780
Germany	19,899

Source: Price Waterhouse

The figures in both tables assume the deduction of Federal income tax, social security (and New York state tax and Ontario provincial tax in the case of the US and Canada respectively).

CALCULATING YOUR TAX LIABILITY IN IRELAND

Example One

Taking an example from the salary ranges provided in the **Salaries and Benefits** chapter, a middle manager in the manufacturing department of a pharmaceuticals company earns a base salary of £35,000 per year. This employee is married and the spouse works at home. They have three children, a fully expensed company car worth £18,000, pay for their own health insurance of £450 and mortgage interest of £5,000. They first claimed this relief in the tax year 1995/96. They contribute 6 per cent of the earning partner's base salary into the company pension scheme — the company pays an additional 6 per cent, but this does not impact their income tax. Since only one person is earning, it makes sense to opt for joint tax assessment.

Income	IR£
Salary	35,000
Benefit-in-kind (Car: 30% of £18,000)	5,400
Less pension contributions (6% of salary)	2,100
Gross Income	**38,300**
Allowances	
Personal (married)	5,800
PAYE (one person only)	800
Mortgage Interest Relief (£3,800 @ 26%)	988
Health Insurance Relief (£450 @ 26%)	117
Other	0
Total Allowances	**7,705**
Taxable Income	**30,595**
Deductions	
First £19,800 @ 26%	5,148
£10,795 @ 48%	5,182
Total PAYE	**10,330**
PRSI @4.5% (first £4,160 exempt, ceiling £23,200)	857
Health levy @1.25%	438
Employment levy @1%	350
Total PRSI	**1,645**
Total Deductions (PAYE and PRSI)*	**11,975 (34% of salary)**
Disposable Income (less pension and deductions)	**20,925 (60% of salary)**

*Note: Pension is not a deduction but a contribution.
This family will also receive Child Benefit of £96 per month — £30 for each of the first two children and £39 for the third.

Example Two

This employee is a single parent with one child whose employer pays for health insurance for the employee and child, worth £300 per year. This person has had a mortgage since 1990 and will pay mortgage interest of £2,000 in 1997/98, and pays 3 per cent into the company's pension plan.

Income	IR£
Salary	20,000
Benefit-in-kind (Health insurance)	300
Less pension contributions (3% of salary)	600
Gross Income	**19,700**
Allowances	
Personal (plus single parent allowance)	5,800
PAYE (one person only)	800
Mortgage Interest Relief (80% less £100)	1,500
Health Insurance Relief (£300 @ 26%)	78
Other	0
Total Allowances	**8,178**
Taxable Income	**11,522**
Deductions	
£11,522 @ 26%	2,996
Total PAYE	**2,996**
PRSI @ 4.5% (first £4,160 exempt)	712
Health levy @1.25%	250
Employment levy @1%	200
Total PRSI	**1,162**
Total Deductions (PAYE and PRSI)*	**4,158** (21% of salary)
Disposable Income (less pension and deductions)	**15,242** (76% of salary)

*Note: Pension is not a deduction but a contribution.
This family will also receive Child Benefit of £30 per month.

Example Three

This employee earns £10,000 working in the claims department of an insurance company, is single, pays rent of £30 per week (£1,560 per year) and does not subscribe to health insurance or pension schemes.

Income	IR£
Salary	10,000
Gross Income	**10,000**
Allowances	
Personal (single)	2,900
PAYE (one person only)	800
Rent Relief (£500 @26%)	130
Total Allowances	**3,830**
Taxable Income	**6,170**
Deductions	
£6,170 @ 26%	1,604
Total PAYE	**1,604**
PRSI @4.5% (first £4,160 exempt)	263
Health levy @1.25%	exempt
Employment levy @1%	exempt
Total PRSI	**263**
Total Deductions	**1,867** (19% of salary)
Disposable Income	**8,133** (81% of salary)

VAT

Value Added Tax (VAT) is a general sales tax charged on goods and services. Prices include VAT — it is not usually stated separately. Businesses are required to register for VAT if their turnover exceeds certain limits (IR£20,000 on the supply of services and IR£40,000 on the supply of goods). VAT is not payable on exports, books, food, children's footwear or children's clothing. Certain activities are also exempt from VAT — for example, education and training, theatre, insurance and banking services and passenger transport. There is a reduced rate of 12.5 per cent, which applies to newspapers, restaurants, cinema admission, heating fuel and electricity (itemised separately on utilities bills). Otherwise, the standard rate of 21 per cent applies, for example on telephone services, petrol and diesel, adults' clothing and footwear.

Key Dates in the Tax Calendar 1998

- 5 April: tax year ends

- 5 April: employers should issue P60s

- 6 April: new tax year commences

- 30 April: employers must submit P35

- 6 July: notify Revenue by this date if you get married to change the way you are assessed.

COST OF LIVING COMPARISONS

Now that you have calculated your potential net income in Ireland, you need to see what you can purchase with it and compare that to your current country of residence. You probably already have an idea of general prices from visits, but you can make a more informed decision with more exact information. There are a number of ways of calculating cost of living comparisons. An entire industry sector is devoted to gathering and comparing cost data from numerous countries and analysing it. Often, assumptions are made about the way you spend your money — for example, it might be assumed that you save a portion of your salary or that a family of a certain size has certain spending priorities. These kinds of assumptions tend to be used where companies expatriate an employee and pay a cost-of-living allowance, whilst continuing to pay salary in the original currency. If you are moving to Ireland on an Irish pound salary, you need to be able to compare your buying power with what you currently have. The following table shows how costs compared between New York City, London, Frankfurt, Paris and Dublin in March 1997. These are purely cost-based and no assumptions are made about spending habits, family size or any other factors.

The comparisons throw up some surprises — for example there is very little difference between Paris and Dublin, except for alcohol and tobacco. You will see this marked difference in all the comparisons for alcohol and tobacco except when comparing to the UK. This reflects the high level of Government duty levied on these items in Ireland and the UK.

Index Categories	Frankfurt	New York	Paris	London
	Index: Dublin mean prices = 100			
Food at home	105	116	102	108
Alcohol and tobacco	60	74	63	97
Domestic supplies	97	93	99	104
Personal care	96	99	109	111
Clothing, footwear	94	97	100	102
Home services	130	143	137	120
Utilities	91	118	114	104
Entertainment	103	103	118	118
Transportation	83	69	88	105
Sports and leisure	105	88	109	103
Total Index	**96**	**98**	**102**	**107**
a) Excluding utilities	97	97	101	97
b) Exc. transportation	99	104	105	107
c) Exc. both above	100	103	104	107

USEFUL CONTACTS

For tax information leaflets contact:

- The Revenue Commissioners, Dublin Castle, Dublin 2. Tel: (01) 679 2777.

- Price Waterhouse produce very informative free literature on taxation, particularly the *Pocket Tax Guide* and *Foreign Citizens Working in the Republic of Ireland*. More information and advice can be obtained by contacting Mark Carter, Senior Manager,

International Assignment Service, Price Waterhouse, Gardner House, Wilton Place, Dublin 2. Tel: (01) 662 6000. Fax: (01) 662 62000/662 6615. E-mail: Mark_P._Carter@Europe.notes.pw.com

Chapter 11

Housing

TRENDS IN PROPERTY

Demographic analysis shows that towns in Ireland with a population of over 10,000 are growing fastest. Between 1951 and 1996 these towns increased their share of the population from 3.6 per cent to 10.5 per cent. The numbers living in country areas with fewer than 50 homes declined from 53 per cent in 1951 to 34.5 per cent in 1996. According to census results, Galway is the fastest growing city in Ireland, with a growth rate of 12.6 per cent from 1991 to 1996. During the same period, Dublin's population grew by 1 per cent and Waterford's by 8 per cent. There was little change in Cork and Limerick. These relatively low increases are probably explained by the rapid expansion of satellite towns. Within a 20-minute drive of Dublin, Leixlip, Celbridge and Lucan have the nearby Intel and Hewlett-Packard plants to thank for the rapid expansion of their towns. Intel's involvement in local environmental improvements has created immeasurable goodwill and there are few objections to the growth. House values in these areas have prospered too. A typical three-bedroom semi-detached that cost £40,000 in 1991 would now expect to fetch £75,000.

Average house prices increased by a record 20 per cent in 1996 and early estimates for 1997 predicted growth of around 7 per cent, later revised to 15 per cent. A report compiled by the Housing Statistics Bulletin on price activity in the first six months of 1997 and published in September suggests these figures are understated. The report shows that the national average cost of a new house rose by 17.5 per cent in the first six months of 1997 to a cost of £78,415. Second-hand houses have also experienced sharp price increases, from just over £72,000 in the first quarter to just over £77,000 at the end of June.

The biggest price increases were recorded in Dublin, where the average price of a new house rose by almost 25 per cent in the first six months, and in June 1997 stood at £94,375. Second-hand houses in Dublin have also increased very significantly — by 19.6 per cent — to an average of £97,920.

Galway City has experienced phenomenal growth in recent years. According to Galway Chamber of Commerce, one in every four houses in Galway today was built after 1960. The growth of Galway is reflected in its house prices and, after Dublin, Galway showed the most significant increases, with the average cost of a new house rising from £78,870 in the first quarter of 1997 to £86,018 at the end of June. Average second-hand prices rose from £70,443 to £76,989 in the same period.

Price increases were not as steep in other parts of the country, rising by an extra £1,000 in Waterford where a new house costs £69,520 on average, and by about £4,000 elsewhere. In Cork, a new house costs £75,966 on average and a second-hand house £67,052. The figures for Limerick are £69,609 and £61,629 respectively.

Summer time sees a lull in the selling season in the Irish residential market, although the high level of demand will probably ensure further increases before the end of the year. Although Ireland has never really experienced a decline in house prices, there is concern about the continued rise in prices and the Minister for the Environment has commissioned a study on the factors influencing house prices. One concern is that continued price rises will push starter homes out of the reach of the first-time buyer, whose demand for homes creates a necessary stimulus at the lower end of the market. Department of Environment figures show that just 2,300 first-time buyers' grants were paid out in the first quarter of 1997, compared with 2,500 in the same period of 1996. However, analysts point out that, particularly in Dublin, the lack of large new developments coming on the market may be a contributing factor. The main reason for this is not a shortage of available land zoned for building but the shortage of a sufficient supply of land already serviced with water and sewerage systems.

Concern prompted by instances of huge differences between guide prices and properties at auction has led to strict new rules being laid down by the Irish Auctioneers and Valuers Institute (IAVI). From autumn 1997, any member handling a property whose guide price differs by more than 10 per cent from the eventual auction sale price will have to explain why. Despite some questions about whether it will be possible to minimise the disparity to 10 per cent in such a buoyant market, the move is generally seen as necessary to restore public confidence in the auction sector.

With more than 1 million homeowners out of a population of just over 3.5 million, home ownership is very important to the Irish, who remain undeterred by rising prices. Given their relative affordability compared to houses, apartments were hugely popular with first-time buyers and parents of grown-up children moving from larger houses. Twenty-one per cent of all new units built in the first six months of 1997 were apartments and there are reports that the number of enquiries at estate agencies have trebled in the past few years. Many apartments are built in tax-designated areas, which means that, provided they are owner-occupied, the owner can claim up to 50 per cent tax relief on the cost of purchasing the apartment for up to ten years. If they sell within that time, the tax relief is not transferable to the new owner, but if the original owner repays the tax relief they received, the new owner can then benefit for ten years.

Though not yet in the market to buy, students and others interested in renting are impacted by the spiralling property market. Where weekly rent at the more modest end of the market was about £30 in 1994, it was closer to £45 in 1997. Houseshares can cost slightly more, depending on location.

OPTIONS

If you are moving to Ireland, an early task will be finding somewhere to live. Those who have family or friends to help out should avail of offers of accommodation, even for a short while. If you do not know anyone here well enough to receive such an offer, you have several alternatives.

For those who can afford quality **temporary accommodation**, Dial-a-Lease can source it for you anywhere in the country. Monthly prices range from £400 for a one-bed apartment, £700 for a two-bed and £1,200 for a four-bed. If you are on a budget, there are excellent hostels in every city, and some addresses are listed at the end of the chapter. More addresses are available from tourist offices or USIT (student travel agency) in Dublin.

In most towns and cities, the best way to find **rental accommodation** is to respond to advertisements in local newspapers and ask around among your friends and acquaintances. The demand in Dublin is such that you will save a lot of shoe leather by using the services of one of the accommodation services. Home Locators offers a free listing (the advertiser pays) which you can collect from their offices. To view a property, you pay a £5 registration fee, which allows you to see as many properties as you like over a one-month period. Accommodation Lettings also offers a list of lettings at no cost to the accommodation seeker. Home Bureau charges a registration fee of £48 but does not guarantee to find you somewhere to live. For a fee of £45, Relocaters will keep you on their books until they find you somewhere suitable to live. Typical offerings in 1997 included:

- Booterstown — One person to share three-bed house with one other. Close to DART. £250 p.m.

- Dublin 6 — One person to share luxury townhouse with one other. £230 p.m.

If you rent, your landlord must provide you with a rent book or written lease that includes the following information:

- Address of the rented dwelling

- Name and address of the landlord and the letting agent, if any

- Name of the tenant and length of the tenancy

- Amount of rent, when and how it is to be paid (cash, standing order, cheque, etc.)

- Details of other payments (telephone, cable television, TV rental)

- Amount and purpose of the deposit and conditions under which you will get it back

- Statement of the basic rights and rules of the landlord and tenant.

Threshold Advice Centres in Dublin, Cork and Galway provide expert free advice on all housing matters.

The Irish Council for Social Housing provides a wide range of service including not-for-profit housing for the elderly, homeless people, families, single people and people with disabilities. It is affiliated to more than 30 other social housing organisations, listed at the end of the chapter.

BUYING A HOME

Finance

Typically, lenders limit the amount they will lend to a multiple of your gross salary and a percentage of the house price. Typically, the maximum homeloan is up to 2.5 times annual gross salary or 90 per cent of the purchase price, whichever is lower. For joint mortgages — that is, two earners — more is available. You can borrow up to two and a half times the higher salary plus once the second salary. For example, a couple earning £35,000 and £20,000 could borrow up to £107,500 (£87,500 plus £20,000) whereas a single person earning £35,000 could borrow £87,500. In both instances, the 90 per cent criterion still applies. Although some institutions will give up to 95 per cent, this practice is strenuously discouraged by the Central Bank and organisations such as

Threshold and, if offered at all, is now likely to be available to people with proven track records at their particular bank. Accordingly, you must have some resources available to pay your deposit. Some purchasers end up borrowing that separately, but this is inadvisable. Experts suggest limiting your expenditure on home purchase to a third of your take home pay. Most lenders will help you to prepare a budget planner before giving you a mortgage to ensure that you are not over-committing yourself.

Interest Rates

Mortgage terms are generally 20 or 25 years, although a few institutions lend for up to 30 years. You can choose to pay either a fixed or variable rate on your mortgage. Two-thirds of people taking out mortgage loans in the second quarter of 1997 opted for fixed-rate mortgages, while the remainder chose variable rate alternatives.

Loans available on 20-year mortgages in September 1997 were at the following rates:

- New business (lower rate): one-year fixed at between 6.25 per cent and 6.75 per cent or two-year fixed at between 6.9 per cent and 7 per cent.

- Variable rate: 7.85 per cent.

The initial costs of buying a home include the following:

- **Application fee**: charged by banks and building societies when they give you a mortgage. Typically around 0.5 per cent of the value for the loan. Some institutions waive this fee, and you should always request a waiver.

- **Stamp duty on the mortgage**: Government tax of 0.1 per cent to an overall maximum of £500 on all mortgages over £20,000.

- **Stamp duty on the purchase deed**: this is a government tax charged on second-hand homes and new homes larger than 1,346 square feet (125 square metres). The duty is charged on a sliding scale as follows:

◊ £0–£60,000:   Between 0% and 5%

◊ £60,000–£150,000   6%

◊ £150,001–£160,000   7%

◊ £160,001– £170,000   8%

◊ £170,000 upwards   9%

- **Legal fees**: there is quite a lot of legal work in the conveyance of a house and costs vary. The Incorporated Law Society of Ireland, which can also provide details of solicitors in your area, recommends a guideline of two per cent of the purchase price.

- **Valuation Report**: this will show how much the property is worth. Your lender will require this and you should use a surveyor who belongs to a recognised professional body. Typical cost is £100.

- **Structural survey:** this will show whether the property is structurally sound, and you should consider it an essential item. Typical cost about £150, though if you use the same surveyor for the valuation report, you can probably work out a reduced fee.

- **Registration of title:** your solicitor will handle this. Check the cost with them.

- **House contents:** unlike other countries, such as the US, it is not possible to rent furniture in Ireland. However, homes do come with fitted bathrooms and kitchens and some built-in wardrobes. Average costs of middle-of-the-range items are:

Kitchen			
Cooker	£200–700	Washing machine	£300
Fridge-freezer	£300	Tumble dryer	£150
Separate refrigerator	£200	Microwave	£100
Separate freezer	£120	Cutlery/dishes	£100
Vacuum cleaner	£120	Window blind	£30

Reception Rooms			
3-piece suite	£1,000	Coffee table	£60
Television	£250	VCR	£220
CD player	£200	Curtains	£150
Bedrooms			
Double bed	£300	Single bed	£150
Duvet, sheets	£100		

If you have good quality items in your current home, it may prove better value to take them with you.

Ongoing costs include your mortgage repayments (monthly), life assurance (can be included in mortgage repayment), buildings insurance, home contents insurance, payment protection plan, mortgage indemnity guarantee, local service charges and utilities. Insurance costs depend on where you live and what additional security measures you take. Alarm systems, smoke detectors, participation in neighbourhood watch schemes and, if you are over 55, your age can all help you qualify for discounts, of up to 50 per cent in some cases.

Without discounts, a three-bedroom house in a Dublin suburb, valued at £90,000, with alarms and smoke detectors, could cost approximately £300 per year to insure and its contents to the value of £10,000, a further £100.

Local service charges are for refuse collection (water rates have been abolished) and cost about £100 per year. You are eligible for tax relief if you pay on time. Electricity and gas costs depend on whether you use either of these as your main source of heating energy. Assuming you use natural gas to heat a four-bedroom house, your combined electricity and gas bills would be about £1,500 a year. Bills are issued every two months; however, as with many kind of services now, you can pay a set monthly amount.

If you are buying a home for the first time, you may be eligible for the Government's first-time buyer's grant of £3,000. The property must be a new house, your primary residence and have a floor area of between 35 square metres and 125 square metres (377 and 1,346 square feet).

Tax relief is also available for those paying mortgage interest; details of how this is calculated can be found in Chapter 10, **Finance and Taxation**.

There are several different types of mortgage available and you are advised to shop around for the best deal. The main types are:

- **Annual or repayment mortgage**: you repay part of the loan each month, together with the interest. In the first few years, you are paying mainly interest.

- **Endowment mortgage:** this combines mortgage repayment with savings through a life assurance policy. Throughout the term of your mortgage, you pay interest on your loan. You also pay monthly contributions into an endowment policy, which includes sufficient life assurance to pay off your loan in the event of your death. The value of the policy should have grown sufficiently by the end of the mortgage term to pay off the mortgage in full and possibly to yield a cash surplus for you.

- **Pension mortgage**: this is available to the self-employed only. Further details of this type of mortgage finance can be obtained from banks or building societies, who are also likely to recommend that you seek independent financial advice because of the complex nature of the product.

Figures for the second quarter of 1997 show that 96.5 per cent of people taking out mortgage loans chose annuity mortgages, while just 3.5 per cent chose endowment mortgages. This is a sharp decline from 1992, when 38 per cent opted for endowment mortgages. There are also a variety of institution-specific mortgage products, some of which are very attractive, so it is well worth investing time in evaluating all the options.

The home-buying process varies greatly from country to country. In Ireland, the seller typically engages an estate agent or an auctioneer and can sell at auction or by private treaty (directly). An estate agent typically charges the seller a certain percentage of the sale price, plus associated costs such as advertising. As a buyer, once you have found a suitable property and have had surveys completed, you make an offer. An offer is not legally binding until the contract has been signed, although you will usually be asked to pay a deposit to show good faith. Although not as prevalent as in the UK, "gazumping" happens in Ireland too. This is where the seller reneges on their agreement to sell by selling to a higher bidder. Deposits are refundable if the sale falls through. If you are buying a new house off the plans, you will be asked to pay a booking deposit. This can be as much as 10 per cent and is deducted from the final price. How the reminder is paid varies around the country. In Dublin, you pay the balance on completion of the contract; in Cork you pay by instalments, so that most of the purchase price is paid prior to completion. Homebond, run by the construction industry, provides limited guarantees on behalf of registered builders against the loss of a deposit and a portion of other payments in the event of the bankruptcy or liquidation of your builder. Their cover also includes some warranties against certain structural defects.

If the possibility of home ownership is one of the factors drawing you to Ireland, some of the information contained in the Appendices on house prices may be a little off-putting. In particular, those of you coming from the UK who may have witnessed the spectre of negative equity of the 1980s may be concerned that the same destructive pattern may take hold in Ireland. You would not be alone in that concern, and in 1997 the Central Bank took the unprecedented step of instructing lenders on their responsibilities in lending affordable amounts — thus the much stricter adherence to the 90 per cent lending guideline.

The current Government is also concerned about maintaining affordability in the housing sector and is commissioning a report on the factors influencing house prices and the implications of those prices for the future. In particular, there is concern about the trend in prices in Dublin, with just cause. Apart from the steady increases to date, rezoning proposals by Dublin Corporation could send prices rocketing.

The very rate of building is staggering in itself. UN research indicates that Ireland has the highest rate of housebuilding in Europe. At 9.5 units per thousand of population, Ireland's rate is almost double the European average (5 units) and three times higher than that in the UK (just under 3.5 units). The second highest ranking is Germany, at just under 7 units per thousand of population. With 1997 the third successive record year for the Irish property market, news that less expensive construction methods are coming on the market is indeed welcome.

An Irish group has acquired the franchise to distribute pre-engineered steel-framed houses, already well known in the US. Claiming a three-fold increase in energy efficiency, these houses can apparently be built in half the time it takes to build a bricks-and-mortar house, with construction cost savings of about a third.

And finally, in a heartening development, the City Housing Initiative in Dublin's Ringsend, a local community effort in conjunction with building company Zoe Developments, which has been building private sector apartments in the area, has resulted in three-bedroom houses coming on the market for just £50,000. Lobbying has started already to ensure that the development of Dublin's Docklands will facilitate more of the same.

USEFUL CONTACTS

- Architects and Surveyors Institute, 7 Woodbine Park, Blackrock, Co. Dublin. Tel: (01) 269 4462.

- Irish Auctioneers and Valuers Institute, 38 Merrion Square, Dublin 2. Tel: (01) 661 1794.

- Irish Council for Social Housing, 50 Merrion Square East, Dublin 2. Tel: (01) 661 8335. Fax: (01) 661 4462.

- Royal Institute of the Architects of Ireland, 8 Merrion Square North, Dublin 2. Tel: (01) 676 1703.

- Threshold, Church Street, Dublin 7. Tel: (01) 872 6311.
  8 Fr Matthew Quay, Cork. Tel (021) 271250. Augustine House,
  St Augustine Street, Galway. Tel: (071) 563080.

Once you are here, contact these numbers for utilities connections:

- Bord Gáis (gas). Tel: (01) 671 2422.
- ESB (electricity). Tel: (01) 677 8855.
- Telecom Eireann. Tel: (01) 661 1111.

Chapter 12

Social Welfare

As the Social Welfare system caters for such a wide range of people in many different circumstances, the amount of information available is vast. The Department of Family, Social and Community Affairs bears responsibility for developing and implementing policies and for administering payments through a network of Social Welfare Offices. In 1993, the Social Welfare (Consolidation) Act was passed, bringing together more than 80 years of social welfare law. The Department of Family, Community and Social Affairs has become very customer-focused over the years and produces a range of literature explaining how the system works at different levels of detail, from leaflets to 200-page books. All of the informational literature is free, available in English and Irish, and in some cases Braille. Each publication is accorded its own identification code, starting with the letters "SW".

The aim of this chapter is to highlight the preparation you need to do before you leave your current country of residence, list relevant contact details and provide a snapshot view of some of the available benefits. Sources of housing assistance are listed in Chapter 11, **Housing**. Where information leaflets are available, the SW number is given in parentheses. If you are already in this country, your local Social Welfare office can provide all relevant information to you. If you are not yet in Ireland and want to receive any of the details mentioned, contact: Information Service, Department of Family, Community and Social Affairs, Aras Mhic Dhiarmada, Store Street, Dublin 1. Tel: (01) 874 8444. No website is available at present.

WHERE TO START

"Social welfare" does not just apply to the "dole", that is, a payment you receive if you have no job. Among the many other areas it covers are additional benefits such as child benefit (formerly children's allowance) to which all parents are entitled, optical and dental benefits, maternity benefits and, of course, pensions. If you have been working outside of Ireland, it is important that you gather details of your records in your current country of residence before you leave.

Since 1 January 1994, EC Regulations on Social Welfare have applied to people who travel and work within any EU country or any of the EFTA countries that participate in the EEA (Iceland, Norway and Liechtenstein). These regulations ensure that if you were entitled to social security benefits in any of these countries, your period of social insurance will contribute towards your qualification for the same benefits in the country to which you move. In other words, provided you are eligible, you will be treated in the same way as nationals of that country.

The qualifying benefits are: disability and maternity, benefits for an accident at work or occupational disease, invalidity pension, old age contributory and retirement pensions, survivors' and orphans' contributory pensions, unemployment benefit, child benefit, death grant and treatment benefit.

If you are coming to Ireland (to work) from any of the countries listed above, you should bring back a record of your contributions on Forms E301 and E304.

Ireland also operates special bilateral agreements with Canada (SW 84), Australia (SW 87), the US (SW 91) and New Zealand (SW 95).

If you are coming from one of these countries, or any country not listed so far, contact: International Operations Section, Social Welfare Services Office, Floor 1, O'Connell Bridge House, D'Olier Street, Dublin 2. Tel: (01) 874 8444.

SOME KEY POINTS

The Department classifies Social Welfare Benefits into three categories:

- **Contributory (social insurance) payments** which are made on the basis of a PRSI (Pay Related Social Insurance) record or the equivalent if transferring from abroad. Each payment requires a certain number of PRSI contributions.

- **Non-contributory (social assistance) payments** which are based on need — successful claimants must pass a means test.

- **Universal Services** such as Child Benefit or Free Travel which are not linked to PRSI or your means.

Anyone can make a claim in their own right, together with a claim for their dependent children and spouse/cohabiting partner.

Claims are decided by Deciding Officers and there is an appeals procedure if you are dissatisfied with your claim. Supplementary Welfare Allowances are decided upon separately by the Health Boards. Many benefits cannot be backdated, so it is important to claim in time.

The tax year runs from 6 April to 5 April. The relevant tax year for social welfare purposes is the last complete tax year before the year in which you claim benefit. For example, if you claim Unemployment Benefit between January and December 1998, the relevant tax year on which your claim is based would be 6 April 1996 to 5 April 1997.

Payments are usually made weekly, and you have a choice of four payment methods. Details of the current levels of payment are contained in the *Rates of Payment Booklet* SW 19.

Extra (Secondary) Benefits are available with many types of social welfare payments — for example pension, unemployment benefit or assistance, lone parent's allowance. You will not receive secondary benefits straight away, and qualifying periods can stretch from 13 weeks up to 15 months. Some examples of secondary benefits are:

- **Rent/Mortgage Interest Supplement** (SW 54): this is a payment from the Community Welfare Officer at your local health centre to help you with your rent or mortgage payments. Contact your local Health Board for more information.

- **Fuel Allowance** (SW 17): a weekly payment paid from mid-October to mid-April to help with heating costs.

- **Smokeless Fuel Allowance**: a weekly payment as above to meet the extra costs of using smokeless fuels in certain areas of Dublin and Cork where the sale of bituminous fuel is banned.

- **Butter Vouchers**: distributed monthly for yourself and your dependants.

- **Back to School Clothing and Footwear Allowance** (SW 75): helps towards the cost of clothing and footwear of children of school-going age and is payable from the beginning to the end of September each year. Contact your local Health Board.

- **Medical Card** if your income is below certain guidelines, you may get a Medical Card. It covers you for free doctor's care, prescriptions, etc. Contact your local Health Board.

UNEMPLOYMENT

There are two types of unemployment payments: Unemployment Benefit and Unemployment Assistance. To receive either of these, you must be fully or partly unemployed (i.e. at least 3 days within 6 days), looking for work, capable of work, available for work and aged under 65.

Unemployment Benefit is based on your PRSI record; the amount payable depends on which PRSI class you fall into. If you are employed and earn £30 per week or more, you will pay PRSI Class A. To qualify you must have:

- 39 weeks PRSI paid since starting work and

- 39 weeks PRSI paid or credited in the relevant tax year (the last complete tax year before the year in which you claim).

If you have received Unemployment Benefit in another qualifying country for at least 4 weeks, you can transfer your payment to Ireland for up to 13 weeks. If after 13 weeks you have not found employment, you can apply for Unemployment Assistance. To transfer your payment, you must complete Form E303 in your current country of residence and bring it to Ireland with you.

If this condition does not apply to you and you return to Ireland (for example, you finish work in a qualifying country and do not make a claim there), you can work and pay PRSI for at least one week, after which any insurance contributions you have made in another qualifying country will count towards eligibility for 15 months of Unemployment Benefit in Ireland.

If you are aged 18 or over, you may be paid **Unemployment Assistance** if you do not qualify for Unemployment Benefit or if you have used up your entitlement to it. It is based on a means test and your means must be below a certain level. In general, your "means" are any income, savings or property (not your own home) that you or your spouse/partner may have. If you live at home with your parents, you may be assessed on some of their income.

SOCIAL WELFARE BENEFITS AND RETURNING TO WORK

Working Part-time or Casually

It is possible to retain your benefits while working. For example, your weekly Unemployment Benefit is paid for six days, so if you work three days per week, you will receive benefit for the other three days. Also, if you work part-time or on a casual basis (i.e. up to three days per week) you will be paid Unemployment Assistance for the full week less 60 per cent of your average net weekly earnings. If you have no child dependants, £10 per day worked is first deducted from your average net weekly earnings and then 60 per cent of the balance is assessed as your weekly means. Your means are then deducted from your weekly Unemployment Assistance payment and you are paid the balance.

Example	
If you have 2 dependent children and work 2 days:	
Average net weekly earnings	= £60.00
Means — 60 per cent of £60	= £36.00
Weekly Unemployment Assistance payment	= £129.40
Less Means	– £36.00
Weekly Payment	= £93.40

Example	
If you have no child dependants and work 3 days per week:	
Average net weekly earnings	= £90.00
Less disregard (£10 per day worked)	= £30.00
Means — 60 per cent of £60	= £30.00
Weekly Unemployment Assistance payment	= £64.50
Less Means	– £36.00
Weekly Payment	= £28.50

- **Systematic Short-time**: If your normal working week is reduced, you may get Unemployment Benefit for the days you do not work. The total number of days at work and on Unemployment Benefit cannot be more than five in a week. For example, if you are on a three-day week, you may receive Unemployment Benefit for two days. If you do not qualify for Unemployment Benefit, you may qualify for Unemployment Assistance instead.

- **Self-employed and Unemployment Assistance**: If you are self-employed, you may be entitled to Unemployment Assistance, depending on your income from your business.

- **Part-time Job Incentive Scheme**: If you are getting the long-term rate of Unemployment Assistance (that is, you have been signing on for at least 15 months), you can take up a part-time job for less than 24 hours per week and get a special income supplement each week. This supplement is governed by the fact that you work under 24 hours and is not impacted by your income from your part-time job.

- **If your spouse or partner works** and earns more than £90 gross per week (this figure was £60 prior to October 1997), you are not entitled to an increase for him or her as a qualifying adult. In this situation, the amount you receive for each child dependant is halved. This applies to both Unemployment Benefit and Unemployment Assistance. If you are receiving Unemployment Assistance, your means may also be assessed and deducted from your payment. An extra allowance may be made for travelling expenses.

  If your spouse/partner earns less than £90 per week, you are entitled to be paid for him or her and at full rate for any children. However, if you are receiving Unemployment Assistance, there could be a small proportion of this means-assessed and deducted from your payment.

- **Continued Child Dependant Payment**: If you have been unemployed for 12 months or more and are being paid full rate for your children, you may continue to be paid for your children for up to 13 weeks if you get work for at least four weeks. Your local Social Welfare Office can provide further details.

- **Work and Your Medical Card**: If you have a medical card and have been unemployed for at least one year and get work or take part in the Back to Work Allowance Scheme, Community Employment, Job Initiative or a development course such as Workplace, you will keep your medical card for three years. Contact your local regional Health Board for more information.

- **Back to Work Allowance** (SW 93A): This weekly payment is for unemployed people who set up their own business or obtain employment. If you are an employee, you may receive both Family Income Support (FIS — see below under "Family Benefits") and the Back to Work Allowance. To qualify for the Back to Work Allowance, you must have been unemployed for at least 12 months and be aged 23 or over. This allowance commences at three-quarters of your social welfare payment for the first year, half for the second year and one-quarter for the third year. There is no income tax or PRSI payable on this allowance. If you qualify for this allowance, you keep your medical card for three years and may also be eligible to keep your fuel allowance, rent or mortgage interest supplement, Christmas bonus and other secondary benefits for three years if your combined income from work and the Back to Work Allowance does not exceed £250 per week. For further details, contact your local Social Welfare office or the Back to Work Allowance Section at (01) 704 3165.

- **FÁS — Community Employment**: If you are aged over 21 and have been receiving either Unemployment Benefit or Unemployment Assistance for 12 months or more, you can work for 39 hours per fortnight on the Community Employment (CE) Scheme. You should receive training and are not restricted from supplementing your income in your time off. You are entitled to keep your medical card and other secondary benefits, provided your income is lower than £250 per week. FÁS coordinates the CE schemes.

- **FÁS — Jobstart**: This programme is designed to help those who have been unemployed (and receiving an unemployment payment) for three years or more to return to the workforce. Under Jobstart, an employer is paid a subsidy of £80 per week for one year towards the cost of employing a person who has been unemployed for three years or more. If you return to work under Jobstart, you can keep your medical card and any secondary benefits for three years, provided your income does not exceed £250 per week. You may also be eligible for FIS.

- **FÁS — Workplace**: If you have been receiving an unemployment payment for six months or more, you may obtain up to five weeks work experience with employers under the Workplace programme. You continue to receive your normal Social Welfare and secondary benefits. In addition, FÁS contributes an extra £15 per week towards your travel and meal expenses.

- **FÁS — Whole Time Jobs Option/Jobs Initiatives**: This programme is designed to assist the return to work of those who are aged over 35 and who have been unemployed for more than five years. The scheme provides full-time work for three years at the going market rate of pay for the job with local sponsor companies. Participants in the scheme are eligible to keep their medical cards and may be entitled to FIS.

- **Area Allowances**: These are administered by Area Partnership Companies (see Chapter 7, **Setting Up in Business**) and are intended to support people who have been unemployed for at least 12 months and who want to set up a business. Enquire at your local Partnership or Social Welfare office.

- **CORI — Part-Time Jobs Opportunities Scheme** (SW 69). This programme offers part-time positions to unemployed people aged over 21 and in receipt of either Unemployment Assistance or Pre-Retirement Allowance. Details from: The Project Manager, Institute for Action and Research on Work and Employment, SMA House, Maynooth, County Kildare. Tel: (01) 629 0044.

SOCIAL WELFARE BENEFITS AND RETURNING TO STUDY (SW 70)

If you are aged 21 or over, you can avail of a VTOS (Vocational Training Opportunities Scheme) course, Second Level Allowance or Third Level Allowance or alternatively maintain your current allowances and attend a part-time course. Briefly, these allowances are:

- **VTOS**: education and training for unemployed adults, covering a wide range of skills and which can lead to third-level education. Participants receive their current rate of allowances and possibly a travel and meal allowance.

- **Second-Level Allowance**: recipients can attend any type of publicly funded second-level school on a full-time course that leads to a recognised certificate e.g. Junior Cert, Leaving Cert or a vocational qualification. The maximum standard rate of Unemployment Benefit and an annual book allowance of £100 are paid.

- **Third-Level Allowance**: conditions are as for Second Level Allowance except that full-time attendance at a Department of Education third-level course is required. Existing graduates aged over 24 can participate by attending a post-graduate course if they can show it will improve their employment prospects. You can keep both second- and third-level allowances during holiday breaks, even if you also work.

FAMILY BENEFITS

- **Child Benefit (SW 42)** is available to all parents with children aged up to 16 (may extend to 18) and is paid monthly. There are no PRSI requirements or means tests. Application forms are available from Social Welfare offices, post offices or from the Child Benefit Section, Social Welfare Services Office, St Oliver Plunkett Road, Letterkenny, County Donegal. Tel: (074) 25566 or (01) 874 8444.

- **Family Income Support (FIS) (SW 22):** You may qualify for this weekly payment if you are working at least 19 hours per week (38 hours per fortnight), have one or more children and an income below the limit for your family size. FIS does not affect your medical card, nor do you have to pay any income tax on this allowance. Further details are available from your local Social Welfare office or by contacting FIS on (01) 704 3842 or (045) 45211.

- **Maternity Benefit**: this is a payment for employed women with their own insurance record who satisfy the PRSI contribution requirements. If you qualify under PRSI conditions, your payment will be 70 per cent of your weekly earnings, subject to an overall maximum of £250. If you are already receiving another benefit, e.g. Lone Parent's Allowance, then a proportion of the maternity benefit is payable to you. You should claim the benefit about ten weeks before your due date, although it is not payable until about four weeks before the birth. If your claim is not made within six months of the child's birth, you may lose your benefit. The Maternity Benefit Section is located at Social Welfare Services Office, Government Buildings, Ballinalee Road, Longford. Tel: (043) 45211 or (01) 874 8444.

- The **Carer's Allowance** is a means-tested payment for carers on low incomes who live with and look after certain people who need full-time care. It is not payable in addition to another Social Welfare payment such as unemployment benefit, but you may qualify for some secondary benefits. If the person you are caring for receives an invalidity pension (from Ireland or a qualifying country), contact the Carer's Allowance Section, Social Welfare Services Office, Government Buildings, Ballinalee Road, Longford. Tel: (043) 45211 or (01) 874 8444. Otherwise contact Carer's Allowance Section, Pension Services Office, College Road, Sligo. Tel: (071) 69800.

- The **Lone Parent's Allowance** is a means-tested payment made to you if you are bringing up a child or children without the financial support of a partner (that is, if you are unmarried, widowed, separated, deserted, a prisoner's spouse). You may also be entitled to some extra benefits. The Lone Parent's Allowance Section is located at Pension Services Office, College Road, Sligo. Tel: (071) 69800.

- **The Survivor's Contributory Pension** (formerly Widow's Pension) (Fact Sheet 5/94) is available to male and female applicants and is based on your own or your late spouse's PRSI contributions. Details of this, the Widow's Non-Contributory Pension, the Prisoner's Wife's Allowance, Deserted Wife's Allowance, Orphan's Contributory Allowance and Non-Contributory Pension, can be obtained from the Pension Services Office, College Road, Sligo. Tel: (071) 69800.

TREATMENT BENEFITS

Dental and optical benefits are not automatically free, although you can qualify through your PRSI records for payment of certain items. Periods of qualifying insured employment outside Ireland may also be taken into account. For more information, contact: Treatment Benefit Section, Social Welfare Services Office, St Oliver Plunkett Road, Letterkenny, Co. Donegal. Tel: (074) 25566.

RETIREMENT

There are several alternatives available for retired or elderly people and the same conditions apply regarding transferring your records from abroad. As early retirement becomes more popular, it is also important to gather as much information as you can. In addition to contacting the Department of Family, Community and Social Affairs, you are also recommended to contact the Retirement Planning Council of Ireland at 27–29 Lower Pembroke Street, Dublin 2. Tel: (01) 661 3139. Fax: (01) 661 1368. The entitlement you receive depends on your age, whether you have paid PRSI, and your means.

- **Retirement Pension**: this applies from age 65. You need to have retired from full-time work (though you can work part-time) and satisfy the PRSI conditions. These are that you must have:

  1. Commenced paying PRSI contributions before reaching age 55, or

2. Paid 156 weeks' contributions and a yearly average of at least 48 weeks PRSI paid or credited from 5 April 1979 to the end of the tax year before you reach pension age, or

3. A yearly average of at least 24 weeks PRSI paid or credited from 1953 (or whenever you started work) to the end of the tax year before you reach age 65.

Your retirement pension is not means tested and is therefore not affected by any other income you have. Retirement pension can be paid to you if you live outside Ireland.

- **Old Age Contributory Pension** applies from age 66. It can also be paid abroad, you do not need to retire, nor is it means-tested. The PRSI conditions are similar to the Retirement Pension except that in point 3 above, you can qualify for this pension with a yearly average of 20 weeks' insured employment.

  From 21 November 1997, qualification for this pension expands in a way that is likely to benefit returned emigrants who worked here for a short time before working for a long time abroad, as well as women who have spent long periods outside the paid workforce. The new pro-rata payment will require a total of 260 contributions over your working life (here or abroad); however, the yearly average will be halved to 10.

- **Old Age Non-contributory Pension** is available to those aged over 66 who do not have sufficient PRSI contributions, who live in Ireland (it cannot be paid abroad) and is means-tested. In the case of both the contributory and non-contributory old-age pensions, additional benefits may be payable if you are aged over 66 and live alone, or are aged over 80. Recipients of all three pensions may be entitled to extra benefits, such as fuel allowance, rent/mortgage interest assistance. Those aged 66 or over are entitled to free travel, and may also qualify for an electricity allowance, television allowance, telephone rental allowance and other benefits. For more information, contact your local post office or the Pension Services Office, College Road, Sligo. Tel: (071) 69800.

- A **Pre-Retirement Allowance** allows people aged over 55 who receive Unemployment Assistance to retire. You continue to receive the same amounts and extra benefits, but no longer have to "sign on". For more information, contact Pre-retirement Allowance Section, Social Welfare Services Office, Government Buildings, Ballinalee Road, Longford. Tel: (043) 45211.

USEFUL CONTACTS

- Department of Family, Community and Social Affairs, Aras Mhic Dhiarmada, Store Street, Dublin 1. Tel: (01) 874 8444 to be transferred to any other Social Welfare office nationwide.

- Combat Poverty Agency, 8 Charlemont Street, Dublin 2. Tel: (01) 478 3355.

Chapter 13

Family Matters

CHILDREN

Infant Needs

If you are travelling with a young infant, it makes sense to take sufficient formula milk with you until you find a match here. Products by Cow & Gate, Milupa and Heinz are among those available. The average cost of a 900 gramme box of baby food is £3.50, while nappies cost around £7.50 per pack for a brand name.

Childcare

The Childcare (Pre-School Services) Regulations 1996 govern the standards of crèches, nurseries and childminders in Ireland. These are part of the 1991 Child Care Act. The provisions of the Regulations include a requirement on Health Boards to promote the development of children attending pre-school services and to supervise and inspect services available. A copy of the Regulations can be obtained from the Health Boards (listed in Chapter 14, **Health Care**). The Regulations do not apply to family members or people caring for three or fewer pre-school children.

The types of childcare available in Ireland are:

- **Sessional Services**: these cater for children in the two to six age group and provide planned pre-school programmes of up to three-and-a-half hours per session. These services are provided by pre-schools, crèches, playgroups, Montessori groups and naionraí (Irish language playgroups). You should enquire in your local community for details about playgroups.

- **Full Day Care**: this refers to the provision of structured day care lasting more than three-and-a-half hours a day. This service is provided by day nurseries and crèches. Operating hours are usually 8.00 a.m. to 6.00 p.m. and they are run by individuals or voluntary groups. If you live near an Area Partnership, it is worth checking whether they are involved in childcare projects. Typical costs are from £50 to £100 per week, which includes meals.

- **Childminders** care for children in the childminder's own home and are not covered by the Regulations, unless they care for more than three children. Costs vary, but around £50 a week is average.

- **Nannies/Au Pairs** will care for your child in your own home, a nanny on a full-time basis, an au pair part-time. Agencies can be found in the Golden Pages and include the Job Options Bureau in Cork.

- **Drop-in Centres**: these are provided in shopping centres and leisure facilities and allow for children to be left for short periods of time while their parents use the other facilities. There is usually no charge.

- **Baby-sitters** care for your children in the evenings, for example. They should be aged over 18, but in practice many teenagers often baby-sit to earn extra pocket-money. Typical cost is about £2 an hour.

Registering Births of Dual Nationals

Anyone born in Ireland is automatically Irish. If you want your child to be a dual national, you should contact your Embassy for details of the procedure for registering its birth.

Useful References

- The Baby Book of Ireland (£5.95) is an annual publication available from newsagents and bookshops.

- *Mother & Baby* Magazine (available from most newsagents).

- The Irish Pre-School Playgroups Association (IPPA) works for the needs of pre-school children.

- The National Children's Nurseries Association (NCNA) is a voluntary organisation which acts as a pressure group to improve standards in the area of childcare.

- Barnardo's focuses on all family issues, with a particular emphasis on those who are disadvantaged or at risk.

- Information on Montessori Schools can be obtained by contacting Association Montessori International (AMI), Mount St Mary's, Dundrum Road, Milltown, Dublin 14. Tel: (01) 269 2499.

- An Comhchoiste Réamhscolaíochta Teo, 7 Cearnóg Mhuirfea, Dublin 2. (Irish language playgroups).

- Disability Federation of Ireland, 2 Sandyford Office Park, Dublin 18. Tel: (01) 295 9344.

- The Irish Sudden Infant Death Association (ISIDA), Carmichael House, 4 North Brunswick Street, Dublin 7. Tel: (01) 873 2711.

LEGAL MATTERS

Adoption

Adoption in Ireland is regulated by the Adoption Board, which was part of the Department of Justice, but now comes under the umbrella of the Department of Health. All adoptions must be approved by the Board. In reality, only adoptions of babies from overseas take place in Ireland now. The most recent figures on Irish babies available for adoption are for 1995, when 100 were adopted. There are unlikely to be nearly that many now. Adoptions of overseas babies are subject to the same regulations and procedures. There are various information and counselling services which you can contact if you require help with an adoption, or if you are adopted yourself and need advice on how to trace your birth mother. A controversy in 1997 about babies being sent to the US for adoption without their birth mothers' knowledge attracted quite a number of enquiries to the Adoption Advice Service. If you are seeking to trace your birth mother, or indeed your child, the Adoption Advice Service is a good place to start.

Marriage Breakdown, Conciliation, Divorce

Although there are some 90,000 separated people in Ireland, the number of applications for divorce since it became an option in February 1997 has been low. This is attributed to the cost — about £2,000, although one campaigner processed her own application for less than £15 — and the fact that many people separated for the required four years have already obtained legal separations. More than 1,000 people are waiting to receive legal assistance with divorce through the Legal Aid Board, which subsidises the cost of civil cases for some 5,000 people a year who pass a means test. McCann Fitzgerald, solicitors, in conjunction with Hamilton Osborne King, auctioneers, have produced a free guide to the financial, legal, tax and property aspects of separation and divorce. Copies are available through their offices or from the Mediators' Institute of Ireland. Mediation services are available through Gingerbread, Aim Group Family Information Centre and the Family Mediation Service.

Making a Will

Regardless of age, it is important that an adult makes a will. If you die without making a will, then your estate will be distributed in accordance with the Succession Act 1965. If you leave a will, its terms will be followed. If you die intestate (no will) the possibilities are:

- If you leave a spouse but no children, your spouse will inherit your entire estate.

- If you leave a spouse and children, your spouse inherits two-thirds and the children one-third divided equally among them.

- If you leave children but no spouse, your estate will be divided equally among them.

- If you leave no relations whatsoever, the State becomes the eventual owner of your property.

Wills must be made in writing, signed by you and witnessed. Neither the witness nor their spouse can be beneficiaries of your will. Beneficiaries of your will — except for your spouse — may have to pay capital acquisitions tax on their inheritance, although a certain amount is exempt — for example, the exemption limits for the children and parents of a deceased person for 1997 were £185,550 each. Probate tax is also payable at two per cent of the net assets of the deceased person over £10,820, after funeral expenses have been paid. The spouse is exempt from this tax. As this is such a complicated area, you are recommended to seek the assistance of a solicitor in making your will. Details of solicitors can be obtained from the Incorporated Law Society, who also sponsor a Make-a-Will Week every year, when you can have a will made for a small fee which goes to charity.

Voting

Everyone aged over 18 by 15 February and who is legally resident on 1 September is entitled to be registered to vote. The right to vote is as follows:

- Irish citizens may vote at every election and referendum

- British citizens may vote at Dáil, European and local elections

- Other EU citizens may vote at European and local elections

- Non-EU citizens may vote at local elections only.

THE THIRD AGE

As more people are retiring earlier, there is a lot of emphasis on enjoying retirement. The Retirement Planning Council of Ireland offers all kinds of advice and workshops and is useful for meeting others in a similar position. The Council emphasises getting as much out of retirement as possible and is well worth contacting.

Details of nursing homes and how they are regulated are dealt with in Chapter 14, **Health Care**, and you should also contact the organisations listed in Chapter 12, **Social Welfare**, for more information about your entitlements.

Many services are discounted for retired people and the over-55s, so do check.

USEFUL CONTACTS

- Adoption Advice Service, Barnardo's Centre, Christchurch Square, Dublin 8. Tel: (01) 454 6388. Operates a telephone service staffed by qualified social workers on Tuesdays from 2.00 p.m. to 5.00 p.m. and on Thursdays from 10.00 a.m. to 2.00 p.m. If you are not yet in Ireland, it may be best to write first.

- Adoption Board, Shelbourne House, Shelbourne Road, Ballsbridge, Dublin 4. Tel: (01) 667 1392.

- AIM Family Services, 6 D'Olier Street, Dublin 2. Tel: (01) 670 8363.

- Directory of Social Service Organisations, National Social Services Board, 7th Floor, Hume House, Pembroke Road, Ballsbridge, Dublin 4. Tel: (01) 605 9000.

- Family Mediation Service, Fifth Floor, Block 1, Irish Life Centre, Lower Abbey Street, Dublin 1. Tel: (01) 872 8277.

- Gingerbread Ireland, 29 Dame Street, Dublin 2. Tel: (01) 671 0291.

- Retirement Planning Council of Ireland, 27–29 Pembroke Street Lower, Dublin 2. Tel: (01) 661 3139. Fax: (01) 661 1368.

Chapter 14

Health Care

CURRENT TRENDS

Maintaining good health has become a priority for many people in Ireland and health education campaigns start in schools. The Health Promotion Unit of the Department of Health and Children reports a high level of interest in its activities, which include promotions such as Healthy Eating Week and No Smoking Days.

Employers are also conscious of the value and cost of good health. Speaking at the Institute of Personnel Development's 1997 annual conference, the acting chief executive of VHI estimated that sick leave is costing companies in Ireland an estimated £11 million per week. VHI indicates that, nationally, 15 per cent of employers provide private health insurance as a standard benefit. However, where companies provide any benefits, health insurance features strongly. In a survey of 194 companies conducted in 1997 by Mercers, 69 per cent indicated that they contribute at some level to employees' private health insurance. Available figures suggest that almost half of the population have private health insurance. At the same time, employers are increasingly encouraging a recreational approach to employee fitness and negotiate company discounts at local fitness clubs, offer reimbursement as part of a flexible benefits package, subsidise club memberships, or in the case of a lucky few, provide on-site sports facilities. Intel, and its neighbour Hewlett-Packard, provide professionally run gyms, while Waterford Crystal's sports facilities and swimming pool are open to all local residents. Even some of the smaller operations, such as Oracle's new international services centre, boast a gym, and Creative Labs have recently opened an on-site gym, as well as a cybercafé to encourage some employee leisure during breaks. Quality fitness clubs with swimming pools continue to spring up around the country with annual costs averaging around £500 per adult. However, less expensive options are available, and many towns offer good quality facilities in community centres, which offer low cost memberships and occasional use. Public swimming pools are run by local county councils and sessions usually cost around £2.

The growing interest in keeping fit is proven by the numbers taking part in organised sports. Events such as the annual Dublin City Marathon at the end of October and the Women's Mini-Marathon every June are hugely popular. Mini-marathons, fun-runs and other family-oriented recreational sports activities are commonplace throughout the country.

Many of the same questions that concern you in your current country of residence also matter here. The AIDS Helpline was established in 1997 and received 1,335 calls in 1996, 70 per cent of which were seeking information and support and 26 per cent of which required referrals to clinics. In the period 1986 to 1997, there have been 593 reported cases of AIDS — 489 males and 104 females. According to recent reports, the majority of these were aged between 25 and 34; 251 were drug-users, 206 homosexual or bisexual and 72 heterosexual. The remainder were accidentally infected.

The anti-smoking movement is growing in Ireland and pressure groups are succeeding in their efforts to further limit cigarette advertising, with a recent decision by the *RTE Guide* (national TV guide) to take only one cigarette advertisement per issue in 1998 and none whatsoever from 1999 on. Cigarette advertising is banned on any electronic media and there are strict rules governing the contents of newspaper or magazine advertisements. However, since it is hard to control readership, lobby groups such as ASH (Action on Smoking and Health) are pushing for a complete ban. They have plenty of unpleasant statistics to substantiate their demands. Some 6,000 people die from tobacco-related diseases in

Ireland every year and although cigarettes cannot be legally sold to anyone under the age of 16, statistics show that the incidence of under-age smoking is high. Pressure groups are likely to press for the prosecution of shops breaking the law. It was reported in September 1997 that the first four cases against tobacco companies in Ireland were being prepared on behalf of individuals with smoking-related illnesses. Meanwhile, in the UK, the first health authorities are preparing actions against the tobacco companies in the wake of further successful settlements in the US. In Ireland, the Department of Health has yet to take any such action, but is said to be reviewing the outcome of US litigation.

While schools in Ireland are far from deteriorating to the same level as reported in the UK as far as drug abuse is concerned, according to a Department of Health survey, 19 per cent of all second-level students have experimented at least once with solvents over the past seven years. The National Parents Council, the Drugs Task Force and the Department of Education are united in their efforts to educate young people about the perils of drugs and to combat the use of Ecstasy and cannabis.

PUBLIC HEALTH CARE

Everyone is entitled to health care in Ireland, and this is partly funded by your PRSI contributions. The health services are administered by eight Regional Health Boards. There are two categories of entitlement to public health care, namely an entitlement to the full range of medical services at no cost, or an entitlement to certain services free with the remainder to be paid for. In addition, there are several schemes to help defray the cost of paying for prescribed medication in certain circumstances.

If you are entitled to free health care, you will receive a Medical Card. Medical cards are issued by the Health Boards and you need to satisfy a means test to qualify. In 1997, the income guidelines for qualification for a medical card were:

	Gross Weekly Income Exclusive of PRSI (£)
Single person living alone (under age 66)	88.00
Single person living alone (66–79)	96.00
Single person living along (80+)	100.50
Single person living with family (under 66)	78.00
Single person living with family (66–79)	83.00
Single person living with family (80+)	86.00
Married couple (under 66)	127.50
Married couple (66–79)	143.00
Married couple (80+)	150.00

There are additional allowances for children and other dependants. It is still possible in certain circumstances to obtain a medical card if you exceed these income levels. If you do qualify for a medical card, you will be entitled to:

- Free treatment from a general practitioner

- Free prescriptions

- All in-patient public hospital services in public wards, including consultant services

- All out-patient public hospital services, including consultant services

- Dental, ophthalmic and aural services and appliances

- Maternity and infant care services.

Elderly people who receive certain kinds of social security pension from another qualifying country (EU/EEA) qualify for a medical card under EU regulations, regardless of their income, provided they do not also receive an Irish social welfare pension or are not employed or self-employed here.

If you do not qualify for a medical card, you will have to pay for visits to your GP, medicines and prescriptions. You would also have to pay for routine dental, optical or aural services. However, you may be entitled to some benefit if you fall into any of the following categories:

If you are:	You must have:
Aged under 21	39 weeks PRSI paid since first starting work
Aged 21–24	39 weeks PRSI paid since first starting work *and* 39 weeks PRSI paid or credited in the relevant tax year, of which a minimum of 13 weeks must be paid contributions
Aged 25–65	260 weeks PRSI paid since first starting work and 39 weeks PRSI paid or credited in the relevant tax year, of which a minimum of 13 weeks must be paid contributions
Aged 66 or over	260 weeks PRSI paid since first starting work and 39 weeks PRSI paid or credited in either the last 2 tax years before reaching age 66 , of which a minimum of 13 weeks must be paid contributions

You would also be entitled to the following services, provided you are an EU national or ordinarily resident in Ireland:

- All in-patient public hospital services in public wards, including consultant services, subject to certain charges. There is a daily charge of £20 for public hospital accommodation, up to a maximum limit of £200 in any consecutive 12 months.

- All other out-patient hospital services, including consultants.

- Accident and Emergency (A&E) departments. If your doctor refers you, there is no charge. Otherwise it costs £12 per visit.

- Maternity and Infant care services including the services of a GP during pregnancy and for up to six weeks after the birth.

- Where hospital charges apply, a bill will be sent to you.

Drugs Refund Scheme

If you spend more than £90 on prescribed drugs and medicines in a specified three-month period, you are eligible to claim a refund in excess of £90. Claim forms are available from pharmacies and must be accompanied by receipts.

Drugs and Medicines for Long-term Illness

If you do not qualify for a medical card but suffer from a long-term illness, the medication needed to treat that condition is free. Your pharmacist provides the medication and you are issued with a long-term illness book. The conditions covered by this scheme are: mental handicap, phenylketonuria, cystic fibrosis, spina bifida, hydrocephalus, diabetes mellitus, diabetes insipidus, haemophilia, cerebral palsy, epilepsy, multiple sclerosis, muscular dystrophies, parkinsonism, acute leukaemia and mental illness for under 16s.

Drugs Cost Subsidisation Scheme (DCSS)

This scheme is to help those who do not hold a medical card or long-term illness book, but who are certified as having a long-term medical condition with an ongoing requirement for prescribed drugs and medicine costing more than £32 per month. To qualify, your doctor needs to certify that the condition is likely to last at least 12 months.

Children

Children are entitled to the following services free of charge:

• Immunisation vaccines up to age 15 months

• Annual dental check-ups whilst at primary school.

Elderly People

The Health Boards provide a range of services to elderly people, including:

• Public health nursing

- Home help and meals on wheels services

- Day care services

- Physiotherapy, occupational therapy and chiropody services

- Hospital services, including assessment and rehabilitation

- Extended and respite care for dependent elderly people and their carers in health board hospitals and homes or in private nursing homes.

Nursing homes, including those catering for the elderly, are regulated and graded by the Department of Health and Children. The demand for places is high and the cost of private nursing homes is high, running to several hundred pounds per week. However, those who require care in a residential home may qualify for assistance, or Nursing Homes Subvention, which is means-tested and administered by the Health Boards. There is a very modest level of tax relief available to those who have dependent relatives living with them (see Chapter 10, **Finance and Taxation**).

PRIVATE HEALTH CARE

There are two providers of private health insurance in Ireland: the Voluntary Health Insurance Board (VHI) and BUPA.

VHI was established in 1957 as a not-for-profit organisation and was given a monopoly of the market, as the Government of the day did not believe there was room for competition. Today, the VHI has almost 1.4 million members.

BUPA is a worldwide not-for-profit health insurance organisation operating in more than 170 countries. Following an EU directive, the Irish health insurance market was deregulated on 1 July 1994 and BUPA first launched its products into the Irish market in November 1996. However, concerns about whether it encompassed community rating caused it to revise its schemes and relaunch them. Accordingly, earlier plans you may have read or heard about — such as cash plans — are no longer on offer. BUPA does not disclose membership figures; however, it was estimated to have about 30,000 members by September 1997. The legislation requires insurers to allow their members to move from one supplier to another without penalty, which should provide an added incentive to maintain competitive prices.

All VHI and BUPA premiums are calculated on the basis of "Community Rating". This means that, except for those under 18 years of age, who are charged a lower "child" premium rate, all members pay the same rate of premium, irrespective of age.

This system is considered to be fairer than a risk or age-based system, whereby as one grows older, the cost of health insurance would increase. As the incidence of ill-health generally increases with age, a risk-based system would mean that the cost of health insurance would increase dramatically at a time in life when people are less financially secure. According to the VHI, which was determined that BUPA would compete on an equal footing, the experience in countries where community rating is not used shows a dramatic decline in the level of insurance of older people.

The essence of community rating is that younger people pay a slightly higher premium than might otherwise be the case. However, this ensures that older people, who are less financially secure, can continue to enjoy the benefits of health insurance. As young members grow older, they in turn are subsidised by new young members who join the scheme. Throughout your lifetime, community rating therefore ensures that health insurance always remains affordable to all age groups.

What's on Offer

The VHI offers five plans: A, B, C, D and E. Plan E is the highest level of cover. BUPA offers three: Essential, Essential Plus and Essential Gold. These are broadly equivalent to the VHI's A, B and E plans respectively, although Essential Gold offers a higher level of benefits than Plan E. Most people subscribe at the Plan B level.

VHI's premiums are higher than those of BUPA, although the benefits vary, so you should read the details of cover provided by each of them. While the VHI announced a nine per cent increase in its premiums, effective from 1 September 1997, BUPA predict only modest increases in 1998 and are reassuring potential customers with the fact that they have valid price agreements in place with consultants until 1 March 1999. While analysts ponder how long BUPA can maintain its lower prices, its strategy makes sense while it is still gaining market share.

The detailed rules and conditions published by both BUPA and VHI merit careful review before you select one company over the other. Some notable comparisons are:

- The range of hospitals covered: 102 by VHI, 74 by BUPA.

- Level of hospital cover provided: BUPA provides full cover while VHI pays between 92 per cent and 97 per cent of bills incurred in certain private hospitals.

- Out-patient cover provided: similar for both companies, although BUPA does contribute towards GP visits.

- The age at which the adult premium applies: with VHI, from age 18. However, BUPA's children's rate applies up to age 21 if the child is in full-time education.

- BUPA pays an allowance if you want to give birth to your child at home and also covers some homeopathic treatments.

Both BUPA and VHI operate group plans (six or more members) and many companies operate these and often contribute to the subscription. Group rates are approximately 10 per cent less expensive than individual rates. Given that most people can access a group scheme, those are the rates shown here.

Annual Premiums, Adult Rates			
VHI	£	*BUPA*	£
Plan A	181.57	Essential	155.04
Plan B	259.56	Essential Plus*	215.04
Plan E	733.27	Essential Gold	770.04
Annual Premiums, Child Rates			
VHI	£	*BUPA*	£
Plan A	60.74	Essential	50.04
Plan B	94.44	Essential Plus*	75.00
Plan E	299.08	Essential Gold	250.08

* To avail of this rate for Essential Plus, you must agree to pay the first £50 of the cost of private hospital treatment. Alternatively you can pay a higher rate and receive full cover.

Tax Relief

Both BUPA and VHI subscriptions are eligible for tax relief at 26 per cent, regardless of what your highest rate of tax is. The original cash plans launched by BUPA would not have been eligible; however, now both companies' products attract the same tax treatment. Therefore the cost of health insurance at a group scheme rate for a family of two adults and 2 children is:

	Total Annual Cost (£)	Annual Cost Net of Income Tax (£)
BUPA (Essential Plus)	580	430
VHI (Plan B)	708	524

USEFUL CONTACTS

- BUPA, 12 Fitzwilliam Square, Dublin 2. Tel: (01) 662 7662.

- Department of Health, Hawkins Street, Dublin 2. Tel: (01) 671 4711.

- Irish Society of Homeopaths, Prospect House, Newcastle, Co. Wicklow. Tel: (01) 281 0030.

- The Homeopathic Association of Ireland, 92 Connolly Street, Nenagh, Co. Tipperary. Tel: (067) 34677.

- VHI, VHI House, Lower Abbey Street, Dublin 1. Tel.: 1 850 444 844. Fax: (01) 799 4091. E-mail: info@vhi.ie.

Health Boards

- Eastern Health Board, Health Board Headquarters, Dr Steevens' Hospital, Dublin 8. Tel: (01) 670 0700. Freephone 1800 520520. Covers Dublin, Kildare and Wicklow.

- Midland Health Board, Arden Road, Tullamore, County Offaly. Tel: (0506) 21868. Covers Offaly, Westmeath, Laois, Longford.

- Mid-Western Health Board, Catherine St, Limerick. Tel: (061) 316655. Covers Limerick, Clare, Tipperary North.

- North-Eastern Health Board, Navan Road, Kells, County Meath. Tel: (046) 40341. Covers Louth, Cavan, Meath, Monaghan.

- North-Western Health Board, Manorhamilton, County Leitrim. Tel: (072) 55123. Covers Donegal, Leitrim, Sligo.

- South-Eastern Health Board, Lacken, Dublin Road, County Kilkenny. Tel: (056) 51702. Covers Kilkenny, Carlow, Waterford, Tipperary, Wexford.

- Southern Health Board, Cork Farm Centre, Dennehy's Cross, County Cork. Tel: (021) 545011. Covers Cork, Kerry.

- Western Health Board, Merlin Park Regional Hospital, Galway, County Galway. Tel: (091) 751131. Covers Galway, Roscommon, Mayo.

Chapter 15

Education and Learning

The European Year of Lifelong Learning (1997) was a particularly good year for education in Ireland. Increases of 50 per cent in college places in specified courses, Government commitment to enhance spending on education and the speed with which a partnership of industry, education and Government representatives have produced results in addressing education and skills needs — all highlight the importance attached to education and learning in Ireland.

Modern Ireland offers a wide spectrum of educational choice. Returning emigrants will see many changes. Curricula at all levels are constantly reviewed and regularly updated. Primary schools are no longer referred to as "national" schools, multi-denominational and co-educational schools are less rare, gaelscoileanna (all tuition through Irish language) are increasingly popular, and from this year, your children may have a chance to learn an additional European language at primary school.

At second level, the Inter Cert and Matric have disappeared and the points system has been enhanced by a fairer and more transparent system of allocating "points" to Leaving Certificate students. Education in the much developed third-level sector is now largely free, while the introduction of modularisation has added new flexibility and added incentive to continue learning.

If you have never lived in Ireland before, you will notice some distinct differences from other systems. For example, there is no nationwide Government subsidised pre-school system, and some of what is covered in pre-schools in other countries is taught in the infant classes in Irish primary schools.

Only you can decide what is best for your child, and before you make any decision you should try to obtain as much first-hand information as you can. Before you make the move, speak to as many parents and teachers as you can and visit as many schools as possible. If you do not know anyone in the area, ask to be put in contact with other parents whose children attend a particular school and who can provide information on what is it like, how much parent/teacher contact is encouraged, what extra-curricular activities are available and any special features.

This Chapter aims to provide a clear explanation of how each level of the Irish education system works, but first, some general background:

- Full time education is compulsory for children from the age of six to 16; however, in practice 65 per cent of four-year-olds and almost all five-year-olds are enrolled in primary school.

- At present, 86 per cent of all children participate in Senior Cycle education. The aim is to increase the numbers staying on until age 18 to at least 90 per cent by the year 2000.

- Education is paid for by the Government, although private options are available.

- Parents must pay for school books and, where required, school uniforms.

- The primary and second-level school curricula are formulated at national level by the Minister for Education, and the Department of Education oversees their implementation through an inspection system in Government-funded schools.

- Primary schools are usually managed by Boards of Management, in which parents play an important role.

EDUCATION — WHO PAYS?

The Government provides free education at both primary and second level. In addition, approved third-level courses are provided at no cost. Parents are responsible for buying books (average cost at primary level is IR£60 per child per year) and uniforms which are often available in chain stores. There is also a private school sector at both primary and second level. These schools do not receive any State funding and the Minister for Education has no control over them. The parents councils of most schools supplement the Government funding with their own activities and at some schools parents may be asked to make a voluntary financial contribution.

PRIMARY (FIRST LEVEL) EDUCATION

Some 500,000 children are currently in the primary education sector, 98 per cent of them in 3,300 primary schools, the remainder in the 115 Special Schools or 79 fee-paying (private) primary schools. Most towns and villages have a school, and more than half of Irish schools at this level have four or fewer teachers. The typical ratio is one teacher to every 25 pupils. In some small rural areas, the arrival of a new family with school-age children can therefore mean saving the local school. Typical school hours at primary level are from 9.30 a.m. to 2.00 p.m. for senior infants and 9.30 a.m. to 3.00 p.m. for the rest of the pupils. Children receive homework throughout primary school; generally it should not take more than an hour in the junior classes. A 15-minute break mid-morning and a 45-minute lunch are typical and children eat a packed lunch in their classroom. In Catholic primary schools, highlights include First Communion for which children must be aged at least eight and Confirmation at age 12. While the ceremonies attached to these events have become more modern in recent years, the cost has not reduced. Despite growing efforts to simplify these occasions, enthusiasm generally seems to overrule, and they can prove expensive.

Although all schools follow the same broad curriculum, parents have a number of choices when it comes to selecting a school. Besides the question of *fee-paying* or *free*, other considerations include: whether to select a *single-sex* or *co-educational* school, one that has a *religious ethos* or is *multi-denominational*, tuition through *English* or *Irish* (in a *Gaelscoil*, which literally means Irish school). There are a number of international schools, as described below.

SECOND LEVEL EDUCATION

There are currently over 370,000 students in the second-level sector which comprises four categories of second-level schools: secondary, vocational, community/comprehensive and fee-paying secondary schools. The table below describes each type:

Type	Number	% of second-level students attending	Description
Secondary	452	61%	Privately owned and managed, the majority by religious communities
Vocational	247 All free	26%	Administered by Vocational Education Committees. Government provides 93% total cost. VEC generates remainder.
Community/ Comprehensive	76 All free	13%	Allocated individual budgets by Government. Adult Education.

Second-level education has been the subject of continuous review over the past number of years and significant changes have been made. While exams continue to be important and entry to third-level remains extremely competitive, second-level education has been adapted to provide a much wider range of both academic, vocational and developmental education with an increased focus on the way in which Ireland's employment market is evolving.

Second level education consists of a three-year *Junior Cycle* leading to the Junior Certificate. In the *Senior Cycle* there is an optional one-year Transition Year Programme, followed by a choice of three two-year Leaving Certificate programmes.

Junior cycle students can take as many subjects as they like, but they must sit exams in the core curriculum which is Irish, English, Maths, and at least four other curriculum subjects such as History, Geography, one of the modern European languages, business, arts, science and social science subjects. Students also take Civics and Physical Education, but these are not exam subjects. Religious Education is also a core subject in many schools, depending on their religious ethos. Most schools prescribe core subjects and ask the student to select others. This ensures that students gain a broad understanding of subjects and can discover which suit them best before making exam choices in the senior cycle. All exam subjects in the Junior Certificate may be taken at either higher or ordinary level.

Senior cycle programmes last two years and there are three choices of programme. In 1997, 86 per cent of all children remained in education to age 18 and the aim is to increase that figure to 90 per cent by the year 2000. Accordingly, a lot of emphasis is placed on providing senior cycle education to facilitate the needs of all students to this age.

Key senior cycle initiatives include the introduction of the optional year-long Transition Programme which students can take between Junior Certificate and commencement of studies for a Leaving Certificate programme. This is very popular, and anecdotal evidence already suggests that students who opt for Transition subsequently score well in their Leaving Certificate. Transition Programmes vary from school to school, as there is a lot of flexibility for teachers to design their own curricula with contributions from students, parents and local enterprise and communities. Programmes may include work experience in different types of companies, team and individual projects. Some schools have won enterprise awards for their projects.

Bonus Points at Leaving Certificate

Students who sit their written exams through Irish can gain an extra 10 per cent. Higher-level Maths used to be awarded extra points by most third-level institutions; however, in 1997, only three did so, and this practice is being phased out. The old-style higher Maths was very difficult and attracted few students. The new syllabus has made a major impact and 60 per cent of Leaving Cert students now take the higher paper.

Exams can become all-consuming, and it is important that students make time to research future career choices. Most second-level schools provide career guidance counselling. *The Irish Times* publishes an education supplement every Tuesday during term time and a top-class "Exam Times" throughout the period of exams and the offering of college places.

International Schools

The introduction of tuition in European languages in primary schools, introduced on a pilot basis in 1997 was broadly welcome. There are a number of international schools — for example, a French school in Dublin, a Japanese school in Kildare and St Killians in Dublin, where the Irish curriculum is taught through English and German. More details on these and other international schools may be obtained by contacting the Irish Embassy in your current country of residence, or the Embassy of the relevant country when you are here.

Questions to Ask about Schools	
• Location	• Type
• Free or fee-paying	• Religious ethos, if any
• Co-educational or single-sex	• Uniform
• Number of pupils	• Number of teachers
• Average age of teachers	• What languages are taught
• Science facilities	• Library facilities
• PCs available to students	• School meals
• Sports facilities	• Transition year
• Application procedure	

Cycle	Options	Duration	Course/Subjects Taken	Description	Exams and Qualifications
Junior Cycle	Compulsory	3 years	Irish, English, Maths and other subjects, higher or ordinary level	Broad-ranging, structured programme. Students will generally take subjects in preparation for more specialised choices in senior cycle.	Junior Certificate exams in June. Results in September.
Senior Cycle	Established Leaving Certificate	2 years	English, Irish, Maths plus 4 other subjects. Best 6 counted for third-level entry	Very structured programme. Students may take any subject at higher or ordinary level. Leads to entry to third-level education.	Leaving Certificate exams in June. Results in August.
	Optional Additional Transition Year	1 year	Wide range of team and individual projects with creative, cultural or business theme.	Very flexible developmental programme with extensive input into curriculum from students, parents, teachers, local business and community.	Depending on school, opportunity to gain extra-curricular qualifications.
	Leaving Certificate Vocational Programme	2 years	(1) Leaving Cert subjects, 2 of which are selected from vocational subjects (2) 1 modern European language (3) 3 compulsory link modules, i.e. Enterprise Education, Preparation for Work and Work Experience	Same as established Leaving Cert, with concentration on technical subjects. Funded by European Social Fund due to vocational content. Leads to further vocational training, e.g. PLC or RTC.	Leaving Certificate.
Options	Leaving Certificate Applied	2 years	(1) General Education (min. 30% of time) (2) Vocational Education (min. 30% of time) (3) Vocational Prep. (min. 25% of time)	Self-contained programme for students who do not choose other Leaving Cert options. Emphasis on person. Covers broad curriculum. Can lead to Post Leaving Cert courses.	Applied Leaving Certificate.

APPLYING FOR A PLACE IN A THIRD-LEVEL COLLEGE

Unlike many other countries, Ireland operates a centralised system for applying to almost all third-level college places. The Central Applications Office (CAO), based in Galway, processes all applications for all universities, Regional Technical Colleges (RTC), the Dublin Institute of Technology (DIT) and Colleges of Education. The CAO produces a handbook each year listing every course in its system. Applicants should request brochures of the different courses from the colleges or their school to find out more about course content. Applications should be made by 1 February with the appropriate fee, although late applications can be submitted for a fee up to 1 July. Offers of places are made in August, about one week after Leaving Certificate results are published. Although entry to third-level courses is extremely competitive, each CAO applicant can list up to ten degree and ten certificate/diploma choices, so very often, good research on the range of courses pays off.

A system of *points* is used for allocating college places. This is a way of converting Leaving Cert exam grades into numbers and comparing results. The points system changed to a much more accurate and fairer way of grading results in 1992 and the old system of straightforward A, B, C, D grades, which could count for as much as 25 per cent each, have been replaced by the following bands:

Leaving Cert Grades	
% Range	*Grade*
90–100	A1
85–89	A2
80–84	B1
75–79	B2
70–74	B3
65–69	C1
60–64	C2
55–59	C3
50–54	D1

Students who take their written exams in Irish gain an extra 10 per cent.

Leaving Cert Grade	Higher Paper	Ordinary Paper	Higher Maths
A1	100	60	140
A2	90	50	125
B1	85	45	115
B2	80	40	105
B3	75	35	95
C1	70	30	85
C2	65	25	75
C3	60	20	65
D1	55	15	—
D2	50	10	—
D3	45	5	—

HIGHER EDUCATION (THIRD LEVEL)

There have been enormous advances in third-level education over the past few years and university is no longer the only option. Students have a wide range of options and the majority of higher education places are now in colleges other than universities. Modularisation has been introduced in most third-level institutions over the past couple of years. While full-time students bemoan the fact that this means two sets of exams per year, for others who want to build up their academic qualifications in steps, it provides the means to do so. It also eliminates the idea of having to repeat a year's tuition. There are no set timeframes for adding modules to your portfolio, although if you are repeating a module, you may have to wait more than a semester for the next scheduled exams.

The table on the following pages describes the type of educational institutions available. It is worth checking the employment prospects for all of them, and noting that while the universities produce excellent results, it does not make any sense to be snobbish about the alternatives, which are by no means second best. In fact, some of them have gained global recognition for what they do. One such example is the PLC, Senior College in Ballyfermot which produces the most sought after animation professionals in Europe and has formed a partnership with Disney.

A total of 690 new places in 1997/98 have also being filled in PLCs to train school leavers over two years in the skills needed for the growing teleservices sector.

The same advice applies when selecting a qualification. The key point is to obtain a certified qualification and you can build on it from there. It is possible to start with a certificate course in an RTC or Institute of Technology and later transfer to a university to obtain a degree. Students are strongly recommended to visit any colleges of interest and read their brochures carefully to find a course that suits. The main types of qualifications are:

Certificate

The national certificate is a two-year course and leads to a technician qualification, which is a job qualification. Technicians are in great demand, particularly in the health care and computer sectors. One-year certificate courses do not have the same status as the year one courses, and you should read carefully each course prospectus to understand in advance what qualification you will obtain.

Diploma

National diploma courses are usually three-year courses, though there are diplomas which certificate-holders can acquire by studying for an extra year. The diploma student acquires a more advanced technician level qualification in areas such as accounting and auctioneering.

Degree

A degree is a full course of academic study leading to a professional qualification. Degree courses usually last four years, although some of the more general degrees last for three. All DCU and UL courses have a significant compulsory element of work placement or attending university overseas if you study languages. Many of the other institutions are now following suit.

Transferring Upward

A student who does not get a sufficient number of points at Leaving Cert to proceed straight to a degree course can first obtain a certificate and a diploma and, provided a distinction is obtained in these, transfer onto a degree course. It might take five years to obtain a degree this way instead of the customary three or four, but is worth it. Bearing this flexibility in the system in mind, it is therefore well worth considering all courses and making sure the CAO form is completed with the maximum number of choices.

Private Colleges

There are a number of well established private colleges to choose from. The range of courses provided is wide — and so is the price range. While students at private colleges do not qualify for grants, some courses are eligible for tax relief. Besides checking this point, your key considerations should be whether the college is *bonded* (operates in the same way as bonds for holiday companies) and also whether the courses are *accredited* and by whom.

Third-level courses are accredited either by a university or the National Council for Educational Awards (NCEA). Always check about accreditation before paying for a private course.

Student Grants are available though local authorities and VECs and qualification is based on a means test. In September 1997, the Minister for Education announced a plan to set up a new central agency to pay grants to third-level students. This move is a result of dissatisfaction with the current system, both in terms of qualifications and payment. Under the new system, grant applications would be processed in advance of the final CAO deadlines and would be means-tested, probably by the Revenue Commissioners.

College Type	Examples	Description	Qualifications	Student Grants
Universities	Dublin City Univ. Univ. College Dublin, Trinity College, Maynooth College	Top-tier third level. Primary, post-graduate and research degrees.	All universities award their own degrees	Yes, where students are eligible
Institutes of Education	DIT (7 colleges) College of Music, Waterford Institute of Ed. (status awarded 1997)	Entry possible at all 3 levels of higher education	Degrees, diplomas, certificates	Yes
Regional Technical Colleges (RTCs)	Athlone, Carlow, Cork, Dundalk, Galway, Sligo, Letterkenny, Limerick	Specialises in engineering, science, construction, art and design	Mainly 2-year cert. courses, can lead to diplomas, degrees	Yes
Colleges of Education		Train primary school teachers	Degree in education	Yes
Colleges of Art & Design	NCAD, Dublin, Crawford, Cork, Dun Laoghaire	Dedicated exclusively to art and design	NCAD up to degree. Other certs, diplomas	Yes
Open University	Open University Business School, Dublin	Distance learning with tutorial backup	Primary & higher degrees, prof. qualifications	No, however tax relief on fees

College Type	Examples	Description	Qualifications	Student Grants
CERT	Locations nationwide	Tourism	Certified in Ireland and the EU	Weekly allowance, books, uniform
Agricultural Colleges	Co-ordinated by Teagasc	1-year courses with practical element	Certificates can lead to RTCs	Allowances
Nursing	17 general and 6 specialised hospitals, all linked to third-level college or university	3 years	Diploma from associated college	Grant for uniform, books
Apprenticeships	FÁS nationwide	2–3 years, 7 phases of training	International crafts certificate	Allowance
Private Colleges	Options nationwide	Variety of courses including degree	Depends on certification	Generally no, some tax relief for courses over 2 years
Distance Education	Oscail, the National Distance Learning Centre	Wide range of degree and post-graduate courses	Degrees, post-grad quals., professional quals.	No

Adult Education

The decision in 1997 to dedicate a Minister of State to adult education for the first time ever signals the growing importance attached to this area. Existing initiatives include the VTOS programme for lone parents and the unemployed, outreach education programmes co-ordinated by Dublin City University, which covers a range of levels including degrees, and a modular BA offered by Maynooth University. For more information, contact these universities directly or AONTAS, the umbrella organisation for adult education.

Learning Languages

The opportunity to learn English as a foreign language attracts large numbers to Ireland every year — some 70,000 teenage and 30,000 mature students in 1997 alone. Meanwhile, anglophones in Ireland are learning other European languages in large numbers, with good cause when you look at the increase in the number of employment opportunities in the international services sector. Alliance Française, the Goethe Institute, the Italian Cultural Institute, the Dutch Society and Gael Linn are among the organisations to contact for further information.

USEFUL CONTACTS

Primary Level

- Department of Education, Marlborough Street, Dublin 1. Tel: (01) 873 4700.

- National Parents' Council, Primary Schools, 16–20 Cumberland Street South, Dublin 2. Tel: (01) 678 9981.

Second Level

- Department of Education, Marlborough Street, Dublin 1. Tel: (01) 873 4700.

- Central Applications Office (CAO), Tower House, Eglinton Street, Galway. Tel: (091) 63318.

- National Parents' Council Post-Primary Schools, Marino Institute of Education, Griffith Avenue, Dublin 7. Tel: (01) 857 0522.

PLC/VEC Sector

- Cavan: Cavan College of Further Studies. Tel: (049) 32633.

- Clare: Ennis Community College, Ennis, Co. Clare. Tel: (065) 29432.

- Cork: College of Commerce, Cork City. Tel: (021) 270777.

- Donegal: Vocational School, Letterkenny. Tel: (074) 21047.

- Dublin: Stillorgan Senior College. Tel: (01) 288 0704.

- Dublin: Ballsbridge College. Tel: (01) 668 4806.

- Dublin: Senior College, Ballyfermot (Dame Street Branch). Tel: (01) 626 9421.

- Dublin: Senior College, Eblana Avenue, Dun Laoghaire. Tel: (01) 280 0385.

- Dublin: Coláiste Íde, Senior College, Finglas. Tel: (01) 834 2333.

- Dublin: Whitehall Senior College. Tel: (01) 837 6011.

- Galway: Galway Technical Institute, Galway City. Tel: (091) 581342.

- Kerry: Community College Killorglin. Tel: (066) 61168.

- Kildare: St Conleth's Vocational School, Newbridge. Tel: (045) 431417.

- Kilkenny: Ormonde College, City Vocational School, Kilkenny. Tel: (056) 22108.

- Limerick: Limerick Senior College, Limerick City. Tel: (061) 414344.

- Louth: Drogheda College of Further Studies. Tel: (041) 37105.

- Monaghan: Monaghan Institute of Further Education. Tel: (047) 84900.

- Waterford: Central Technical Institute, Waterford City. Tel: (051) 874053.

- Wicklow: Abbey Community College, Wicklow. Tel: (0404) 67567.

- Wicklow: Bray Senior College, County Wicklow. Tel: (01) 282 9668.

Technology Sector

- Athlone RTC, Althone, County Westmeath. Tel: (0902) 24400.

- Carlow RTC, County Carlow. Tel: (0503) 70400.

- Cork RTC, County Cork. Tel: (021) 545222.

- Dundalk RTC, Dundalk, County Louth. Tel: (042) 34785.

- Galway RTC, County Galway. Tel: (091) 753161.

- Letterkenny RTC, County Donegal. Tel: (074) 24888.

- Limerick RTC, County Limerick. Tel: (061) 327688.

- Sligo RTC, County Sligo. Tel: (071) 43261.

- Tallaght RTC, Dublin 24. Tel: (01) 404 2000.

- Tralee RTC, County Kerry. Tel: (066) 24666.

- Dun Laoghaire College of Art & Design, County Dublin. Tel: (01) 280 1138.

- Dublin Institute of Technology, Dublin City. Tel: (01) 402 3000.

- Waterford Institute of Technology, County Waterford. Tel: (051) 302000.

University Sector

- Admissions Office, University College, Cork. Tel: (021) 276871.

- Admissions Office, University College, Belfield, Dublin 4. Tel: (01) 706 7777/269 3244.

- Dublin City University, Glasnevin, Dublin 9. Tel: (01) 704 5000.

- Admissions Office, University College, Galway. Tel: (091) 524411.

- University of Limerick, Limerick. Tel: (061) 333644.

- Admissions Office, St Patrick's College, Maynooth, County Kildare. Tel: (01) 628 5222.

- Admissions Office, Trinity College, Dublin 2. Tel: (01) 677 2941.

Chapter 16

Transport and Travel

A Ha'penny's Worth

One halfpenny in every motor tax pound is all that it would take to make a decisive and permanent improvement in Dublin's traffic problems, according to the Automobile Association. Or perhaps a little more discipline on the part of drivers. Contrary to appearances, Dublin is not the car-swamped city that many people believe. In fact, according to an AA survey of 16 European cities — including 14 capitals — Dublin has the second lowest density of cars per capita with a car-to-people ratio of 1:3.18. Experts believe that the solution to reducing traffic congestion and commuting times lies in a better public transport system, combined with more stringent law enforcement measures on traffic violations. Operation Freeflow was a police initiative launched in December 1996 in Dublin and involved just 100 additional gardaí on the streets monitoring illegal parking and other breaches of traffic rules. A seasonal initiative, there is pressure to have it implemented all year.

Half a penny hardly merits a mention when you look at the total cost of driving which, according to the AA, rose by 5.9 per cent from 1996 to 1997. The increase was prompted by a sharp increase in the cost of motor insurance and a rise in the price of petrol from an average of 57 pence per litre to over 60 pence per litre by May 1997. The cost of related items such as servicing and parts rose in line with inflation.

The AA calculates the total cost of motoring for different categories of car based on an annual mileage of 10,000 miles. Included are all related costs, from depreciation and interest on capital to servicing and fuel. The figures are then broken down into "cost per mile". Using this method, the AA puts the cost per mile for a small car (1251–1500cc) at 59.6 pence in 1997, up from 56.3 pence in 1996. Higher rates may only be used by agreement with the Revenue Commissioners.

DRIVING IN IRELAND

Rules of the Road

The Rules of the Road are available from any post office for £1. You will need to study this booklet carefully, particularly if you have not driven in Ireland for some time.

Insurance

You must be insured to drive in Ireland. You need to show proof of insurance to obtain your motor tax and are legally required to display a valid insurance disc on your car. Uninsured driving is a serious breach of the law, while failure to display a valid insurance can result in a fine of £50.

There are different kinds of motor insurance available in Ireland. "Fully comprehensive" insurance covers you for all damage to your own car and a third party in the case of an accident, whereas "third party, fire and theft" does not. There are discounts known as "no claims bonuses" for accident-free driving and you are recommended to obtain written confirmation of your driving record from your current insurer in order to obtain these here.

Following are examples of insurance costs:

Insurance Premium Costs, September 1997 (£)				
Comprehensive	*Female (35)*	*Male (35)*	*Female (45)*	*Male (45)*
PMPA	316	363	335	334
Guardian Direct	280	321	260	301
AA Car Insurance	289	295	274	290
Premier Direct	291	357	272	367
Hibernian	305	341	323	305

Comprehensive	Female (35)	Male (35)	Female (45)	Male (45)
First Call Direct	317	353	339	265
Celtic International	272	262	262	272
General Accident	410	448	448	448
Quinn Direct	343	459	387	295
Norwich Union	374	427	451	335

Notes: Prices are for comprehensive cover on a 1992 1.1 litre Ford Fiesta valued at £5,000. All drivers have sedentary type occupations, full licences and live and work in Dublin. Premiums are based on a full driving licence and a maximum no claims discount. Benefits vary from one policy to another. It should also be noted that the cost of insurance rises for drivers under 25, and rises sharply for those on provisional licences only.

Source: AA Insurance costs survey, by Lansdowne Research

Driver's Licence

There are two types of driver's licence in Ireland: provisional and full. A provisional licence is valid for one year and is available to anyone over 17. The purpose of this licence is to give the driver an opportunity to learn how to drive and take the driving test. A learner driver is obliged to take the driving test on or before their fourth provisional licence. A full licence can be obtained on passing the test.

Certain EU and Australian licences can be exchanged for an Irish licence within one year of arrival. Holders of all other licences must take a practical and oral test. An international licence obtained in your current country of residence may be used for a limited period of time; however, you should check with your insurer about any implications of this.

Motor Tax

If you are taxing a newly imported car, you need to take it to the regional licensing authority with a Vehicle Registration Certificate and an IF100 Import Form, which you obtain from Customs and Excise at the time of importation.

Private cars are taxed at an annual rate which is calculated according to the cubic capacity (cc) of the vehicle. The rates are as follows:

cc	£	cc	£	cc	£
1000 or less	92	1001–1100	138	1101–1200	150
1201–1300	163	1301–1400	175	1401–1500	188
1501–1600	232	1601–1700	247	1701–1800	288
1801–1900	304	1901–2000	320	2001–2100	410
2101–2200	429	2201–2300	449	2301–2400	468
2401–2500	488	2501–2600	572	2601–2700	594
2701–2800	616	2801–2900	638	2901–3000	660
Over 3000	800				

ROAD SAFETY

Drinking and Driving

The legal alcohol limit is 100 milligrams of alcohol per 100 millilitres of blood. Garda checkpoints and a variety of safe driving programmes have greatly stemmed the trend in drinking and driving, for which the penalties include disqualification from driving for a specified period of time and a heavy fine. You would also expect to pay more for motor insurance and may have difficulty obtaining insurance.

Garda National Traffic Policy Bureau

The current establishment of this group is an indication of how serious the police force is about making Ireland's roads safer. One of its aims is to make speeding and failure to wear seat-belts as socially unacceptable as drinking and driving has become. Its plans include training garda officers in media skills so they can participate in road safety education on local radio stations.

Accidents

Despite safety efforts, accidents do happen and these are the AA guidelines on what you should do.

You *must* stop immediately, remain at the scene of the accident for a reasonable period of time and give your name, address (and that of the owner of the vehicle if it does not belong to you), vehicle registration number and insurance details to the other driver. In cases of injury, you are obliged to inform the Gardaí. In cases where there are no injuries but there is damage to property, you should still inform the Gardaí; however, they will not necessarily attend the scene.

To speed up your subsequent insurance claim, you should gather details of the driver and owner of the other vehicle (name, address, vehicle registration, insurance), contact details of any witnesses, description of any injuries, name of attending garda, accident details (time, date, location). You should also note the speed of the vehicles, road markings and conditions and whether seat-belts were worn. If you can photograph or sketch the scene, you should do so.

PUBLIC TRANSPORT

Ireland's public transport system has improved greatly over the years. What used to be CIE has been divided into three companies: Irish Rail (nation-wide train service), Bus Éireann (nation-wide provincial bus service) and Dublin Bus (urban bus service). Reduced price single day, weekly and monthly tickets are available on public transport services. Dublin city services include the Dublin Area Rapid Transit (DART) system which runs along the coastline from Greystones to Howth, and Nitelink buses which run until 2.00 a.m. at weekends.

To date, cyclists have fared least well in the battle for space on Ireland's roads. There are relatively few cycle lanes, although this has not stopped people getting on their bikes. However, there has been a significantly visible increase in safety awareness, and it is the sight of a cyclist without a helmet that will catch your attention now.

Chapter 17

Irish Culture

Much has been written about Ireland's beauty, culture and welcoming people. These accolades are richly deserved, and a wealth of information describing Ireland is available from Bord Fáilte tourist information offices, listed at the end of this chapter. Once you are in Ireland, the newspapers devote plenty of space to covering events in sports, arts, culture and entertainment. In particular, *The Irish Times* "Weekend" supplement on a Saturday is an excellent guide. *Hot Press* is a unique fortnightly magazine that covers pop music, film and entertainment. It sells about 21,000 copies per issue, mainly to the 16–30 age group. Most cities provide events and entertainment guides. Over one million people live in the greater Dublin area and some 44 per cent of Ireland's population of 3.6 million are aged under-25. These facts influence the trends in modern culture. The following is just a taste of what's on offer.

ART

The National Gallery in Dublin boasts an excellent collection, while the Irish Museum of Modern Art caters for contemporary Irish and international artists. There are a number of other quality galleries around the country, such as the Crawford Gallery in Cork. Painting has grown in popularity as a leisure pursuit and there are numerous classes available in summer schools and locally in many towns. Sculpting too has gained considerable prominence. There were a number of events in Autumn 1997, including the *Ireland and Europe Exhibition*, which saw sculptures on display in public places right across Dublin and the *Temple Bar*

Street Art Symposium where the challenge for some 50 contemporary artists was to make work that would stand out from bill-
boards and shop-fronts and be appreciated by passers-by.

RELIGION

Although Ireland's society has all the appearances of being quite a
secular one, the reality is that religion is part of the fabric of Irish
life, partly because it has played such a powerful role for so long.
According to academics at the 1997 National Conference of Priests
in Ireland, recent European studies on values show that Irish attitudes to the Catholic Church have changed considerably. Increasingly, individual Catholics (who make up 91 per cent of the
population according to the 1991 census) make their own decisions on moral issues and feel less obliged to follow the Church's
teaching. The statistics indicate that people are not necessarily
abandoning their religious faith. The figures quoted show an increase in the proportion of people who said they took comfort
from prayer from 80 per cent in 1980 to 82 per cent in 1990, although church attendance decreased from 83 per cent to 81 per
cent in the same period. However, these figures belie the true state
of affairs in the late 1990s, where a series of scandals has shattered
the Church's credibility and Church representatives and commentators freely recount stories of the abuse that is now hurled at
priests in the streets in some places. While the Church is striving
to improve its image, religion remains an integral part of Irish society, and those of you returning or moving from abroad may be
surprised at the extent of its influence, particularly in schools.

COLOURFUL LANGUAGE

You will notice on returning to Ireland the somewhat casual attitude to expletives. The first point is that swear words have a different (and often less strong) meaning in Ireland, so you cannot
even be sure you have understood what you have heard. The second is that swearing is not considered offensive by everyone, although it is also not true that everyone approves of it. The best

advice is to be aware that unexpected people may swear; try not to be offended, find out from someone you trust what it means and avoid falling into the same habit.

CRAIC

If the "craic" is good enough it defies definition. Formerly "crack", until ambiguous meaning necessitated a change, "craic" is an Irish sounding pronunciation of an English word, the kind of thing linguistic purists hate. However, they don't mind having craic. Craic is a good time, good company, good atmosphere and conversation. If you are enjoying yourself, it is good craic.

DANCE

You can learn or practice just about any kind of dance in Ireland, and this country embraces dancing crazes as happily as anywhere else. Thankfully, line-dancing seems to be losing its appeal, but the enthusiasm generated for traditional Irish dancing by *Riverdance* continues to grow. Many children learn Irish dancing at school; extracurricular classes are available just about everywhere, including for adults. Some pubs have dancing sessions, typically where traditional Irish music is played.

DATING

Dating is one of those subjects that interests everyone. It is also something that varies greatly across cultures, so it is important to learn to read social situations correctly, to avoid misunderstanding or embarrassment. It is easy to be glib about this subject. However, meeting people matters, and many claim it is not always easy if you have a busy working life. Still, a lot of people make an effort and you will find plenty of media coverage about the latest "in" places. At the time of writing, the five-week long Lisdoonvarna Matchmaking festival (for the over-40s) reported excellent results — at least financially — yielding in excess of £5 million for the local community. Meanwhile, new branches of the farmers' social organisation Macra na Feirme are thriving in city areas amid reports of great social success. (There is no known link between this development and the training of an additional 2,500 farmers by Teagasc in 1997).

EATING AND DRINKING

A lot of socialising goes on in Ireland's pubs, with conversation an integral part of an evening in most locals. Stricter laws on drinking and driving do not seem to have altered the numbers in pubs — just what the customers are drinking. Recent reports say that it has now become fashionable for men to drink bottled water (40 million litres are consumed overall every year) when they are to drive home. The range of food in restaurants has benefited from chefs returning from all over the world. A 1997 survey by the Food Products Development Centre of 90 Dublin restaurants found a sharp increase in demand for ethnic cuisine. If you want to cook for yourself, try the Saturday morning Temple Bar Market in Dublin, described as food heaven by those who frequent it, for organic produce, fresh food and a huge range of ethnic products from Indian spices to Moroccan specialities. Cork's "English" market is also well worth a visit.

BSE did not hit Ireland as badly as other countries, although there have been cases found in animals. Screening is vigorous and needs to be so, as Irish farmers are heavily dependent on their beef exports. Teagasc, the farm advisory, research and training organisation, is currently compiling a database on the food purity of Irish products and establishing a food safety consultancy for Irish food companies. Meanwhile, the Irish Organic Farmers and Growers Association publish a magazine listing developments in organic food production and suppliers.

FILM

During 1996, Ireland celebrated a centenary of film. Over that century, many leading international film-makers have worked here. Alfred Hitchcock filmed O'Casey's *Juno and the Paycock* with the Abbey Theatre Players in 1930. John Ford directed *The Informer* in 1935 and *The Quiet Man* in 1952. John Huston, who made his home in Ireland, made many films here including his last film, James Joyce's *The Dead*, in 1987. David Lean made his epic *Ryan's Daughter* in County Kerry in 1970.

Over the last 20 years, however, Ireland has made its own mark on the world of film, with directors like Jim Sheridan and Neil Jordan winning Oscars for films such as *My Left Foot* and *The Crying Game*. *Michael Collins* and *The Commitments* are also well-known Irish films. The recent release *I Went Down* has already started winning awards.

The wealth of locations and film-making skills available in Ireland has brought directors from all over the world to film in Ireland. *Braveheart* was made here. Steven Spielberg filmed in Wexford in the summer of 1997 and *Dancing at Lughnasa*, starring Meryl Streep, was shot at various locations around Ireland. This film activity is matched by the growth of the cinema business, and the quality and choice of cinemas has improved enormously. In addition, film festivals are held in Cork and Dublin every year.

HUMOUR

This is one of those things that does not always travel well. The problem may not lie in having the humour of where you are coming from understood, but trying to establish an understanding of the Irish humour. Irish people are known for their quick-witted one-liners, and it would be a mistake to interpret these as an attempt to put you down. It is more a case of sending each other up. The rise of the comedy club and the emergence of some Irish comedians on the international circuit provide ample evidence of how seriously Irish people take their humour.

LANGUAGE

There are two official languages in Ireland. Irish is the national language and English the language of the majority of the population. Irish is a Celtic language, closely related to Scottish Gaelic, Welsh and Breton. It was the language of the vast majority of the population until the early nineteenth century. The subsequent shift to English was swift, 1891 and by it was being spoken by over 85 per cent of the population. The early twentieth century saw a national cultural revival as well as the establishment of an independent Irish State. Subsequent promotion of the Irish language by the state has preserved existing usage and increased bilingualism. Irish is the principal language in areas known as Gaeltachts, situated mainly along the western seaboard. A State authority, Údarás na Gaeltachta, promotes industrial development in these areas. Bord na Gaeilge (the Irish Language Board), also a State agency, promotes the use of Irish throughout the country and as a core school subject.

A growing number of schools, known as Gaelscoil (all-Irish School — Gaelscoileanna in the plural), offer tuition exclusively through the Irish language. Radio na Gaeltachta broadcasts nationally in Irish, and a new Irish language television service, Telefís na Gaeilge, was launched in November 1996. Latest available figures show that 32 per cent of adults claim some knowledge of the Irish language. Gael Linn reports a surge in the numbers of people enrolling in courses to improve their Irish language skills, many from overseas.

LITERATURE

Ireland's writers and poets — both through English and Irish — are well known. Jonathan Swift, W. B. Yeats, Lady Gregory, Samuel Beckett, John Millington Synge, James Joyce, Patrick Kavanagh, Elizabeth Bowen, George Bernard Shaw, Sean O'Casey, Brendan Behan, Brian Friel, Seamus Heaney, Maeve Binchy, Hugh Leonard and Roddy Doyle are just some of those whose work is known internationally. Beckett, Shaw, Yeats and Heaney were all awarded the Nobel Prize for Literature. Novelist Roddy Doyle is a Booker Prize winner.

Ireland is a good place to be if you want to write. Tax incentives aside, you will find plenty of encouragement here. As with so many other elements of Irish culture, there is a lot of activity among writing groups in local communities.

MUSIC

Music has always been important in Irish cultural life. One of the earliest Irish composers whose work has survived is Turlough O'Carolan (1670–1738), known as "The Blind Harpist", who was one of the last in the ancient Bardic tradition. Eighteenth-century Dublin attracted many composers and saw the first performance of Handel's Messiah in 1742. In this century, traditional Irish music has inspired modern composers such as Seán Ó Ríada, A. J. Potter, Brian Boydell, Seoirse Bodley, Shaun Davey and Mícheál Ó Súilleabháin, to name but a few.

Comhaltas Ceoltoirí Éireann promotes Irish traditional music and culture and has more than 400 branches all over the world, including Europe, Japan and the US, attracting many followers, not all of Irish extraction. In Ireland, it runs more than 600 classes teaching Irish traditional music around the country and organises more than 40 "fleadhanna". A fleadh is an Irish music competition and the Fleadh Cheoil is the musical equivalent of an All-Ireland Final.

Since the 1960s, traditional Irish music has grown in popularity, both in Ireland and abroad, through groups as diverse as The Clancy Brothers, The Dubliners, Clannad, The Chieftains, De Dannan and Altan, who have put traditional music into a modern context. Another example of this phenomenon in Irish culture is the international hit show "Riverdance", which presents a modern picture of Irish song, dance and music.

Ireland also has an international reputation for other musical styles, with artists like Van Morrisson, U2, Sinéad O'Connor, Enya and The Cranberries. Numerous newer bands include Therapy, Ash and The Corrs.

Planning restrictions have curbed the fabulous rock concerts at Slane Castle for the moment. However, The Point in Dublin provides a home for countless events, and U2's promoters did manage to overcome planning obstacles in 1997 to include Dublin in the group's Pop Mart tour. The "Trip to Tipp", which began in the early 1990s as a weekend rock festival, has now become a day trip, again due to planning restrictions.

Opera lovers are well catered for, with Dublin's National Concert Hall, the Cork Opera House, Limerick University's concert hall and the annual Wexford Opera Festival to choose from.

NEWSPAPERS

Newspapers have been published in Ireland for over 300 years. Today, there are four morning (*The Irish Independent, The Irish Times, The Examiner* and *The Star*) and two evening (*The Evening Herald* and *The Evening Echo*) daily national papers. The Irish Business Readership Survey 1997 shows the percentage of readership among business people as: *Irish Times* (83 per cent), *Irish Independent* (56 per cent), *Financial Times* (33 per cent — a UK paper).

There are five Sunday newspapers: *The Sunday Tribune, The Sunday Independent, The Sunday World, The Sunday Business Post* and *Ireland on Sunday*, a new paper launched in September 1997. Readership numbers for the first half of 1997 were: *Sunday Independent* (333,966), *Sunday Tribune* (84,148), *Sunday Business Post* (41,890).

Dublin Sport is a new weekly tabloid paper devoted to all the sports played in the capital.

There are also about 100 local newspapers, usually published weekly, and a wide variety of magazines dealing with current affairs, economic issues and leisure interests. *Business and Finance* and *Magill* are examples. Newspapers and magazines from many other countries are widely available.

SPORTS

Golf, fishing, horse riding, walking, cycling and water-sports are all well catered for in Ireland, are easily accessible and very popular. Michelle Smith, Sonia O'Sullivan and Eamonn Coughlan all achieved their early sporting success at the Community Games, one of the sporting highlights of the year for many young people and more than half-a-million children participated nationwide in 1997, with more than 6,000 competing at the finals.

Michelle Smith's remarkable feat of winning three gold and one bronze medal for swimming in the 1996 Atlanta Olympics, followed by European success in 1997, has resulted in the expected upsurge in interest in swimming, although Ireland has yet to build an Olympic-size swimming pool.

Ireland's able-bodied do not hold the monopoly on international sporting achievements. Bridie Lynch captured a gold and a bronze medal for track and field events at the 1996 Paralympic Games, at which the Irish team won a total of ten medals.

Soccer is an obsession with many Irish people, particularly when the national team is playing well. In 1990, for example, Ireland reached the quarter-finals of the Soccer World Cup for the first time and the Taoiseach of the day, now remembered less favourably, declared a half-day national holiday during the finals.

Gaelic football, hurling and camogie remain hugely popular, and the GAA has almost three-quarters of a million members country-wide. Clare won the All-Ireland hurling final in 1997, with the Sam McGuire Cup for Gaelic football going to Kerry.

Horse racing followers are delighted with the success of top jockeys Richard Dunwoody, Charlie Swan and Michael Kinane. Racing is a hugely popular social activity and there are more than 250 days of race meetings every year. Some highlights are the Irish Grand National in March, Punchestown in April, the Budweiser Derby in June and the Galway Races in July.

News that the Ryder Cup will be hosted by Ireland in 2005 will ensure that golf retains its status. Philip Walton, Darren Clarke, Paul McGinley and Pádraig Harrington have achieved international success playing golf in recent years and the sport is growing in popularity in Ireland all the time. Waiting lists for club memberships are not uncommon. Straffan's K Club and Mount Juliet in Kilkenny are among the favourites to host the Ryder cup, where for a fee of half a million pounds to the European organisers, they are effectively guaranteed that their course will become one of the ten most famous in the world. Meanwhile, 1998's golfing highlights include the Smurfit European Open Golf Tournament at the K Club.

Other individuals whose international success ensures the popularity of their sport at home include motor racing's Eddie Irvine, snooker champion Ken Doherty, Catriona McKiernan and Sonia O'Sullivan in athletics, Ian Wiley and Gary Mawer in canoeing and Anthony O'Connor and Neville Maxwell in rowing. Wayne McCullough and Steven Collins are world professional boxing champions, and news that the latter plans to retire has been greeted with dismay. Given the excitement of these sports — for example, the exhilarating experience of following the course of the Liffey Descent canoeing race in the Autumn — it is hardly surprising that they attract an active supportive as well as participant following.

TELEVISION AND RADIO

National radio and television services are operated by Radio Telefís Éireann (RTE), the public broadcasting company which transmits on three television (RTE 1, Network 2 and TnaG) and four radio channels (Radio One, 2FM, FM3, Radio Cork). The annual licence fee is £75. UK radio and television programming and satellite channels (including CNN) are also widely available.

Irish speakers are served by RTE's dedicated radio channel Radio na Gaeltachta (FM3) and Telefís na Gaeilge (TnaG), the Irish language television station which was launched in October 1996. Less than a year later, TnaG claims to attract more viewers than any of the other minority channels available, such as Sky News or MTV.

Radio Ireland, the nationwide third channel, is not yet a year old and still trying to find its niche. RTE's Radio One and 2FM are hugely popular, and if you want to discover Irish attitudes and concerns, listen in to any of the daytime programmes on Radio One and the morning programmes on 2FM.

The 1988 Radio and Television Act established the Independent Radio and Television Commission which has responsibility for licensing and overseeing independent radio and television broadcasting. In recent years, quite a number of independent local and community radio initiatives have emerged across the country, gaining substantial audiences. At the time of writing, former Boomtown Rat and Live Aid organiser Bob Geldof was trying to persuade the IRTC to allow him to establish a channel called Atomic TV to provide a showcase for new bands and music, at least 40 per cent of which would be Irish-based.

THEATRE

Oliver Goldsmith, Richard Brinsley Sheridan and Oscar Wilde brought Irish theatrical works to prominence as far back as the eighteenth and nineteenth centuries. Twentieth century playwrights such as Seán O'Casey, Brendan Behan, Brian Friel and Sebastian Barry have copper-fastened Ireland's place in international theatre. Theatre is well represented all over Ireland today and includes many international as well as Irish works. The Galway Arts Festival (July) celebrates its twenty-first anniversary in 1998 and Kilkenny Arts Week (August) its twenty-fifth, while the Dublin Theatre Festival (October) provided an excellent range of productions on its fortieth anniversary in 1997. Galway-based Macnas can be credited with bringing theatre to the streets; its transforming contribution to Dublin's 1996 St Patrick's Day parade was particularly memorable.

Youth theatre is very popular and theatres such as the Gaiety in Dublin offer coaching from acting professionals during the summer holidays. New efforts to provide training opportunities for aspiring young actors include the opening of the first Limerick Youth Theatre by Belltable Arts Centre in 1997, which will enable 25 young people to train for two years. Meanwhile, amateur dramatics continues to thrive as a leisure pursuit throughout Ireland.

HIGHLIGHTS FOR 1998

Ireland is never short of an excuse to generate some craic and 1998 provides plenty of opportunity. In addition to countless festivals and events, just a few of which have been mentioned, these are some to the highlights:

- Commemorations of the United Irish Rising of 1798 will take place all over the country. County Wexford is staging a year-long commemoration, which includes drama, exhibitions and other events. An international academic conference, "1798, A Bicentenary Perspective", takes place in the Ulster Museum, Belfast and Dublin Castle in late May.

- The third biggest sporting event in the world, the Tour de France, starts in Dublin on 11 July 1998, and over three days competitors will cycle from Dublin through Wicklow and from County Wexford to Cork.

- Up to 90 spectacular sailing vessels with a combined crew of more than 5,000 are expected in Dublin Port in August on the last leg of the international Cutty Sark Tall Ships race, which begins in England and includes Portugal and Spain before setting sail for Dublin. The planned festivities promise to be as spectacular as the ships.

The contribution of new cultures enriches the range of things to do in Ireland. It is a small island — just 170 miles (275 kilometres) at its widest point and 301 miles (486 kilometres) at its longest — but you are certain to find something to do, wherever you go. Enjoy it.

For further information about Ireland, contact the Irish Tourist Board/Bord Fáilte at:

- Bord Fáilte, Head Office, Baggot Street, Dublin 2. Tel: (01) 602 4000.

- 5th Level, 36 Carrington Street, Sydney, NSW 2000, Australia, Tel: 00-61-2-299-6177. Fax: 00-61-2-299-6323.

- Libellenweg 1, 1040 Vienna, Austria. Tel: 00-431-914-1351. Fax: 00-431-911-3765.

- Avenue de Beaulieu 25, 1160 Brussels, Belgium. Tel: 0032-2-673-9940. Fax: 00 322-672-1066.

Appendices

APPENDIX 1: NON-EXECUTIVE SALARIES

	1–2 Years' Experience (£)	3–5 Year' Experience (£)
Accountancy (refer also to the financial categories in the executive salaries listed in Chapter 4)		
Qualified Management Accountant	21,497	25,521
Qualified Financial Accountant	17,451	27,005
Accounts Assistant	11,632	12,987
Accounting Technician	12,647	13,784
Book-keeper	10,356	12,897
Credit Controller	11,897	14,956
Financial Controller (industry)	29,687	34,452
Audit Manager (practice)	30,473	34,006
Administration		
Secretary	9,017	11,996
Senior Secretary/PA	10,528	15,562
Receptionist/Telephonist	9,134	11,492
Administrator	9,008	12,564
Office Manager	11,165	15,928
Legal Secretary	7,533	12,065
Banking/Finance Secretary	9,056	12,574
Graphic Artist	10,078	14,158
DTP Operator	8,240	11,163
More experienced and senior administration staff (e.g. PA to senior management) can earn up to £25,000 per year.		

	1–2 Years' Experience (£)	3–5 Year' Experience (£)
Customer Service		
Customer Service Rep.	10,243	13,147
Customer Service Rep. (multi-lingual)	12,295	14,595
Customer Service Supervisor	15,556	18,345
Customer Service Manager	31,326	33,015
Sales Order Administrator	10,168	12,997
Telemarketing Executive	9,534	13,246
Telemarketing Executive (with languages)	12,436	15,943
Reservations Supervisor	18,478	20,489
Call Centre Manager	36,965	42,458
Telemarketing Supervisor	20,879	22,587
Chemicals and Plastics		
Injection Moulding Engineer	10,034	14,321
Polymer Technician	10,123	14,442
Polymer Engineer	14,009	22,786
Chemical Engineer	16,328	25,005
Laboratory Technician	10,000	18,032
Laboratory Manager	25,064	34,649
Validation Engineer	16,056	26,165
Validation Technician	12,432	20,326
Computing (refer also to the executive categories given in Chapter 4)		
Computer Operations		
Operator	13,893	15,775
Shift Leader	16,238	18,831
Operations Manager	27,035	28,222
PC Client Server Environment		
Programmer	17,751	23,329
Analyst Programmer	18,320	24,517
Team Leader	25,700	28,103
Systems Analyst	25,400	27,955
Project Leader	26,952	29,486
Business Analyst	23,957	26,076
DP/MIS Manager	34,334	38,750

	1–2 Years' Experience (£)	3–5 Years' Experience (£)
Localisation		
Software Tester	13,229	17,432
Software Q.A. Engineer	17,249	22,331
Software Localisation Engineer	16,978	21,005
Localisation Manager	24,223	35,000
UNIX		
Programmer	17,835	24,520
Analyst Programmer	18,535	24,749
Team Leader	26,123	29,053
Systems Analyst	25,876	28,335
Project Leader	27,569	30,560
Business Analyst	23,892	27,726
DP/MIS Manager	35,136	43,005
Digital/Vax		
Programmer	17,136	20,372
Analyst Programmer	17,944	22,035
Team Leader	26,056	30,078
Systems Analyst	27,898	31,992
Project Leader	27,927	32,064
Business Analyst	25,397	27,779
MIS Manager	35,026	39,743
IBM Mainframe		
Programmer	16,965	20,165
Analyst Programmer	18,223	22,087
Team Leader	26,238	28,945
Systems Analyst	27,875	31,863
Project Leader	27,886	31,987
Business Analyst	25,146	27,863
DP/MIS Manager	36,089	43,286
IBM Midrange		
Programmer	16,575	19,761
Analyst Programmer	17,275	21,371
Team Leader	25,254	29,219
Systems Analyst	26,831	30,524
Project Leader	26,801	30,555
Business Analyst	22,331	26,549
MIS Manager	34,512	38,750

	1–2 Years' Experience (£)	3–5 Years' Experience (£)
Systems Support		
Systems Administrator	16,561	19,297
Systems Manager	19,750	23,456
Networking		
Network Support Executive	15,151	16,752
Network Administrator	16,356	18,188
Network Supervisor	18,541	21,399
Network Engineer	17,459	20,563
Network Manager	21,752	25,304
Help Desk/Support		
Help Desk/Support Executive	14,255	16,758
Help Desk/Support Supervisor	17,899	20,265
Software Trainer	14,887	17,124
Customer Service Manager	25,036	29,564
Design/Test		
Hardware Design Engineer	17,235	25,017
Firmware Design Engineer	15,654	24,301
Electrical Design Engineer	15,890	24,036
Mechanical Design Engineer	16,223	24,014
Software Design Engineer	18,124	26,770
CAD Design Draughtperson	14,003	18,641
CAD Manager	18,146	25,046
Electronic Test Technician	13,599	18,734
Electronic Test Engineer	16,422	21,143
Financial Services (refer also to Banking and Insurance executive salaries in Chapter 4)		
Banking Executive	11,254	14,344
Financial Analyst	15,231	20,014
Pensions Administrator	12,254	15,882
Fund Administrators	13,677	17,265
Settlements Clerk	10,342	12,789
Treasury Clerk	12,019	14,365
Credit Analyst	12,664	15,923

	1–2 Years' Experience (£)	3–5 Years' Experience (£)
Hotel & Catering		
Head Chefs (Hotels)	16,104	26,483
Sous Chefs (Hotels)	14,223	18,241
Chef de Partie (Hotels)	12,063	14,536
Commis Chefs 4th Year	10,204	12,134
Kitchen Porters	6,621	8,529
Catering Manager	15,219	18,002
Restaurant Manager	15,021	18,078
General Manager	24,281	35,716
Bar Staff	8,281	14,186
Human Resources (refer to executive salaries for Senior HR Officer, Managers and Directors in Chapter 4)		
HR Officer	16,645	22,003
Recruitment Specialist	22,165	23,898
HR Administrator	13,189	16,556
Training Officer	18,196	22,000
Employee Relations Specialist	18,978	22,478
Health & Safety Officer	18,534	21,759
Compensation & Benefits Officer	16,449	18,032
Industrial Management		
Purchasing Manager	26,589	30,236
Warehouse Manager	19,897	25,036
Materials Manager	28,791	36,331
Production Manager	24,899	33,452
Operations Manager	38,264	44,654
General Manager	40,364	57,463
Quality Manager	26,113	33,462
Maintenance Manager	24,423	32,461
Facilities Manager	25,000	32,006
Industrial Tradespeople (apprenticeships already served)		
Electrician	13,058	18,000
Fitter	13,000	18,000
Welder	12,000	16,424
Machine Operator	11,124	13,010
Toolmaker	14,000	22,000

	1–2 Years' Experience (£)	3–5 Years' Experience (£)
Maintenance Engineering		
Maintenance Technician — Mechanical	13,045	16,151
Maintenance Technician — Electrical	13,024	16,189
Maintenance Technician — Electro-mechanical	13,110	16,089
Maintenance Supervisor	16,010	20,110
Maintenance Engineer	16,119	23,145
Utilities/Facilities Engineer	13,246	20,221
Materials		
Buyer	14,192	22,874
Production Scheduler	15,326	24,021
Planner	15,114	22,350
Logistics Scheduler	14,874	20,845
Logistics Clerk	11,100	14,560
Distribution/Dispatch Clerk	11,320	13,891
Stock Controller	11,460	16,543
Materials Expediter	11,452	16,896
Store Person	11,365	15,613
Fork Lift Driver	12,664	15,986
Quality		
Quality Inspector	9,876	11,231
Quality Technician	11,015	15,006
Quality Engineer	14,223	25,176
Quality Supervisor	18,312	25,311
Quality Manager	27,327	33,879
Technical		
Production Supervisor	16,245	24,000
Manufacturing Engineer	18,000	25,143
Automation Engineer	13,550	18,213
Automation Technician	13,550	18,213
Instrumentation Technician	12,001	22,789
Industrial Engineer	14,265	23,167

	1–2 Years' Experience (£)	3–5 Years' Experience (£)
Temporary Contracts		
Accounts	£200 to £320 per week	
Assembly Operatives	£4 to £5 per hour	
Customer Service	£155 to 260 per week	
Drivers (artic/rigid/van/ Hazchem licenses)	£12,200 to £17,000 per year	
Industrial Tradespeople	£6 to £7.50 per hour	
Warehouse Operatives	£4.50 to £6 per hour	

Source: The Marlborough Group

APPENDIX 2: HOME PURCHASE PRICE GUIDE

Location	Type of Accommodation	Price
County Cork		
Glanmire	3 bed semi-detached dormer bungalow	£60,000
County Carlow		
Carlow	3 bed semi-detached with garden	£38,000–45,000
County Clare		
Kilmore	4 bed, half acre	£65,000
County Cavan		
Cootehill	5 bed house on 3 acres	£75,000
County Dublin		
Apartments		
Dublin	new 1 bedroom	£50,000–75,000
Dublin	new 2 bedroom	£75,000–90,000
Dublin 1	second-hand, 1 bedroom first floor with car space	£55,000
Dublin 1	second-hand, 2 bed top floor with car space	£86,000
Houses		
Ballyfermot	3 bed, garden	£48,000
Clondalkin	4 bed semi, 2 bath, garden	£73,000
Clonsilla	3 bed semi	from £72,000
Clontarf	3 bed terraced garden	£120,000
Clontarf	4 bed semi with gardens	£220,000
Clontarf	4 bed bungalow with conservatory on half an acre	£325,000
Dun Laoghaire	3 bed semi with garden	£90,000-120,000
Lucan	3 bed semi-detached with garden	£74,000
Palmerstown	3 bed semi-detached with conservatory and garden	£79,500
Location	*Type of Accommodation*	*Price*
Raheny	3 bed semi with gardens	£85,000
Rathfarnham	4 bed detached with gardens	£140,000-200,000
Sandymount	2 bed townhouse with gardens	£135,000

Santry	3 bed semi with gardens	£90,000
Swords	4 bed detached, 2 baths, gardens	£170,000
Tallaght	3 bed semi, garden	£68,000
Templeogue	4 bed detached	£140,000-500,000
County Galway		
Galway	3 bed end house	£69,000
County Kerry		
Killarney	New 3 bed semi	£85,000
County Kildare		
Celbridge	4 bed detached, 2 bath, gardens	£90,000-130,000
Leixlip	4 bed semi with gardens	£86,000
Maynooth	3 bed detached bungalow, gardens	£90,000
Naas	4 bed semi-detached, 2 bath, gardens	£90,000-170,000
Straffan	3 bed, 3 bath, half acre in grounds of K Club, includes membership	£675,000
County Kilkenny		
Kilkenny	8 bed, 2 baths, rural location	£85,000
County Laois		
Dundalk	5 bed, 1 bath, Georgian home, 40 acres	£295,000+
County Limerick		
Limerick	Terrace end house, 3 bed, 3 floors	£110,000
Limerick	4 bed semi-detached	£85,000+
Limerick	3 bed, 2 bath, conservatory	£80,000
County Leitrim		
Carrick on Shannon	3 bed, semi-detached	£62,950
Carrick on Shannon	Large 4 bed, 2 bath, lake view	£135,000
Location	*Type of Accommodation*	*Price*
County Longford		
Longford town	3 bed semi	£75,000
County Louth		
Drogheda	3 bed semi-detached	£69,000

County Mayo		
Near Mayo town	5 bed, 2 reception, 42 acres, outbuildings	£190,000
County Meath		
Kells	5 bed, 2 bath, own grounds	£155,000
Navan	3 bed semi-detached cottage on 1 acre	£66,000
County Offaly		
Near Tullamore	3 bed semi	£70,000
County Roscommon		
Roscommon	3 bed semi	£45–65,000
County Sligo		
Near Sligo town	3 bed semi	£45–£70,000
County Tipperary		
Tipperary	6 bed, 2 bath, 1 acre, conservatory, jacuzzi, sauna	£270,000
County Monaghan		
Castleblaney	3 bed detached bungalow with gardens	£50,000
County Waterford		
Waterford	4 bed town house	£68,000
Waterford	3 bed detached with gardens	£59,000
Wexford		
Bunclody	4 bed bungalow, three-quarters of an acre	£78,000
County Westmeath		
Mullingar	3 bed cottage on 1 acre	£42,000
County Wicklow		
Blessington	Near lakes, 3 reception, bungalow, 1.5 acres	£190,000
Bray	Detached 5 bed, 2 bath, gardens	£200,000
Laragh	Cottage on 7 acres	£118,000

APPENDIX 3: PERSONAL PAYE INCOME TAX TABLES
(1997/98 TAX YEAR)

Allowances	*IR£*
Personal allowance	
Single	2,900
Married	5,800
Widowed person	3,400
Widowed person bereaved in year of assessment	5,800
Additional allowances for one parent family	
Single	2,900
Widowed	
— First tax year after bereavement	3,900
— Next year	3,400
— Next year	2,900
— Subsequent years	2,400
Incapacitated child	700
Employed person taking care of incapacitated child	7,500
Blind person's allowance	
Single/one spouse blind	700
Married (both blind)	1,600
Dependent relative	110
Age allowance	
Single	400
Married	800
Special PAYE allowance	800
Business Expansion Scheme (BES)	
Maximum relief per annum	25,000
Approved profit sharing scheme	
Maximum value of shares per annum	10,000
Employee share subscription	
Maximum lifetime deduction	5,000
Health expenses	
VHI/BUPA subscription (previous year amount — the relief is only allowed by way of tax credit at standard 26%)	In full
Medical expenses in excess of	
£100 for an individual	In full
£200 for a family	In full

Allowances	IR£
Employee pensions (AVCs)	
Maximum % of relevant earnings	15%
Maximum % if aged 55 or over	20%
Permanent health benefit schemes	
Maximum % of statutory income	10%
Eligible fees to private colleges	
The relief is by a tax credit at standard rate of 26%	In full

APPENDIX 4: SAMPLE CV AND COVER LETTER

Curriculum Vitae

John Murphy
Apt. 201A, 1122 Fifth Avenue
New York,
NY 19002
Tel: (212) xxx-xxxx
Fax: (212) xxx xxxx
e-mail: xxxx@xxxxx

Born 1 May 1966
Fluent French and German

Education:

1984–1988
Dublin City University
Applied Languages (French and German)
Result: 1st Class Honours

1982–1988
Oak Tree Co-educational Community School, Dublin
Leaving Certificate (Maths, Irish, English, French, German,
Chemistry, Economics) — All at higher level

Work Experience:

1994 to date
Software Spectacular, London.
European HQ of software localisation and resale specialists.
Localisation co-ordinator for French and German.

Responsibilities include supervision of team of translators,
customer service and client liaison departments, project
management.

1993 to 1994
Travelled and worked in Australia

1988–1992

WorldWide Translations, Paris.
Global translation company with clients in 120 countries.
Commercial Translator

Summers 1984–1988
Worked and travelled in USA, Germany and France, mainly in customer service roles

Skills:
Lotus, Microsoft Word and Excel

Names of referees on request.

Cover Letter

Your name
Your address
Your phone number
(sometimes letters and CVs get separated)

Person and company name and address

Date

Dear (find out the person's name),

I am an (engineer with four years' experience in the US/
native German speaker with customer service experience, etc.)
and am writing to apply for a position with (company name).

My CV is enclosed for your consideration, and I would
appreciate an opportunity to attend interview to discuss how
my skills and experience match your requirements. I will be in
Ireland from (date). In the meantime, please contact me at
(phone number) should you require any more information.

Yours sincerely

(sign)

Print Name

Index

ALSO FROM OAK TREE PRESS

THE CELTIC TIGER:
Ireland's Economic Miracle Explained

Paul Sweeney

The Celtic Tiger is a must-read for anyone — in Ireland or abroad — who wants a better understanding of the Irish miracle.

Ireland's recent success is in stark contrast to almost eighty years of relative decline, today it has one of the fastest growing economies in the world. This growth has been sustained over a long period, is well-balanced and, according to most economists, is likely to continue for the foreseeable future.

But how did this remarkable turnaround come about? What were the factors and policies that led to this success story? Will the economic boom continue into the 21st century? Paul Sweeney clearly examines the important role economic policymakers played in turning around the economy, the role of investment in education and training, foreign investment, new forms of work and other factors which helped to generate phenomenal growth rates.

The author also shows that it is not all good news. There remain serious problems yet to be addressed. On balance, however, *The Celtic Tiger* argues that this economic regeneration has been phenomenal.

Paul Sweeney is an economist with SIPTU, Ireland's largest trade union. His primary work deals with corporate restructuring of leading multinationals and large state companies.

220 pages
£12.95 pb
ISBN 1-86076-081-3